T0256081

Applied Natural Language Processing in the Enterprise
Teaching Machines to Read, Write, and Understand

Ankur A. Patel and Ajay Uppili Arasanipalai

Beijing · Boston · Farnham · Sebastopol · Tokyo

Applied Natural Language Processing in the Enterprise

by Ankur A. Patel and Ajay Uppili Arasanipalai

Published by O'Reilly Media, Inc., 1005 Gravenstein Highway North, Sebastopol, CA 95472.

O'Reilly books may be purchased for educational, business, or sales promotional use. Online editions are also available for most titles (*http://oreilly.com*). For more information, contact our corporate/institutional sales department: 800-998-9938 or *corporate@oreilly.com*.

Acquisitions Editor: Jonathan Hassell	**Indexer:** nSight, Inc.
Development Editor: Melissa Potter	**Interior Designer:** David Futato
Production Editor: Deborah Baker	**Cover Designer:** Karen Montgomery
Copyeditor: Kim Cofer	**Illustrator:** Kate Dullea
Proofreader: Piper Editorial Consulting, LLC	

June 2021:   First Edition

Revision History for the First Edition

2021-05-11:   First Release

See *http://oreilly.com/catalog/errata.csp?isbn=9781492062578* for release details.

978-1-492-06257-8

[LSI]

Table of Contents

Part I.   Scratching the Surface

Part II. The Cogs in the Machine

Preface

What Is Natural Language Processing?

Many of you work with numerical data on a daily basis, either in a spreadsheet program like Microsoft Excel or in a programming environment such as Jupyter Notebook. When you work with numbers, you leave the number-crunching up to the computer. There is almost no reason for you not to.

Computers are fast and precise with number-crunching, whereas the human brain gets bogged down easily. If asked to calculate $24 \times 36 \times 48$, humans would not hesitate for a second to pull out a calculator or a computer and let the machines do the heavy lifting.

But, when it comes to analyzing textual data, the mighty number-crunching machines have not been so good, historically speaking. Humans use computers to crunch numbers but rely on the human brain to analyze documents with text. To date, this inability to work with text has limited the scope of work machines could handle.

This is about to change. In many ways, this change is already well underway. Machines are now able to process text and audio in ways that most humans would have considered magical just two decades ago.

Consider just how much you rely on computers to analyze and make sense of textual data in the everyday world around you. Here are several examples:

Google Search
   Search the entire web and surface relevant search results.

Google Gmail
   Auto-complete sentences as you write emails.

Google Translate
   Convert text and audio from one language to another.

Amazon Alexa, Apple Siri, Google Assistant, Microsoft Cortana
Give voice commands and control your home devices.

Customer Service Chatbots
Ask account-related questions and get (mostly reasonable) answers.

These technologies have become ingrained in our daily lives so gradually and seamlessly that we almost forget just how much we use them day to day. The story of machines being able to work with textual data is just getting started. Over the past few years, there have been pretty dramatic advances in this field, and, over time, we will see computers handle more and more of the work that only humans were capable of doing in the past.

Why Should I Read This Book?

Natural language processing (NLP) is one of the hottest topics in AI today. Having lagged behind other deep learning fields such as computer vision for years, NLP only recently gained mainstream popularity. Even though Google, Facebook, and OpenAI have open sourced large pretrained language models to make NLP easier, many organizations today still struggle with developing and productionizing NLP applications. This hands-on guide helps you learn the field quickly.

What Do I Need to Know Already?

This book is not for complete beginners. We are going to assume that you already know a bit about machine learning and that you have used Python and libraries such as NumPy, pandas, and matplotlib before.

For more on Python, visit the official Python website (*https://www.python.org*), and for more on Jupyter Notebook, visit the official Jupyter site (*https://jupyter.org*). For a refresher on college-level calculus, linear algebra, probability, and statistics, read Part I of the textbook *Deep Learning* (MIT Press) by Ian Goodfellow, Yoshua Bengio, and Aaron Courville. For a refresher on machine learning, read *The Elements of Statistical Learning* (Springer) by Jerome H. Friedman, Robert Tibshirani, and Trevor Hastie.

What Is This Book All About?

If you have basic-to-intermediate understanding of machine learning and programming experience with Python, you'll learn how to build and deploy real-world NLP applications in your organization.

We will walk you through the process without bogging you down in theory.

After reading this book and practicing on your own, you should be able to do the following:

- Understand how state-of-the-art NLP models work.
- Learn the tools of the trade, including the most popular frameworks today.
- Perform NLP tasks such as text classification, semantic search, and reading comprehension.
- Solve problems using new transformer-based models and techniques such as transfer learning.
- Develop NLP models with performance comparable or superior to out-of-the-box systems.
- Deploy models to production and monitor and maintain their performance
- Implement a suite of NLP algorithms using Python and PyTorch.

Our book's goal is to outline the concepts and tools required for you to develop the intuition necessary to apply this technology to everyday problems that you work on. In other words, this is an applied book, one that will allow you to build real-world applications. This book will not have every bit of theory that is relevant to NLP, and you will have to supplement your knowledge in the space using other resources over time, but we will get you started and well underway in this field.

The book will use a hands-on approach, introducing some theory but focusing mostly on applying natural language techniques to solving real-world problems. The datasets and code are available online as Jupyter Notebooks on our GitHub repo (*https://github.com/nlpbook/nlpbook*).

How Is This Book Organized?

This book is organized into three parts.

Part I (Chapters 1–3)
> These chapters focus on a high-level overview of NLP, including the history of NLP, the most popular applications in the field, and how to use pretrained models to perform transfer learning and solve real-world problems quickly.

Part II (Chapters 4–8)
> In these chapters, we'll dive into the low-level details of NLP including preprocessing text, tokenization, and word embeddings. While not the sexiest topics, these are foundational to the field of NLP. We then explore the most effective modeling approaches in NLP today such as transformers, attention mechanisms, vanilla recurrent neural networks, long short-term memory (LSTM), and gated recurrent units (GRUs). Finally, we tie everything together to present the watershed year in NLP—the so-called ImageNet moment in 2018 when large, pretrained language models shattered previous performance records and became widely available for use by both researchers and applied engineers.

Part III (Chapters 9–11)

Here we'll cover the most important aspect of applied NLP—how to production-ize models that have been developed so the models deliver tangible value to organizations. We discuss the landscape of tools available today, and share our opinions on them. We also cover special topics that are, strictly speaking, not related to NLP but may affect how NLP models are productionized.

While we will not be able to cover every NLP topic in this book, including the more advanced topics for seasoned veterans, we will continue to support our community with new and updated material (including code) online via our official book website (*https://www.appliednlpbook.com*) and GitHub. Please tune in for updates after you finish reading this book!

As a side note, it's worth mentioning that this book was written entirely in Jupyter Notebooks. You can find the code for this book on our GitHub repository. We encourage you to run the experiments in the notebooks as you read to get familiar with implementing the ideas presented in real code (but also because we have omitted some outputs in this book due to space constraints).

Conventions Used in This Book

The following typographical conventions are used in this book:

Italic
Indicates new terms, URLs, email addresses, filenames, and file extensions.

`Constant width`
Used for program listings, as well as within paragraphs to refer to program elements such as variable or function names, databases, data types, environment variables, statements, and keywords.

`Constant width bold`
Shows commands or other text that should be typed literally by the user.

`Constant width italic`
Shows text that should be replaced with user-supplied values or by values determined by context.

 This element signifies a tip or suggestion.

This element signifies a general note.

 This element indicates a warning or caution.

Using Code Examples

Supplemental material (code examples, exercises, etc.) is available for download at *https://github.com/nlpbook/nlpbook*.

If you have a technical question or a problem using the code examples, please send email to *bookquestions@oreilly.com*.

This book is here to help you get your job done. In general, if example code is offered with this book, you may use it in your programs and documentation. You do not need to contact us for permission unless you're reproducing a significant portion of the code. For example, writing a program that uses several chunks of code from this book does not require permission. Selling or distributing examples from O'Reilly books does require permission. Answering a question by citing this book and quoting example code does not require permission. Incorporating a significant amount of example code from this book into your product's documentation does require permission.

We appreciate, but generally do not require, attribution. An attribution usually includes the title, author, publisher, and ISBN. For example: "*Applied Natural Language Processing in the Enterprise* by Ankur A. Patel and Ajay Uppili Arasanipalai (O'Reilly). Copyright 2021 Human AI Collaboration, Inc. and Taukren, LLC, 978-1-492-06257-8."

If you feel your use of code examples falls outside fair use or the permission given above, feel free to contact us at *permissions@oreilly.com*.

O'Reilly Online Learning

 For more than 40 years, *O'Reilly Media* has provided technology and business training, knowledge, and insight to help companies succeed.

Our unique network of experts and innovators share their knowledge and expertise through books, articles, conferences, and our online learning platform. O'Reilly's online learning platform gives you on-demand access to live training courses, in-depth learning paths, interactive coding environments, and a vast collection of text and video from O'Reilly and 200+ other publishers. For more information, please visit *http://oreilly.com*.

How to Contact Us

Please address comments and questions concerning this book to the publisher:

> O'Reilly Media, Inc.
> 1005 Gravenstein Highway North
> Sebastopol, CA 95472
> 800-998-9938 (in the United States or Canada)
> 707-829-0515 (international or local)
> 707-829-0104 (fax)

You can access the web page for this book, where we list errata and any additional information, at *https://oreil.ly/Applied_NLP_in_the_Enterprise*.

Email *bookquestions@oreilly.com* to comment or ask technical questions about this book.

For news and more information about our books and courses, visit our website at *http://www.oreilly.com*.

Find us on Facebook: *http://facebook.com/oreilly*

Follow us on Twitter: *http://twitter.com/oreillymedia*

Watch us on YouTube: *http://youtube.com/oreillymedia*

Acknowledgments

We would like to thank the entire team at O'Reilly for helping make this project possible, starting with Jonathan Hassell for championing and green-lighting this book in the summer of 2019. We want to send a huge shout-out to our editor, Melissa Potter. She really helped us stay on schedule throughout 2020, despite all the challenges of COVID-19.

Big thanks to Jeremy Howard for providing valuable advice early on and for sharing the source code for FastDoc, an incredible tool for converting Jupyter Notebooks to AsciiDoc that we used throughout the development process. His work with Rachel Thomas, Sylvain Gugger, Zach Mueller, Hamel Husain, and many fastai contributors to make deep learning accessible and practical has been a huge source of inspiration for this book.

Our production editor, Deborah Baker, and the Content Services Manager, Kristen Brown, helped polish this book to its final form with the help of Kim Cofer, David Futato, Karen Montgomery, Kate Dullea, and the teams at Piper Editorial Consulting, LLC, and nSight, Inc. They made the final stretch of the writing process a breeze.

Special thanks to Artiom Tarasiuk, Victor Borges, and Benjamin Muskalla for spending countless hours reading and reviewing the book and providing critical feedback along the way. We are so grateful for their kinship and generosity in making this project what it is today.

Ajay

First and foremost, I would like to thank my parents, Uppili and Hema, who have worked tirelessly to support me through a raging pandemic, and my sister, Anika, who I have the highest hopes for.

There are many others to whom I owe an immeasurable debt of gratitude. Gayathri Srinivasan, who mentored me all those years ago and **was** the person kind enough to give a random high-schooler access to a supercomputer that first introduced me to the idea that machines can learn. Ganesan Narayanaswamy, for his generosity in providing the computational resources and infrastructure needed to support my research through the OpenPOWER Foundation. Diganta Misra, Trikay Nalamada, Himanshu Arora, and my other collaborators at Landskape, who have spent countless hours running experiments and joining me for the 2 AM discussions about attention mechanisms out of nothing but a shared passion for deep learning and a desire to contribute back to the research community. Their encouragement and enthusiasm for the book and my work in general have been inordinately valuable.

Ankur

I am so happy to be part of an incredibly generous and supportive family, to whom I owe everything. I want to thank my parents, Amrat and Ila, for their sacrifices over the years and for investing in me and my education; I simply would not be here doing what I'm doing today without them. I want to thank my sister, Bhavini, and my brother, Jigar, for championing me, always. And, I am so grateful to my beautiful girlfriend, Maria Koval, and our golden retriever, Brody, both of whom patiently put up with many late nights and weekends of writing and coding. Thank you!

I also want to thank my cofounders at Glean, Howard Katzenberg and Alexander Jia, and my good friend and cofounder at Mellow, Nate Collins, for being incredibly patient and supportive through the entire writing process. I am truly fortunate to have such amazing friends and colleagues—they bring happiness to my life every day.

## PART I

Scratching the Surface

This first section of the book covers NLP at a high level. This is a somewhat subjective term, so to be more specific, when we say "high level" we mean little to no math and little to no PyTorch code.

## CHAPTER 1

Introduction to NLP

What do you think your computer can do? Show you emails? Edit some files? Spin up an Excel sheet maybe?

But what if we told you your computer could read?

```
from transformers import pipeline
classifier = pipeline('sentiment-analysis')
classifier('I am reading the greatest NLP book ever!')

[{'label': 'POSITIVE', 'score': 0.9996862411499023}]
```

And write:

```
text_generator = pipeline("text-generation")
text_generator("Welcome to the ", max_length=5, do_sample=False)
```

And, most impressively, understand:

```
nlp = pipeline("question-answering")
context = """
Natural language processing (NLP) is a subfield of linguistics,
computer science, and artificial intelligence concerned with the
interactions between computers and human language, in particular
how to program computers to process and analyze large amounts of
natural language data. The result is a computer capable of
"understanding" the contents of documents, including the contextual
nuances of the language within them. The technology can then accurately
extract information and insights contained in the documents as well
as categorize and organize the documents themselves.
"""
nlp(question="What is NLP?", context=context)

{'score': 0.9869255423545837,
 'start': 1,
 'end': 28,
 'answer': 'Natural language processing'}
```

What was once the fantasy of a distant future is not only here but is accessible to anyone with a computer and an internet connection. The ability to understand and communicate in natural language, one of the most valuable assets that humanity has developed over the course of our existence, is now practical to do on machines.

"Of course!" you proclaim. "Technology always gets better, and we've had speech recognition and Google Translate for ages!"

But even just five years ago, "NLP" was something better suited to TechCrunch articles than actual production codebases. In the last three years, we've seen an exponential growth in progress in the field; models being deployed in production *today* are vastly superior to the most obscure research leaderboards from the days past.

But we're getting ahead of ourselves. Before we delve deeper, let's start with a high-level overview of the field. Once we cover the basics, we will introduce more advanced topics. Our goal is to help you build intuition and experience working with NLP, chapter by chapter, so that by the end of the book, you'll be able to build *real applications* that add *real value* to the world.

In the first half of this chapter, we will define NLP, explore some commercial applications of the technology, and walk through how the field has evolved since its origins in the 1950s.

In the second half of the chapter, we will introduce a very performant NLP library that is popular in the enterprise and use it to perform basic NLP tasks. While these tasks *are* elementary, when combined together, they allow computers to process and analyze natural language data in complex ways that make amazing commercial applications such as chatbots and voicebots possible.

In some ways, the process of machines learning how to process language is similar to how toddlers begin to learn language by mumbling and fumbling over words, only to later speak in full sentences and paragraphs. As we move through the book, we will build on the basic NLP tasks covered in this chapter.

What Is NLP?

Let's begin by defining what natural language processing is. Here is how NLP is defined on Wikipedia (accessed March 2021) (*https://oreil.ly/MRzEp*):

> Natural language processing (NLP) is a subfield of linguistics, computer science, information engineering, and artificial intelligence concerned with the interactions between computers and human (natural) languages, in particular how to program computers to process and analyze large amounts of natural language data.
>
> Challenges in natural language processing frequently involve speech recognition, natural language understanding, and natural language generation.

Let's unpack this definition. When we say "natural language," we mean "human language" as opposed to programming languages. Natural language refers to not only textual data, but also to speech and audio data.

Great, but so what if computers can now work with large amounts of text, speech, and audio data? Why is this so important?

Imagine for a second the world without language. How would we communicate via text or speech? How would we read books, listen to music, or comprehend movies and TV shows? Life as we know it would cease to exist; we would be stuck in caveman days, able to process information visually but unable to share our knowledge with each other or communicate in any meaningful way.[1]

Likewise, if machines can work with only numerical and visual data but cannot process natural language, they would be limited in the number and variety of applications they would have in the real world. Without the ability to handle natural language, machines will never be able to approach general artificial intelligence or anything that resembles human intelligence today.

Fortunately, machines can now finally process natural language data reasonably well. Let's explore what commercial applications are possible because of this relatively new-found ability of computers to work with natural language data.

Popular Applications

Because of the advances in NLP, machines are able to handle a broad array of natural language tasks, at least in a rudimentary way. Here are some common applications of NLP today:

Machine translation
> Machine translation is the process of using machines to translate from one language to another without any human intervention. By far the most popular example of this is Google Translate, which supports over 100 languages and serves over 500 million people daily. When it was first launched in 2006, the performance of Google Translate was notably worse than what it is today. Performance today is fast approaching human expert level.[2]

---

1 One of the major leaps in human history was the formation of a human (aka "natural") language, which allowed humans to communicate with one another, form groups, and operate as collective units of people instead of as solo individuals.

2 For more, read *The New York Times Magazine* article from 2016 on Google's neural machine translation (*https://oreil.ly/olGqC*).

Speech recognition

It may sound shocking, but voice recognition technology has been around for over 50 years. None of the voice recognition software had good performance or had gone mainstream until very recently, driven by the rise of deep learning. Today, Amazon Alexa, Apple Siri, Google Assistant, Microsoft Cortana, digital voice assistants in your car, and other software are now able to recognize speech with such a high level of accuracy that the software is able to process the information in real time and answer in a mostly reasonable way. Even as little as 15 years ago, the ability of such machines to recognize speech and respond in a coherent manner was abysmal.

Question answering

For these digital assistants to deliver a delightful experience to humans asking questions, speech recognition is only the first half of the job. The software needs to (a) recognize the speech and (b), given the speech recognized, retrieve an appropriate response. This second half is known as *question answering* (QA).

Text summarization

One of the most common tasks humans do every day, especially in white collar desk jobs, is read long-form documents and summarize the contents. Machines are now able to perform this summarization, creating a shorter summary of a longer text document. Text summarization reduces the reading time for humans. Humans who analyze lots of text daily (i.e., lawyers, paralegals, business analysts, students, etc.) are able to sift through the machine-generated short summaries of long-form documents and then, based on the summaries, choose the relevant documents to read more thoroughly.

Chatbots

If you have spent some time perusing websites recently, you may have realized that more and more sites now have a chatbot that automatically chimes in to engage the human user. The chatbot usually greets the human in a friendly, non-threatening manner and then asks the user questions to gauge the purpose and intent of the visit to the site. The chatbot then tries to automatically respond to any questions the user has without human intervention. Such chatbots are now automating digital customer engagement.

Text-to-speech and speech-to-text

Software is now able to convert text to high-fidelity audio very easily. For example, Google Cloud Text-to-Speech is able to convert text into human-like speech in more than 180 voices across over 30 languages. Likewise, Google Cloud Speech-to-Text is able to convert audio to text for over 120 languages, delivering a truly global offering.

Voicebots

Ten years ago, automated voice agents were clunky. Unless humans responded in a fairly constrained manner (e.g., with yes or no type responses), the voice agents on the phone could not process the information. Now, AI voicebots like those provided by VOIQ are able to help augment and automate calls for sales, marketing, and customer success teams.

Text and audio generation

Years ago, text generation relied on templates and rules-based systems. This limited the scope of application. Now, software is able to generate text and audio using machine learning, broadening the scope of application considerably. For example, Gmail is now able to suggest entire sentences based on previous sentences you've drafted, and it's able to do this on the fly as you type. While natural language generation is best at short blurbs of text (partial sentences), soon such systems may be able to produce reasonably good long-form content. A popular commercial application of natural language generation is data-to-text software, which generates textual summaries of databases and datasets. Data-to-text software includes data analysis as well as text generation. Firms in this space include Narrative Science and Automated Insights.

Sentiment analysis

With the explosion of social media content, there is an ever-growing need to automate customer sentiment analysis, dissecting tweets, posts, and comments for sentiment such as positive versus negative versus neutral or angry versus sad versus happy. Such software is also known as *emotion AI*.

Information extraction

One major challenge in NLP is creating structured data from unstructured and/or semi-structured documents. For example, named entity recognition software is able to extract people, organizations, locations, dates, and currencies from long-form texts such as mainstream news. Information extraction also involves relationship extraction, identifying the relations between entities, if any.

The number of NLP applications in the enterprise has exploded over the past decade, ranging from speech recognition and question and answering to voicebots and chatbots that are able to generate natural language on their own. This is quite astounding given where the field was a few decades ago.

To put the current progress in NLP into perspective, let's walk through how NLP has progressed, starting from its origins in 1950.

History

The field of natural language processing has been around for nearly 70 years. Perhaps most famously, Alan Turing laid the foundation for the field by developing the Turing test in 1950. The Turing test is a test of a machine's ability to demonstrate intelligence that is indistinguishable from that of a human. For the machine to pass the Turing test, it must generate human-like responses such that a human evaluator would not be able to tell whether the responses were generated by a human or a machine (i.e., the machine's responses are of human quality).[3]

The Turing test launched significant debate in the then-nascent artificial intelligence field and spurred researchers to develop natural langugage processing models that would serve as building blocks for a machine that someday may pass the Turing test, a search that continues to this day.

Like the broader field of artificial intelligence, NLP has had many booms and busts, lurching from hype cycles to AI winters. In 1954, Georgetown University and IBM successfully built a system that could automatically translate more than 60 Russian sentences to English. At the time, researchers at Georgetown University thought machine translation would be a solved problem within three to five years. The success in the US also spurred the Soviet Union to launch similar efforts. The Georgetown-IBM success coupled with the Cold War mentality led to increased funding for NLP in these early years.

However, by 1966, progress had stalled, and the Automatic Language Processing Advisory Committee (known as ALPAC)—a US government agency set up to evaluate the progress in computational linguistics—released a sobering report. The report stated that machine translation was more expensive, less accurate, and slower than human translation and unlikely to reach human-level performance in the near future. The report led to a reduction in funding for machine translation research. Following the report, research in the field nearly died for almost a decade.

Despite these setbacks, the field of NLP reemerged in the 1970s. By the 1980s, computational power had increased significantly and costs had come down sufficiently, opening up the field to many more researchers around the world.

In the late 1980s, NLP rose in prominence again with the release of the first statistical machine translation systems, led by researchers at IBM's Thomas J. Watson Research Center. Prior to the rise of statistical machine translation, machine translation relied on human handcrafted rules for language. These systems were called *rules-based machine translation*. The rules would help correct and control mistakes that the machine translation systems would typically make, but crafting such rules was a

---

3 For more, refer to the Wikipedia article about the Turing test (*https://oreil.ly/sN3ch*).

laborious and painstaking process. The machine translation systems were also brittle as a result; if the machine translation systems encountered edge-case scenarios for which rules had not been developed, they would fail, sometimes egregiously.

Statistical machine translation helped reduce the need for human handcrafted rules, and it relied much more heavily on learning from data. Using a bilingual corpus with parallel texts as data (i.e., two texts that are identical except for the language they are written in), such systems would carve sentences into small subsets and translate the subsets segment-by-segment from the source language to the target language. The more data (i.e., bilingual text corpuses) the system had, the better the translation. Statistical machine translation would remain the most widely studied and used machine translation method until the rise of neural machine translation in the mid-2010s.

By the 1990s, such successes led researchers to expand beyond text into speech recognition. Speech recognition, like machine translation, had been around since the early 1950s, spurred by early successes by the likes of Bell Labs and IBM. But speech recognition systems had severe limitations. In the 1960s, for example, such systems could take voice commands for playing chess but not do much else.

By the mid-1980s, IBM applied a statistical approach to speech recognition and launched a voice-activated typewriter called Tangora, which could handle a 20,000-word vocabulary.

DARPA, Bell Labs, and Carnegie Mellon University also had similar successes by the late 1980s. Speech recognition software systems by then had larger vocabularies than the average human and could handle continuous speech recognition, a milestone in the history of speech recognition.

In the 1990s, several researchers in the space left research labs and universities to work in industry, which led to more commercial applications of speech recognition and machine translation.

Today's NLP heavyweights, such as Google, hired their first speech recognition employees in 2007. The US government also got involved then; the National Security Agency began tagging large volumes of recorded conversations for specific keywords, facilitating the search process for NSA analysts.

By the early 2010s, NLP researchers, both in academia and industry, began experimenting with deep neural networks for NLP tasks. Early deep learning–led successes came from a deep learning method called *long short-term memory* (LSTM). In 2015, Google used such a method to revamp Google Voice.

Deep learning methods led to dramatic performance improvements in NLP tasks, spurring more dollars into the space. These successes have led to a much deeper integration of NLP software in our everyday lives.

For example, cars in the early 2010s had voice recognition software that could handle a limited set of voice commands. Cars now have tech that can handle a much broader set of natural language commands, inferring context and intent much more clearly.

Looking back today, progress in NLP was slow but steady, moving from rules-based systems in the early days to statistical machine translation by the 1980s and to neural network–based systems by the 2010s. While academic research in the space has been fierce for quite some time, NLP has become a mainstream topic only recently. Let's examine the main inflection points over the past several years that have helped NLP become one of the hottest topics in AI today.

Inflection Points

NLP and computer vision are both subfields of artificial intelligence, but computer vision has had more commercial successes to date. Computer vision had its inflection point in 2012 (the so-called "ImageNet" moment) when the deep learning–based solution AlexNet decimated the previous error rate of computer vision models.

In the years since 2012, computer vision has powered applications such as auto-tagging of photos and videos, self-driving cars, cashier-less stores, facial recognition–powered authentication of devices, radiology diagnoses, and more.

NLP has been a relatively late bloomer by comparison. NLP made waves from 2014 onward with the release of Amazon Alexa, a revamped Apple Siri, Google Assistant, and Microsoft Cortana. Google also launched a much-improved version of Google Translate in 2016, and now chatbots and voicebots are much more commonplace.

That being said, it wasn't until 2018 that NLP had its very own ImageNet moment with the release of large pretrained language models trained using the Transformer architecture; the most notable of these was Google's BERT, which was launched in November 2018.

In 2019, generative models such as OpenAI's GPT-2 made splashes, generating new content on the fly based on previous content, a previously insurmountable feat. In 2020, OpenAI released an even larger and more impressive version, GPT-3, building on its previous successes.

Heading into 2021 and beyond, NLP is now no longer an experimental subfield of AI. Along with computer vision, NLP is now poised to have many broad-based applications in the enterprise. With this book, we hope to share some concepts and tools that will help you build some of these applications at your company.

A Final Word

There is not one single approach to solving NLP tasks. The three dominant approaches today are rule-based, traditional machine learning (statistical-based), and neural network–based.

Let's explore each approach:

Rule-based NLP

Traditional NLP software relies heavily on human-crafted rules of languages; domain experts, typically linguists, curate these rules using things like regular expressions and pattern matching. Rule-based NLP performs well in narrowly scoped-out use cases but typically does not generalize well. More and more rules are necessary to generalize such a system, and this makes rule-based NLP a labor-intensive and brittle solution compared to the other NLP approaches. Here are examples of rules in a rule-based system: words ending in *-ing* are verbs, words ending in *-er* or *-est* are adjectives, words ending in *'s* are possessives, etc. Think of how many rules we would need to create by hand to make a system that could analyze and process a large volume of natural language data. Not only would the creation of rules be a mind-bogglingly difficult and tedious process, but we would also have to deal with the many errors that would occur from using such rules. We would have to create rules for rules to address all the corner cases for each and every rule.

Traditional (or classical) machine learning

Traditional machine learning relies less on rules and more on data. It uses a statistical approach, drawing probability distributions of words based on a large annotated corpus. Humans still play a meaningful role; domain experts need to perform feature engineering to improve the machine learning model's performance. Features include capitalization, singular versus plural, surrounding words, etc. After creating these features, you would have to train a traditional ML model to perform NLP tasks; e.g., text classification. Since traditional ML uses a statistical approach to determine when to apply certain features or rules to process language, traditional ML-based NLP is easier to build and maintain than a rule-based system. It also generalizes better than rule-based NLP.

Neural networks

Neural networks address the shortcomings of traditional machine learning. Instead of requiring humans to perform feature engineering, neural networks will "learn" the important features via representation learning. To perform well, these neural networks just need copious amounts of data. The amount of data required for these neural nets to perform well is substantial, but, in today's internet age, data is not too hard to acquire. You can think of neural networks as very powerful function approximators or "rule" creators; these rules and features are several degrees more nuanced and complex than the rules created by humans, allowing for more automated learning and more generalization of the system in processing natural language data.

Of these three, the neural network–based branch of NLP, fueled by the rise of very deep neural networks (i.e., deep learning), is the most powerful and the one that has led to many of the mainstream commercial applications of NLP in recent years.

In this book, we will focus mostly on neural network–based approaches to NLP, but we will also explore traditional machine learning approaches, too. The former has state-of-the-art performance in many NLP tasks, but traditional machine learning is still actively used in commercial applications.

We won't focus much on rule-based NLP, but, since it has been around for decades, you will not have difficulty finding other resources on that topic. Rule-based NLP does have a room among the other two approaches, but usually only to deal with edge cases.

Basic NLP

Now that we've defined NLP, explored applications in vogue today, covered its history and inflection points, and clarified the different approaches to solve NLP tasks, let's start our journey by performing the most basic tasks in NLP.

We will leverage one of the most popular open source libraries for use in commercial applications of NLP to perform these tasks: `spacy`.

Before we use `spacy`, let's discuss these most basic NLP tasks. As we said in the chapter introduction, they are pretty elementary, akin to teaching a child the basics of language. But, these basic NLP tasks, once combined, help us accomplish more complex tasks, which ultimately power the major NLP applications today.

Machines, like us, must walk before they run.

Defining NLP Tasks

Earlier in the chapter, we explored several NLP applications in vogue today, including the following:

- Machine translation
- Speech recognition
- Question answering
- Text summarization
- Chatbots

- Text-to-speech and speech-to-text conversion
- Voicebots
- Text and audio generation
- Sentiment analysis
- Information extraction

For machines to perform these complex applications, they need to perform several smaller, more bite-sized NLP tasks. In other words, to build successful commercial NLP applications, we must master the NLP tasks that serve as building blocks for those applications.

It is important to note that modern neural network–based NLP models perform these "tasks" automatically through training the neural network; that is, the neural network learns on its own how to perform some of these tasks. We, the operators, do not need to perform these tasks explicitly.

These tasks are a bit outdated for this reason, but they are still relevant today both for building greater intuition around how machines learn to work with natural language and for working with non-neural network–based NLP models. Classical, non-neural network–based NLP is still commonplace in the enterprise even if it is out of favor in state-of-the-art research today. For these reasons, it is worthwhile to learn these tasks.

Without further ado, here are some of these NLP tasks:

Tokenization

Tokenization is the process of splitting text into minimal meaningful units such as words, punctuation marks, symbols, etc. For example, the sentence "We live in Paris" could be tokenized into four tokens: We, live, in, Paris. Tokenization is typically the first step of every NLP process. Tokenization is a necessary step because the machine needs to break down natural language data into the most basic elements (or tokens) so that it can analyze each element in context of the other elements. Otherwise, it would have to analyze a long piece of text or audio as if it were one singular element, making the problem intractable for the machine. Just like a beginner student of a language breaks down a sentence into smaller bits to learn and process the information word by word, a machine needs to do the same. Even with complex numerical calculations, machines break down the problem into basic elements, performing tasks such as addition, subtraction, multiplication, and division of two sets of numbers. The major advantage that the machine has is that it can do this at a pace and scale that no human can. After tokenization breaks down the text into minimal meaningful units, the machine needs to assign metadata to each unit, providing it more information on how to process each unit in the context of other units.

Part-of-speech tagging

Part-of-speech (POS) tagging is the process of assigning word types to tokens, such as noun, pronoun, verb, adverb, adjective, conjunction, preposition, interjection, etc. For "We live in Paris," the parts of speech are: pronoun, verb, preposition, and noun. This part-of-speech tagging gives each token a bit more metadata, making it easier for the machine to assign relationships between each token and every other token. In the sentence, "I kick the ball," "I" and "ball" are both nouns and "kick" is a verb. Using this metadata, we can infer that "kick" somehow connects "I" and the "ball," allowing us to form a relationship among the words. This is why the parts of speech are so important. Without knowing that some words are nouns and other are verbs, etc., the machine would not be able to map the relationships among the tokens.

Dependency parsing

Dependency parsing involves labeling the relationships between individual tokens, assigning a syntactic structure to the sentence. Once the relationships are labeled, the entire sentence can be structured as a series of relationships among sets of tokens. It is easier for the machine to process text once it has identified the inherent structure among the text. Think how difficult it would be for you to understand a sentence if you had all the words in the sentence presented to you out of order and you had no prior knowledge of the rules of grammar. In much the same way, until the machine performs dependency parsing, it has little to no knowledge of the structure of the text that it has converted into tokens. Once the structure is apparent, processing the text becomes a little bit easier.

Dependency parsing can get tricky so the best way to understand it is to visualize the relationships using a parse tree. AllenNLP has a great dependency parsing demo (*https://oreil.ly/yAgAZ*), which we used to generate the dependency graph in Figure 1-1. This dependency graph allows us to visualize the relationships among the tokens. As you can see from the figure, "We" is the personal pronoun (PRP) and the nominal subject (NSUBJ) of "live," which is the non-third person singular present verb (VBP). "Live" is connected to the prepositional phrase (PREP) "in Paris." "In" is the preposition (IN), and "Paris" is the object of the preposition (POBJ) and is itself a singular proper noun (NNP). These relationships are very complex to model, and one reason why it is very difficult to be truly fluent in any language. Most of us apply the rules of grammar on the fly, having learned language through years of experience. A machine does the same type of analysis, but to perform natural language processing it has to crunch these operations one after the other at blazingly fast speeds.

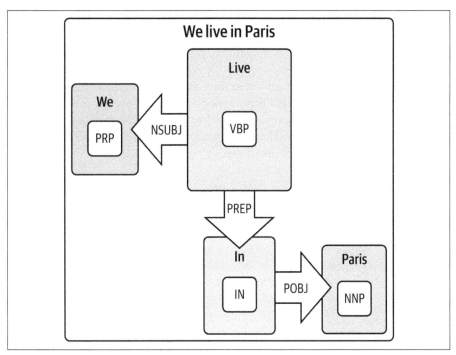

Figure 1-1. Dependency parsing

Chunking

Chunking involves combining related tokens into a single token, creating related noun groups, related verb groups, etc. For example, "New York City" could be treated as a single token/chunk instead of as three separate tokens. Chunking is the process that makes this possible. Chunking is important to perform once the machine has broken the original text into tokens, identified the parts of speech, and tagged how each token is related to other tokens in the text. Chunking combines similar tokens together, making the overall process of analyzing the text a bit easier to perform. For example, instead of treating "New," "York," and "City" as three separate tokens, we can infer that they are related and group them together into a single group (or chunk). Then, we can relate the chunk to other chunks in the text. Once we've done this for the entire set of tokens, we will have a much smaller set of tokens and chunks to work with.

Lemmatization

Lemmatization is the process of converting words into their base forms. For example, lemmatization converts "horses" to "horse," "slept" to "sleep," and "biggest" to "big." It allows the machine to simplify the text processing work it has to perform. Instead of working with a variant of the base word, it can work directly with the base word after it has performed lemmatization.

Stemming

Stemming is a process related to lemmatization, but simpler. Stemming reduces words to their word stems. Stemming algorithms are typically rule-based. For example, the word "biggest" would be reduced to "big," but the word "slept" would not be reduced at all. Stemming sometimes results in nonsensical sub-words, and we prefer lemmatization to stemming for this reason. Lemmatization returns a word to its base or canonical form, per the dictionary. But, it is a more expensive process compared to stemming, because it requires knowing the part of speech of the word to perform well.

Tokenization, part-of-speech tagging, dependency parsing, chunking, and lemmatization and stemming are tasks to process natural language for downstream NLP applications; in other words, these tasks are means to an end. Technically, the next two "tasks"—named entity recognition and entity linking—are not natural language tasks but rather are closer to NLP applications. Named entity recognition and entity linking can be ends themselves, rather than just means to an end. But, since they are also used for downstream NLP applications, we will include them in the "tasks" section here.

Named entity recognition

Named entity recognition (NER), is the process of assigning labels to known objects (or entities) such as person, organization, location, date, currency, etc. In "We live in Paris," "Paris" would be marked as the location. NER is very powerful. It allows machines to tag the most important tokens with named entity tags, and this is very important for informational retrieval applications of NLP. For example, if we want to search for former US President George W. Bush in a set of documents, we would want the machine to tag all persons in all the documents using named entity recognition, and then we would search within this list of persons to find the relevant set of documents for us to investigate further.

Entity linking

Entity linking is the process of disambiguating entities to an external database, linking text in one form to another. This is important both for entity resolution applications (e.g., deduping datasets) and information retrieval applications. In the George W. Bush example, we would want to resolve all instances of "George W. Bush" to "George W. Bush," but not to "George H. W. Bush," George W. Bush's father and also a former US President. This resolution and linking to the correct version of President Bush is a tricky, thorny process, but one that a machine is capable of performing given all the textual context it has. Once a machine has performed entity recognition and linking, information retrieval becomes a cinch, which is one of the most commercially relevant applications of NLP today.

This is just a quick-and-dirty overview of the most basic NLP tasks. You will want to research these tasks further; there are ample resources available online. But, for now, this is plenty of information for us to get started.

Now that you know the basic NLP tasks that serve as building blocks for more ambitious NLP applications, let's use the open source NLP library spacy to perform some of these basic NLP tasks.

Set Up the Programming Environment

To perform the basic NLP tasks, we first will need to set up our programming environment.

In this book, we will use one of these easiest to use programming environments available to data scientists today: Google's Colaboratory (*https://oreil.ly/8dJLj*). Google Colab is a free Jupyter Notebook environment that runs entirely in the cloud. In Chapter 2, we will discuss Google Colab and alternative programming environments in more detail.

We will use GitHub as our coding repository.[4]

If you prefer to run the code locally on your machine, we have instructions for setting up your local environment on our GitHub repo.

With that, let's get started with coding the basic NLP tasks.

spaCy, fast.ai, and Hugging Face

In this book, we will use open source software libraries offered by three major companies: spacy, fast.ai, and Hugging Face—to perform NLP. These libraries are high-level, abstracting away a lot of the low-level work that we would otherwise have to do. Think of these libraries as beautiful wrappers for us to quickly apply NLP. All three libraries are performant and commercially viable, and you can pick any of the three to do your own applied work; you do not have to choose all three. That being said, it is wise to be well-versed in all three because they do have their respective strengths and weaknesses, and sometimes one will be quicker at adopting the latest advances in NLP than the others. Let us quickly introduce each of the three before we move forward with spacy in this chapter. In Chapter 2, we will work with fast.ai and Hugging Face.

---

4 For more on GitHub, visit the GitHub website (*https://github.com*) and Google Colab's instructions (*https://oreil.ly/wQTjQ*) on integrating with GitHub.

spaCy

First released in 2015, spacy (*https://spacy.io*) is an open source library for NLP with blazing fast performance, leveraging both Python and Cython. Prior to spacy, the Natural Language Toolkit (NLTK) (*https://www.nltk.org*) was the leading NLP library among researchers, but NLTK was dated (it was initially released in 2001) and scaled poorly. spacy was the first modern NLP library intended for commercial audiences; it was built with scaling in production in mind. Now one of the go-to libraries for NLP applications in the enterprise, it supports more than 64 languages and both Tensor-Flow and PyTorch.

Prior to 2021, spacy 2.x relied on recurrent neural networks (RNNs), which we will cover later in the book, rather than the industry-leading transformer-based models. But, as of January 2021, spacy now supports state-of-the-art transformer-based pipelines, too, solidifying its positioning among the major NLP libraries in use today.

spacy's creator and parent company, Explosion AI (*http://explosion.ai*), also offers an excellent annotation platform called Prodigy (*https://prodi.gy*), which we will use in Chapter 3. Among the three libraries, spacy is the most mature and most extensible given all the integrations its creators have created and supported over the past six-plus years. It is the one best suited for production usage today.

fast.ai

fast.ai (*https://www.fast.ai*) (the company) released its open source library fastai in 2018, built on top of PyTorch. fast.ai, the company, built its reputation by offering massive open online courses (MOOCs) to coders that want a more practical introduction to machine learning, and the fastai library reflects this ethos. It has high-level components that allow coders to quickly and easily produce state-of-the-art results. At the same time, fastai has low-level components for researchers to mix and match to solve custom problems. The creators of fastai also created ULMFiT (*https://oreil.ly/TJaxc*), one of the first transfer learning methods in NLP, which we will use in Chapter 2. For those who would like course work and videos alongside a fast and easy-to-use library, fastai is a great option. However, it is less mature and less suited to production work than both spacy and Hugging Face.

Hugging Face

Founded in 2016, Hugging Face (*https://huggingface.co*) is the newest comer on the block but likely the best funded and the fastest-growing of the three today; the company just raised a $40 million Series B in March 2021. Hugging Face focuses exclusively on NLP and is built to help practitioners build NLP applications using state-of-the-art transformers. Its library, called transformers, is built for PyTorch and TensorFlow and supports over 100 languages. In fact, it is possible to move from PyTorch and TensorFlow for development and deployment pretty seamlessly.

Hugging Face also has a pipeline API for productionizing NLP models. We are most excited for the future of Hugging Face among the three libraries and highly recommend you spend sufficient time familiarizing yourself with it.

Perform NLP Tasks Using spaCy

Let's now use spacy for our NLP tasks.

First, we'll install spacy. For more on installation, visit the official spaCy website (*https://spacy.io/usage*). If you haven't installed spacy already, these commands will give you everything you need (if you're running them in a notebook, prefix each line with a ! character):

```
pip install -U spacy[cuda110,transformers,lookups]==3.0.3
pip install -U spacy-lookups-data==1.0.0
pip install cupy-cuda110==8.5.0
python -m spacy download en_core_web_trf
```

Download pretrained language models

spacy has pretrained language models for out-of-the-box use. Pretrained models are models that have been trained on lots of data already and are ready for us to perform inference with.

These pretrained language models will help us solve the basic NLP tasks, but more advanced users are welcome to fine-tune them on more specific data of your choosing. This will deliver even better performance for your specific tasks at hand.

Fine-tuning is the process of taking a pretrained model and training it some more (i.e., fine-tuning the model) on a more specific corpus of text that is relevant to the domain of the user.[5] For example, if we worked in finance, we may decide to fine-tune a generic pretrained language model on financial documents to generate a finance-specific language model. This finance-specific language model would have even better performance on finance-related NLP tasks versus the generic pretrained language model.

spacy breaks out its pretrained language models into two groups: core models and starter models. The core models are general-purpose models and will help us solve the basic NLP tasks. The starter models are base models useful for transfer learning; these models have pretrained weights, which you could use to initialize and fine-tune for your own models. Think of the core models as ready-to-go models and the base models as do-it-yourself starter kits.

---

5 The operation of taking a model developed for one task and using it as a starting point for a model on a second task is known as *transfer learning*.

We will use the ready-to-go core models to perform the basic NLP tasks. Let's first import the core model:[6]

```
# Import spacy and download language model
import spacy
nlp = spacy.load("en_core_web_sm")
```

Now, let's perform the first of the NLP tasks: tokenization.

Tokenization

Tokenization is where all NLP work begins; before the machine can process any of the text it sees, it must break the text into bite-sized tokens. Tokenization will segment text into words, punctuation marks, etc.

spacy automatically runs the entire NLP pipeline when you run a language model on the data (i.e., nlp(SENTENCE)), but to isolate just the tokenizer, we will invoke just the tokenizer using nlp.tokenizer(SENTENCE).

Then, we will print the length of the tokens and the individual tokens:

```
# Tokenization
sentence = nlp.tokenizer("We live in Paris.")

# Length of sentence
print("The number of tokens: ", len(sentence))

# Print individual words (i.e., tokens)
print("The tokens: ")
for words in sentence:
    print(words)
The number of tokens:  5
The tokens:
We
live
in
Paris
.
```

The length of tokens is 5, and the individual tokens are "We, live, in, Paris, .". The period at the end of the sentence is its own token.

Note that the spacy tokenizer will treat new lines (\n), tabs (\t), and whitespace characters beyond a single space (") as tokens.

Let's try the tokenizer on a slightly more complex example.

---

6 A spacy language model is not the same thing as what we generally refer to in the NLP literature as a *language model*. For more information on language modeling, see Chapter 2.

We will load in publicly available *Jeopardy* questions and then run the entire spacy language model on a few of the questions:

```python
import pandas as pd
import os
cwd = os.getcwd()

# Import Jeopardy Questions
data = pd.read_csv(cwd+'/data/jeopardy_questions/jeopardy_questions.csv')
data = pd.DataFrame(data=data)

# Lowercase, strip whitespace, and view column names
data.columns = map(lambda x: x.lower().strip(), data.columns)

# Reduce size of data
data = data[0:1000]

# Tokenize Jeopardy Questions
data["question_tokens"] = data["question"].apply(lambda x: nlp(x))
```

We have now created tokens for each of the 1,000 *Jeopardy* questions.

To make sure this worked right, let's view the first question and the tokens created:

```python
# View first question
example_question = data.question[0]
example_question_tokens = data.question_tokens[0]
print("The first questions is:")
print(example_question)
```

```
The first questions is:
For the last 8 years of his life, Galileo was under house arrest for espousing
 > this man's theory
```

```python
# Print individual tokens of first question
print("The tokens from the first question are:")
for tokens in example_question_tokens:
    print(tokens)
```

```
The tokens from the first question are:
For
the
last
8
years
of
his
life
,
Galileo
was
under
house
arrest
```

```
for
espousing
this
man
's
theory
```

This is the first basic NLP task that machines perform; now we can move on to the other NLP tasks. Well done!

Part-of-speech tagging

After tokenization, machines need to tag each token with relevant metadata, such as the part-of-speech of each token. This is what we will perform now.

Since we applied the entire spacy language model to the *Jeopardy* questions, the tokens generated already have a lot of the meaningful attributes/metadata we care about.

spacy uses preloaded statistical models to predict the part of speech of each token. We loaded the English language statistical model earlier using this code: spacy.load("en_core_web_sm").

Let's take a look at the POS tagging attributes for the tokens in the first question:

```
# Print Part-of-speech tags for tokens in the first question
print("Here are the Part-of-speech tags for each token in the first question:")
for token in example_question_tokens:
    print(token.text,token.pos_, spacy.explain(token.pos_))
```

```
Here are the Part-of-speech tags for each token in the first question:
For ADP adposition
the DET determiner
last ADJ adjective
8 NUM numeral
years NOUN noun
of ADP adposition
his PRON pronoun
life NOUN noun
, PUNCT punctuation
Galileo PROPN proper noun
was AUX auxiliary
under ADP adposition
house NOUN noun
arrest NOUN noun
for ADP adposition
espousing VERB verb
this DET determiner
man NOUN noun
's PART particle
theory NOUN noun
```

The first token "For" is marked as an adposition (e.g., in, to, during); the second token "the" is a determiner (e.g., a, an, the); the third token "last" is an adjective, the fourth token "8" is a numeral; the fifth token "years" is a noun; and so on.

Table 1-1 displays the full list of all possible POS tags, including descriptions and examples of each.[7]

Table 1-1. Universal part-of-speech tags

POS	Description	Example
ADJ	Adjective	Big, old, green, incomprehensible, first
ADP	Adposition	In, to, during
ADV	Adverb	Very, tomorrow, down, where, there
AUX	Auxiliary	Is, has (done), will (do), should (do)
CONJ	Conjunction	And, or, but
CCONJ	Coordinating conjunction	And, or, but
DET	Determiner	A, an, the
INTJ	Interjection	Psst, ouch, bravo, hello
NOUN	Noun	Girl, cat, tree, air, beauty
NUM	Numeral	1, 2017, one, seventy-seven, IV, MMXIV
PART	Particle	's, not
PRON	Pronoun	I, you, he, she, myself, themselves, somebody
PROPN	Proper noun	Mary, John, London, NATO, HBO
PUNCT	Punctuation	., (,), ?
SCONJ	Subordinating conjunction	If, while, that
SYM	Symbol	×, %, §, ©, +, -, ×, ÷, =, :),
VERB	Verb	Run, runs, running, eat, ate, eating
X	Other	Sfpksdpsxmsa
SPACE	Space	

Now that we have used the tokenizer to create tokens for each sentence and part-of-speech tagging to tag each token with meaningful attributes, let's label each token's relationship with other tokens in the sentence. In other words, let's find the inherent structure among the tokens given the part-of-speech metadata we have generated.

---

7 Visit the spacy POS documentation (*https://oreil.ly/RzTvP*) for more.

Dependency parsing

Dependency parsing is the process of finding these relationships among the tokens. Once we have performed this step, we will be able to visualize the relationships using a dependency parsing graph.

First, let's view the dependency parsing tags for each of the tokens in the first question:

```
# Print Dependency Parsing tags for tokens in the first question
for token in example_question_tokens:
    print(token.text,token.dep_, spacy.explain(token.dep_))
```

```
For prep prepositional modifier
the det determiner
last amod adjectival modifier
8 nummod numeric modifier
years pobj object of preposition
of prep prepositional modifier
his poss possession modifier
life pobj object of preposition
, punct punctuation
Galileo nsubj nominal subject
was ROOT None
under prep prepositional modifier
house compound compound
arrest pobj object of preposition
for prep prepositional modifier
espousing pcomp complement of preposition
this det determiner
man poss possession modifier
's case case marking
theory dobj direct object
```

The first token "For" is marked as a prepositional modifier; the second token "the" is a determiner; the third token "last" is an adjectival modifier; the fourth token "8" is a numeric modifier; the fifth token "years" is the object of preposition; and so on.

Table 1-2 lists all the possible syntactic dependency tags, including descriptions and examples of each.[8]

Table 1-2. Universal dependency labels

Label	Description
ac1	Clausal modifier of noun (adjectival clause)
advc1	Adverbial clause modifier
advmod	Adverbial modifier

---

8 Visit the spacy documentation (*https://oreil.ly/EJ2Mg*) for more.

Label	Description
amod	Adjectival modifier
appos	Appositional modifier
aux	Auxiliary
case	Case marking
cc	Coordinating conjunction
ccomp	Clausal complement
clf	Classifier
compound	Compound
conj	Conjunction
cop	Copula
csubj	Clausal subject
dep	Unspecified dependency
det	Determiner
discourse	Discourse element
dislocated	Dislocated element
expl	Expletive
fixed	Fixed multiword expression
flat	Flat multiword expression
goeswith	Goes with
iobj	Indirect object
list	List
mark	Marker
nmod	Nominal modifier
nsubj	Nominal subject
nummod	Numeric modifier
obj	Object
obl	Oblique nominal
orphan	Orphan
parataxis	Parataxis
punct	Punctuation
reparandum	Overridden disfluency
root	Root
vocative	Vocative
xcomp	Open clausal complement

These tags help define the relationships among the tokens; using these tags, we can understand the relationship structure among the tokens that make up the sentence.

Dependency parsing is hard to unpack, so let's use `spacy`'s built-in visualizer to get a better sense of the dependencies across the tokens:

```
# Visualize the dependency parse
from spacy import displacy

displacy.render(example_question_tokens, style='dep',
                jupyter=True, options={'distance': 120})
```

Figure 1-2 displays the first part of the sentence parsed.

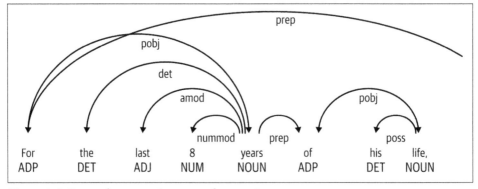

Figure 1-2. Dependency parsing example, part 1

Notice the importance of "For" and "years" in the prepositional phrase—multiple tokens map to these two.

Figure 1-3 displays the second part of the sentence parsed.

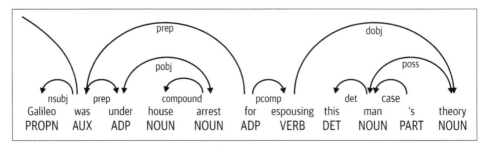

Figure 1-3. Dependency parsing example, part 2

The token "was" connects to the nominal subject "Galileo" and two prepositional phrases: "under house arrest" and "for espousing this man's theory."

These figures show how certain tokens can be grouped together and how the groups of tokens are related to one another. This is an essential step in NLP. First, the machine breaks the sentence apart into tokens. Then it assigns metadata to each token (e.g., part of speech), and then it connects the tokens based on their relationship to one another.

Let's move on to chunking, which is another form of grouping of related tokens.

Chunking

Let's perform chunking on the sentence "My parents live in New York City":

```
# Print tokens for example sentence without chunking
for token in nlp("My parents live in New York City."):
    print(token.text)

My
parents
live
in
New
York
City
.
```

Chunking combines related tokens into a single token.

With chunking, the spacy language model will identify "My parents" and "New York City" as noun chunks, much like a human would when parsing a sentence:

```
# Print chunks for example sentence
for chunk in nlp("My parents live in New York City.").noun_chunks:
    print(chunk.text)

My parents
New York City
```

By grouping related tokens into chunks, the machine will have an easier time processing the sentence. Instead of viewing each token in isolation, the machine now recognizes that certain tokens are related to others, a necessary step in NLP.

Lemmatization

Now, let's go a step further and perform lemmatization. If you recall, lemmatization is the process of converting words into their base (or canonical) forms; for example, "horses" to "horse," "slept" to "sleep," and "biggest" to "big." Just like part-of-speech tagging, dependency parsing, and chunking, lemmatization helps the machine "process" the tokens. With lemmatization, the machine is able to simplify the tokens by converting some of them into their most basic forms.

Stemming is a related concept, but stemming is simpler. Stemming reduces words to their word stems, often using a rule-based approach.

Lemmatization is a more difficult process but generally results in better outputs; stemming sometimes creates outputs that are nonsensical (nonwords). In fact, spacy does not even support stemming; it supports only lemmatization.

We will create a DataFrame to store and view the original and lemmatized versions of tokens side-by-side:

```
# Print lemmatization for tokens in the first question
lemmatization = pd.DataFrame(data=[], \
  columns=["original","lemmatized"])
i = 0
for token in example_question_tokens:
    lemmatization.loc[i,"original"] = token.text
    lemmatization.loc[i,"lemmatized"] = token.lemma_
    i = i+1
```

```
lemmatization
```

	Original	Lemmatized
0	For	for
1	the	the
2	last	last
3	8	8
4	years	year
5	of	of
6	his	his
7	life	life
8	,	,
9	Galileo	Galileo
10	was	be
11	under	under
12	house	house
13	arrest	arrest
14	for	for
15	espousing	espouse
16	this	this
17	man	man
18	's	's
19	theory	theory

As you can see, words such as "years," "was," and "espousing" are lemmatized to their base forms. The other tokens are already their base forms, so the lemmatized output is the same as the original. Lemmatization simplifies tokens into their simplest forms, where possible, to simplify the process for the machine to parse sentences.

Named entity recognition

When combined together, everything we've done so far—tokenization, part-of-speech tagging, dependency parsing, chunking, and lemmatization—makes it possible for machines to perform more complex NLP tasks. One example of a complex NLP task is *named entity recognition* (also known as "NER"), which parses notable entities in natural language and labels them with their appropriate class label. For example, NER labels names of people with the label "Person" and names of cities with the label "Location."

NER is possible only because the machine is able to perform text classification using the metadata generated by the earlier NLP tasks we've covered. Without the metadata from the earlier NLP tasks, the machine would have a very difficult time performing NER because it would not have enough features to classify names of people as "Person," names of cities as "Location," etc.

NER is a valuable NLP task because many organizations need to process lots and lots of documents in volume, and the simple act of labeling notable entities with the appropriate class label is a meaningful first step in analyzing the textual information, particularly for information retrieval tasks (e.g., finding information that you need as quickly as possible).

These documents include contracts, leases, real estate purchase agreements, financial reports, news articles, etc. Before named entity recognition, humans would have had to label such entities by hand (at many companies, they still do). Now, named entity recognition provides an algorithmic way to perform this task.

spacy's NER model is able to label many types of notable entities ("real-world objects"). Table 1-3 displays the current set of entity types the spacy model is able to recognize.

Table 1-3. spaCy NER entity types

Type	Description
PERSON	People, including fictional
NORP	Nationalities or religious or political groups
FAC	Buildings, airports, highways, bridges, etc.
ORG	Companies, agencies, institutions, etc.
GPE	Countries, cities, states
LOC	Non-GPE locations, mountain ranges, bodies of water
PRODUCT	Objects, vehicles, foods, etc. (not services)

Type	Description
EVENT	Named hurricanes, battles, wars, sports events, etc.
WORK_OF_ART	Titles of books, songs, etc.
LAW	Named documents made into laws
LANGUAGE	Any named language
DATE	Absolute or relative dates or periods
TIME	Times smaller than a day
PERCENT	Percentage, including %
MONEY	Monetary values, including unit
QUANTITY	Measurements, as of weight or distance
ORDINAL	"First," "second," etc.
CARDINAL	Numerals that do not fall under another type

It's very important to note that NER is, at its very core, a classification model. Using the context around the token of interest, the NER model predicts the entity type of the token of interest. NER is a statistical model, and the corpus of data the model has trained on matters a lot. For better performance, developers of these models in the enterprise will fine-tune the base NER models on their particular corpus of documents to achieve better performance versus the base NER model.

Let's try the spacy NER model. We will perform NER on the first sentence of the Wikipedia article (accessed March 2021) (*https://oreil.ly/SmNV2*) describing George Washington, the first president of the United States. Here's the sentence:

> George Washington was an American political leader, military general, statesman, and Founding Father who served as the first president of the United States from 1789 to 1797.

As you can see, there are several real-world objects to recognize here, including "George Washington" and "the United States":

```
# Print NER results
example_sentence = "George Washington was an American political leader, \
military general, statesman, and Founding Father who served as the \
first president of the United States from 1789 to 1797.\n"

print(example_sentence)

print("Text Start End Label")
doc = nlp(example_sentence)
for token in doc.ents:
    print(token.text, token.start_char, token.end_char, token.label_)

George Washington was an American political leader, military general, statesman,
 > and Founding Father who served as the first president of the United States
 > from 1789 to 1797.
```

```
Text Start End Label
George Washington 0 17 PERSON
American 25 33 NORP
first 119 124 ORDINAL
the United States 138 155 GPE
1789 to 1797 161 173 DATE
```

There are four elements to the output. First, the text that comprises the entity; note that the text could be a single token or a set of tokens that makes up the entire entity. Second, the start position of the text in the sentence. Third, the end position of the text in the sentence. Fourth, the label of the entity.

To make the value of NER even more apparent, let's use spacy's built-in visualizer to visualize this sentence with the relevant entity labels:

```
# Visualize NER results
displacy.render(doc, style='ent', jupyter=True, options={'distance': 120})
```

As you can see in Figure 1-4, the spacy NER model does a great job labeling the entities. "George Washington" is a person, and the text starts at index 0 and ends at index 17. His nationality is "American." "First" is labeled as an ordinal number, "the United States" is a geopolitical entity, and "1789 to 1797" is a date.

Figure 1-4. Visualize NER results

The sentence is beautifully rendered with color-coded labels based on the entity type. This is a powerful and meaningful NLP task; you can see how doing this machine-driven labeling at scale without humans could add a lot of value to enterprises that work with a lot of textual data. Of course, to train such a model in the first place, you do need to have a lot of humans that annotate textual data. And you may need humans in the loop to deal with edge cases in production. You are never really human-free, but perhaps you could ultimately get to a mostly human-free process.

Named entity linking

Another complex yet very useful NLP task in the enterprise is *named entity linking* (NEL). NEL resolves a textual entity to a unique identifier in a knowledge base. In other words, NEL resolves the entity in your source text to a canonical version in a knowledge database. Let's try to link all entities that are named persons to Google's

Knowledge Graph. We will make a Google Knowledge Graph API call to perform this named entity linking.[9]

Here is the function to perform this API call:

```
# Import libraries
import requests

# Define Google Knowledge Graph API Result function
def returnGraphResult(query, key, entityType):
    if entityType=="PERSON":
        google = f"https://kgsearch.googleapis.com/v1/entities:search\
         ?query={query}&key={key}"
        resp = requests.get(google)
        url = resp.json()['itemListElement'][0]['result']\
         ['detailedDescription']['url']
        description = resp.json()['itemListElement'][0]['result']\
         ['detailedDescription']['articleBody']
        return url, description
    else:
        return "no_match", "no_match"
```

Let's perform entity linking on our George Washington example:

```
# Print Wikipedia descriptions and URLs for entities
for token in doc.ents:
    url, description = returnGraphResult(token.text, key, token.label_)
    print(token.text, token.label_, url, description)
```

Here is the output:

George Washington
PERSON *https://en.wikipedia.org/wiki/George_Washington* George Wash ington was an American political leader, military general, states man, and Founding Father, who also served as the first President of the United States from 1789 to 1797.

American
NORP no_match no_match

first
ORDINAL no_match no_match

the United States
GPE no_match no_match

---

9 You'll need your own Google Knowledge Graph API key (*https://oreil.ly/Juu8j*) to perform this API call on your machine. We will perform this using our own API key for illustrative purposes.

1789 to 1797
```
DATE no_match no_match
```

As you can see, George Washington is a PERSON and is linked successfully to the "George Washington" Wikipedia URL and description. The rest are not of entity type PERSON and are not linked. If desired, we could link the other named entities, such as the United States, to relevant Wikipedia articles, too.

NEL has many use cases in the enterprise, especially since the need to link information to a taxonomy comes up over and over again (e.g., linking stock tickers, pharmaceutical drugs, publicly traded companies, consumer products, etc., to canonical versions in a taxonomy or knowledge base).

Conclusion

In this chapter, we defined NLP and covered its origins, including some of the commercial applications that are popular in the enterprise today. Then, we defined some basic NLP tasks and performed them using the very performant NLP library known as spacy. You should spend more time using spacy, including reviewing documentation that is available online, to hone what you have learned in this chapter.

While the tasks we performed are very basic, when combined, NLP tasks such as tokenization, part-of-speech tagging, dependency parsing, chunking, and lemmatization make it possible for machines to perform even more complex NLP tasks such as NER and entity linking. We hope our walkthrough of these tasks helped you build some intuition on just how machines are able to unpack and process natural language, demystifying some of the space.

Today, most complex NLP applications do not require practitioners to perform these tasks manually; rather, neural networks learn to perform these tasks on their own. In the next chapter, we will dive into some of the state-of-the-art approaches using the Transformer architecture and large, pretrained language models from fast.ai and Hugging Face to show just how easy it is to get up and running with NLP today. Later in the book, we will return to the basics (which we just teased you with briefly in this chapter) and help you build more of your foundational knowledge of NLP.

## CHAPTER 2

Transformers and Transfer Learning

Now that you've been introduced to the field of natural language processing, there's something important you need to understand. It's not actually a very long journey from where you start to state of the art.

Eventually, we *will* return to the basics, discuss the fundamentals, and understand all the details, of course. But we're going to show you the promised land before we venture on the long and hard journey to get there.

One of the most important ideas to implement if you want to get deep learning working in the real world is *transfer learning*, which is the process of taking a model that has already been trained on another dataset and fine-tuning it to fit your new dataset. For example, if you're training a language model to generate compelling short stories in the style of Hemingway, you could fine-tune a model trained on a wide variety of books instead of training on just the text samples of Hemingway, of which there may not be many.

A nice analogy in object-oriented programming is the concept of inheritance in classes. Suppose we're making some sort of zoo management video game, where each animal is represented by a class. The animals have properties like weight and height, as well as functions like eat and sleep. In theory, we could just create a new class for each animal and replicate those shared functions, but in practice, we usually refactor our code so that we have a superclass for a generic animal and a subclass for each species to avoid duplication in our code, making it easier to read.

Who's That Pokémon? Language Models

A language model is a function that takes in a sequence of words and returns a probability distribution over all the possible next words in that sequence. This task is considered one of the most important in NLP because, as the reasoning goes, to predict the next word in a sentence, you *must* have a good understanding of the language. Language models learn the features and characteristics of language to guess what the next word should be after any given phrase or sentence. They are the backbone of NLP today because they do not require explicit annotations (labels) and can be trained on massive corpuses without material data preparation. Once they learn the properties of language well, language models can be fine-tuned to perform more specific NLP tasks such as text classification, which is what we're going to do in this chapter.

By training on the larger dataset, the model essentially inherits a large amount of extra knowledge, which it can use to perform better on the task you care about. From a practical standpoint, transfer learning helps you get better performing models faster since fine-tuning, if done correctly, is often computationally cheaper than training from scratch.[1]

The other big advancement we'll discuss is the use of a new kind of model architecture called the *transformer*. Training transformers can be complicated and does not always work well without some fine-tuning. So, instead of training a transformer from scratch, we'll show you the pretraining technique on another architecture, and use a popular pretrained transformer to perform inference.

When we refer to pretrained models throughout this book, we are generally referring to large, pretrained *language* models that have been trained to perform language modeling on large corpuses.

For this chapter, it's important that you have your compute environment set up since we'll be training models. Check out our GitHub page (*https://oreil.ly/UHmBF*) for more information on how to do this.

---

1 Assuming that the original dataset you're transferring *from* is much larger than the dataset you're using for fine-tuning. If your fine-tuning dataset is larger, perhaps you should be applying transfer learning the other way around! But in practice, it's very hard to prepare natural language text datasets that are of comparable size to the ones used for pretraining.

Training with fastai

First, we'll use `fastai` for transfer learning. We're going to fine-tune a language model and then transform it into a text classifier that categorizes text based on sentiment. We'll start with the simplest working implementation, and progressively train our network using the ULMFiT (*https://oreil.ly/luXdk*) technique. The following example is adapted from the official fastai documentation, and is a great demonstration of how the library makes it easy to great results very quickly.

The dataset we're going to use here is the IMDb movie review dataset. It's not very fun, but it's simple and small, which is what we want when starting off:

Using the fastai Library

`fastai` is more than your standard deep learning library. It includes tools that help you solve the problem at hand end-to-end as fast as possible. One of those tools is a built-in set of common datasets that can be easily downloaded:

```
from fastai.text.all import *
path = untar_data(URLs.IMDB)
```

We can set up our dataset and prepare for training by using the `TextDataLoad ers.from_folder` method built into `fastai`:

```
dls = TextDataLoaders.from_folder(path, valid='test')
```

Another useful method is `show_batch`, which lets us take a quick glimpse at our data to make sure everything looks OK:

```
dls.show_batch()
```

	Text	Category
0	xxbos xxmaj match 1 : xxmaj tag xxmaj team xxmaj table xxmaj match xxmaj bubba xxmaj ray and xxmaj spike xxmaj dudley vs xxmaj eddie xxmaj guerrero and xxmaj chris xxmaj benoit xxmaj bubba xxmaj ray and xxmaj spike xxmaj dudley started things off with a xxmaj tag xxmaj team xxmaj table xxmaj match against xxmaj eddie xxmaj guerrero and xxmaj chris xxmaj benoit . xxmaj according to the rules of the match , both opponents have to go through tables in order to get the win . xxmaj benoit and xxmaj guerrero heated up early on by taking turns hammering first xxmaj spike and then xxmaj bubba xxmaj ray . a xxmaj german xxunk by xxmaj benoit to xxmaj bubba took the wind out of the xxmaj dudley brother . xxmaj spike tried to help his brother , but the referee restrained him while xxmaj benoit and xxmaj guerrero	pos
1	xxbos xxmaj titanic directed by xxmaj james xxmaj cameron presents a fictional love story on the historical setting of the xxmaj titanic . xxmaj the plot is simple , xxunk , or not for those who love plots that twist and turn and keep you in suspense . xxmaj the end of the movie can be figured out within minutes of the start of the film , but the love story is an interesting one , however . xxmaj kate xxmaj winslett is wonderful as xxmaj rose , an aristocratic young lady betrothed by xxmaj cal (billy xxmaj zane) . xxmaj early on the voyage xxmaj rose meets xxmaj jack (leonardo dicaprio) , a lower class artist on his way to xxmaj america after winning his ticket aboard xxmaj titanic in a poker game . xxmaj if he wants something , he goes and gets it	pos

	Text	Category
2	xxbos xxmaj warning : xxmaj does contain spoilers . \n\n xxmaj open xxmaj your xxmaj eyes \n\n xxmaj if you have not seen this film and plan on doing so , just stop reading here and take my word for it . xxmaj you have to see this film . i have seen it four times so far and i still have n't made up my mind as to what exactly happened in the film . xxmaj that is all i am going to say because if you have not seen this film , then stop reading right now . \n\n xxmaj if you are still reading then i am going to pose some questions to you and maybe if anyone has any answers you can email me and let me know what you think . \n\n i remember my xxmaj grade 11 xxmaj english teacher quite well . xxmaj	pos
3	xxbos i thought that xxup rotj was clearly the best out of the three xxmaj star xxmaj wars movies . i find it surprising that xxup rotj is considered the weakest installment in the xxmaj trilogy by many who have voted . xxmaj to me it seemed like xxup rotj was the best because it had the most profound plot , the most suspense , surprises , most xxunk the ending) and definitely the most episodic movie . i personally like the xxmaj empire xxmaj strikes xxmaj back a lot also but i think it is slightly less good than than xxup rotj since it was slower - moving , was not as episodic , and i just did not feel as much suspense or emotion as i did with the third movie . \n\n xxmaj it also seems like to me that after reading these surprising reviews that	pos
4	xxbos xxup myra xxup breckinridge is one of those rare films that established its place in film history immediately . xxmaj praise for the film was absolutely nonexistent , even from the people involved in making it . xxmaj this film was loathed from day one . xxmaj while every now and then one will come across some maverick who will praise the film on philosophical grounds (aggressive feminism or the courage to tackle the issue of xxunk) , the film has not developed a cult following like some notorious flops do . xxmaj it 's not hailed as a misunderstood masterpiece like xxup scarface , or trotted out to be ridiculed as a camp classic like xxup showgirls . \n\n xxmaj undoubtedly the reason is that the film , though outrageously awful , is not lovable , or even likable . xxup myra xxup breckinridge is just	neg
5	xxbos xxmaj my xxmaj comments for xxup vivah : - xxmaj its a charming , idealistic love story starring xxmaj shahid xxmaj kapoor and xxmaj amrita xxmaj rao . xxmaj the film takes us back to small pleasures like the bride and bridegroom 's families sleeping on the floor , playing games together , their friendly banter and mutual respect . xxmaj vivah is about the sanctity of marriage and the importance of commitment between two individuals . xxmaj yes , the central romance is naively visualized . xxmaj but the sneaked - in romantic moments between the to - be - married couple and their stubborn resistance to modern courtship games makes you crave for the idealism . xxmaj the film predictably concludes with the marriage and the groom , on the wedding night , tells his new bride who suffers from burn injuries : " come let me	pos
6	xxbos xxmaj that word ' true ' in this film 's title got my alarm bells ringing . xxmaj they rang louder when a title card referred to xxmaj america 's xxmaj civil xxmaj war as the ' war xxmaj between the xxmaj states ' (the xxunk preferred by die - hard southerners) . xxmaj jesse xxmaj james -- thief , slave - holder and murderer -- is described as a quiet , gentle farm boy . \n\n xxmaj how dishonest is this movie ? xxmaj there is xxup no mention of slavery , far less of the documented fact that xxmaj jesse xxmaj james 's poor xxunk mother owned slaves before the war , and that xxmaj jesse and his brother xxmaj frank actively fought to preserve slavery . xxmaj according to this movie , all those xxmaj civil xxmaj war soldiers were really fighting to decide	neg
7	xxbos " fever xxmaj pitch " is n't a bad film ; it 's a terrible film . \n\n xxmaj is it possible xxmaj american movie audiences and critics are so numbed and lobotomized by the excrement that xxmaj hollywood churns out that they 'll praise to the skies even a mediocre film with barely any laughs ? xxmaj that 's the only reason i can think of why this horrible romantic comedy (and i use that term loosely because there 's nothing funny in this film) is getting good reviews . \n\n i sat through this film stunned that screenwriters xxmaj lowell xxmaj ganz and xxmaj babaloo xxmaj mandel would even for an instant think their script was funny . \n\n xxmaj the brilliant xxmaj nick xxmaj hornby usually translates well to film . xxmaj he adapted " fever xxmaj pitch " for a xxmaj british film	neg

	Text	Category
8	xxbos xxmaj to be a xxmaj buster xxmaj keaton fan is to have your heart broken on a regular basis . xxmaj most of us first encounter xxmaj keaton in one of the brilliant feature films from his great period of independent production : ' the xxmaj general ' , ' the xxmaj navigator ' , ' sherlock xxmaj jnr ' . xxmaj we recognise him as the greatest figure in the entire history of film comedy , and we want to see more of his movies . xxmaj here the heartbreak begins . xxmaj after ' steamboat xxmaj bill xxmaj jnr ' , xxmaj keaton 's brother - in - law xxmaj joseph xxmaj xxunk pressured him into signing a contract that put xxmaj keaton under the control of xxup mgm . xxmaj keaton became just one more actor for hire , performing someone else 's scripts . xxmaj	neg

If you looked closely, you might have noticed a bunch of strange words like "xxmaj" and "xxbos" interspersed throughout the text samples. These are not actually part of the original samples, but were added in through a process called tokenization, which we'll discuss in Chapter 4. These tokens represent special words that are designed to be interpreted by the language model. For example, "xxmaj" indicates that the next word should start with a capitalized character.

fastai uses an object called a Learner for doing pretty much everything. We can construct one for text classification in one line of code:

```
learn = text_classifier_learner(dls, AWD_LSTM, drop_mult=0.5, metrics=accuracy)
```

Instead of the transformer model that we've been raving about so far in this book (and will continue to discuss), we're going to use the AWD-LSTM (*https://oreil.ly/ K2a6J*) architecture for now, since it's easier and faster to train.

There are a few other details: drop_mult is a hyperparameter that controls the magnitude of all dropouts in that model, and we use accuracy to track down how well we are doing. But you don't need to worry too much about these parameters just yet.

With the Learner defined, we can now fine-tune our pretrained model, using a method with an unsurprising name:

```
learn.fine_tune(4, 1e-2)
```

epoch	train_loss	valid_loss	accuracy	time
0	0.587251	0.386230	0.828960	01:35

epoch	train_loss	valid_loss	accuracy	time
0	0.307347	0.263843	0.892800	03:03
1	0.215867	0.226208	0.911800	02:55
2	0.155399	0.231144	0.913960	03:12
3	0.129277	0.200941	0.925920	03:01

```
learn.fine_tune(4, 1e-2)
```

epoch	train_loss	valid_loss	accuracy	time
0	0.594912	0.407416	0.823640	01:35

epoch	train_loss	valid_loss	accuracy	time
0	0.268259	0.316242	0.876000	03:03
1	0.184861	0.246242	0.898080	03:10
2	0.136392	0.220086	0.918200	03:16
3	0.106423	0.191092	0.931360	03:15

Ninety-three percent accuracy looks good! But let's see how well it's actually doing:

```
learn.show_results()
```

	text	category	category_
0	xxbos xxmaj there 's a sign on xxmaj the xxmaj lost xxmaj highway that says : \n\n * major xxup spoilers xxup ahead * \n\n (but you already knew that , did n't you ?) \n\n xxmaj since there 's a great deal of people that apparently did not get the point of this movie , xxmaj i 'd like to contribute my interpretation of why the plot makes perfect sense . xxmaj as others have pointed out , one single viewing of this movie is not sufficient . xxmaj if you have the xxup dvd of xxup md , you can " cheat " by looking at xxmaj david xxmaj lynch 's " top 10 xxmaj hints to xxmaj unlocking xxup md " (but only upon second or third viewing , please .) ;) \n\n xxmaj first of all , xxmaj mulholland xxmaj drive is	pos	pos
1	xxbos (some spoilers included :) \n\n xxmaj although , many commentators have called this film surreal , the term fits poorly here . xxmaj to quote from xxmaj encyclopedia xxmaj xxunk 's , surreal means : \n\n " fantastic or incongruous imagery " : xxmaj one need n't explain to the unimaginative how many ways a plucky ten - year - old boy at large and seeking his fortune in the driver 's seat of a red xxmaj mustang could be fantastic : those curious might read xxmaj james xxmaj kincaid ; but if you asked said lad how he were incongruous behind the wheel of a sports car , he 'd surely protest , " no way ! " xxmaj what fantasies and incongruities the film offers mostly appear within the first fifteen minutes . xxmaj thereafter we get more iterations of the same , in an	pos	neg
2	xxbos xxmaj hearkening back to those " good xxmaj old xxmaj days " of 1971 , we can vividly recall when we were treated with a whole xxmaj season of xxmaj charles xxmaj chaplin at the xxmaj cinema . xxmaj that 's what the promotional guy called it when we saw him on somebody 's old talk show . (we ca n't recall just whose it was ; either xxup merv xxup griffin or xxup woody xxup woodbury , one or the other !) xxmaj the guest talked about xxmaj sir xxmaj charles ' career and how his films had been out of circulation ever since the 1952 exclusion of the former " little xxmaj tramp ' from xxmaj los xxmaj xxunk xxmaj xxunk on the grounds of his being an " undesirable xxmaj alien " . (no xxmaj schultz , he 's xxup not from another	pos	pos

	text	category	category_
3	xxbos " buffalo xxmaj bill , xxmaj hero of the xxmaj far xxmaj west " director xxmaj mario xxmaj costa 's unsavory xxmaj spaghetti western " the xxmaj beast " with xxmaj klaus xxmaj kinski could only have been produced in xxmaj europe . xxmaj hollywood would never dared to have made a western about a sexual predator on the prowl as the protagonist of a movie . xxmaj never mind that xxmaj kinski is ideally suited to the role of ' crazy ' xxmaj johnny . xxmaj he plays an individual entirely without sympathy who is ironically dressed from head to toe in a white suit , pants , and hat . xxmaj this low - budget oater has nothing appetizing about it . xxmaj the typically breathtaking xxmaj spanish scenery around xxmaj almeria is nowhere in evidence . xxmaj instead , xxmaj costa and his director of photography	pos	pos
4	xxbos xxmaj if you 've seen the trailer for this movie , you pretty much know what to expect , because what you see here is what you get . xxmaj and even if you have n't seen the previews , it wo n't take you long to pick up on what you 're in for-- specifically , a good time and plenty of xxunk from this clever satire of ` reality xxup tv ' shows and ` buddy xxmaj cop ' movies , ` showtime , ' directed by xxmaj tom xxmaj dey , starring xxmaj robert xxmaj de xxmaj niro and xxmaj eddie xxmaj murphy . \n\n\t xxmaj mitch xxmaj preston (de xxmaj niro) is a detective with the xxup l.a.p.d . , and he 's good at what he does ; but working a case one night , things suddenly go south when another cop	pos	pos
5	xxbos * xxmaj some spoilers * \n\n xxmaj this movie is sometimes subtitled " life xxmaj everlasting . " xxmaj that 's often taken as reference to the final scene , but more accurately describes how dead and buried this once - estimable series is after this sloppy and illogical send - off . \n\n xxmaj there 's a " hey kids , let 's put on a show air " about this telemovie , which can be endearing in spots . xxmaj some fans will feel like insiders as they enjoy picking out all the various cameo appearances . xxmaj co - writer , co - producer xxmaj tom xxmaj fontana and his pals pack the goings - on with friends and favorites from other shows , as well as real xxmaj baltimore personages . \n\n xxmaj that 's on top of the returns of virtually all the members	neg	neg
6	xxbos (caution : several spoilers) \n\n xxmaj someday , somewhere , there 's going to be a post - apocalyptic movie made that does n't stink . xxmaj unfortunately , xxup the xxup postman is not that movie , though i have to give it credit for trying . \n\n xxmaj kevin xxmaj costner plays somebody credited only as " the xxmaj postman . " xxmaj he 's not actually a postman , just a wanderer with a mule in the wasteland of a western xxmaj america devastated by some unspecified catastrophe . xxmaj he trades with isolated villages by performing xxmaj shakespeare . xxmaj suddenly a pack of bandits called the xxmaj holnists , the self - declared warlords of the xxmaj west , descend upon a village that xxmaj costner 's visiting , and their evil leader xxmaj gen . xxmaj bethlehem (will xxmaj patton	neg	neg
7	xxbos xxmaj in a style reminiscent of the best of xxmaj david xxmaj lean , this romantic love story sweeps across the screen with epic proportions equal to the vast desert regions against which it is set . xxmaj it 's a film which purports that one does not choose love , but rather that it 's love that does the choosing , regardless of who , where or when ; and furthermore , that it 's a matter of the heart often contingent upon prevailing conditions and circumstances . xxmaj and thus is the situation in ` the xxmaj english xxmaj patient , ' directed by xxmaj anthony xxmaj minghella , the story of two people who discover passion and true love in the most inopportune of places and times , proving that when it is predestined , love will find a way . \n\n xxmaj it 's xxup	pos	pos

	text	category	category_
8	xxbos xxmaj no one is going to mistake xxup the xxup squall for a good movie , but it sure is a memorable one . xxmaj once you 've taken in xxmaj myrna xxmaj loy 's performance as xxmaj nubi the hot - blooded gypsy girl you 're not likely to forget the experience . xxmaj when this film was made the exotically beautiful xxmaj miss xxmaj loy was still being cast as foreign vixens , often xxmaj asian and usually sinister . xxmaj she 's certainly an eyeful here . xxmaj it appears that her skin was darkened and her hair was curled . xxmaj in most scenes she 's barefoot and wearing little more than a skirt and a loose - fitting peasant blouse , while in one scene she wears nothing but a patterned towel . i suppose xxmaj i 'm focusing on xxmaj miss xxmaj loy	neg	neg

We can also run prediction on individual sentences one at a time:

```
learn.predict("That movie was wicked cool!")

('pos', tensor(1), tensor([0.0092, 0.9908]))
```

Our model predicts that the review is positive, as expected.

 fastai also has another way to load datasets and run this pipeline —the data block API. This can be very useful if your data is not in a standard format like IMDb was, in the preceding example. For more information on the data block, data loaders, and more, see the fastai documentation (*https://docs.fast.ai*).

ULMFiT for Transfer Learning

The language model we used in the previous section was trained to guess the next word on a set of Wikipedia articles after reading all the words before. We got great results by directly fine-tuning this language model to a movie review classifier, but with one extra step, we can do even better.

Wikipedia English is slightly different from IMDb English. So instead of jumping directly to the classifier, we could fine-tune our pretrained language model to the IMDb dataset and then use *that* as the base for our classifier instead of the Wikipedia language model.

This intuitively makes sense—if you, as a literate human being, get some context on what movie reviews generally sound like, you'd probably do a better job of classifying them. It's kind of like getting access to the SAT reading passages a few days before you actually take the test. Only here, we won't call the language model out for cheating, since we're friends.[2]

---

2 See, we said it right here. Please don't eat us, robot overlords in the future.

But beyond that, another very important reason why this is useful is that we often have more *raw* data than we have *labeled* text data. Labeling is expensive and generally requires human time and effort, so it's not uncommon to have a large database of text records where only a small subset of them are used for, say, document tagging. But with this fine-tuning approach, we can still use the unlabeled data to fine-tune the *language model* even before we train the classifier.

At the risk of dragging on a flawed analogy, this is almost like getting access to years of previous SAT passages. None of them will show up on the test *exactly*, but practicing them will help get a sense of what the SAT is like.

This approach is called ULMFiT, introduced by Jeremy Howard[3] and Sebastian Ruder in 2018. The process is summarized in Figure 2-1.

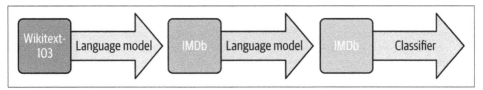

Figure 2-1. ULMFiT

Arrows and boxes make everything so much simpler, don't they?

Since we already have the pretrained Wikipedia language model, we can start with step 2 of the pipeline in Figure 2-1—fine-tuning the IMDb language model.

Fine-Tuning a Language Model on IMDb

We can get our text data in a `DataLoaders` suitable for language modeling very easily:

```
dls_lm = TextDataLoaders.from_folder(path, is_lm=True, valid_pct=0.1)
dls_lm.show_batch(max_n=5)
```

	text	text_
0	xxbos xxmaj about thirty minutes into the film , i thought this was one of the weakest " xxunk ever because it had the usual beginning (a murder happening , then xxmaj columbo coming , inspecting everything and interrogating the main suspect) squared ! xxmaj it was boring because i thought i knew everything already . \n\n xxmaj but then there was a surprising twist that turned this episode into	xxmaj about thirty minutes into the film , i thought this was one of the weakest " xxunk ever because it had the usual beginning (a murder happening , then xxmaj columbo coming , inspecting everything and interrogating the main suspect) squared ! xxmaj it was boring because i thought i knew everything already . \n\n xxmaj but then there was a surprising twist that turned this episode into a

---

3 Who also happens to be the creator of `fastai`!

	text	text_
1	yeon . xxmaj these two girls were magical on the screen . i will certainly be looking into their other films . xxmaj xxunk xxmaj jeong - ah is xxunk cheerful and hauntingly evil as the stepmother . xxmaj finally , xxmaj xxunk - su xxmaj kim gives an excellent performance as the weary , broken father . \n\n i truly love this film . xxmaj if you have yet to see	. xxmaj these two girls were magical on the screen . i will certainly be looking into their other films . xxmaj xxunk xxmaj jeong - ah is xxunk cheerful and hauntingly evil as the stepmother . xxmaj finally , xxmaj xxunk - su xxmaj kim gives an excellent performance as the weary , broken father . \n\n i truly love this film . xxmaj if you have yet to see '
2	tends to be tedious whenever there are n't any hideous monsters on display . xxmaj luckily the gutsy killings and eerie set designs (by no less than xxmaj bill xxmaj paxton !) compensate for a lot ! a nine - headed expedition is send (at hyper speed) to the unexplored regions of space to find out what happened to a previously vanished spaceship and its crew . xxmaj	to be tedious whenever there are n't any hideous monsters on display . xxmaj luckily the gutsy killings and eerie set designs (by no less than xxmaj bill xxmaj paxton !) compensate for a lot ! a nine - headed expedition is send (at hyper speed) to the unexplored regions of space to find out what happened to a previously vanished spaceship and its crew . xxmaj bad
3	movie just sort of meanders around and nothing happens (i do n't mean in terms of plot - no plot is fine , but no action ? xxmaj come on .) xxmaj in hindsight , i should have expected this - after all , how much can really happen between 4 teens and a bear ? xxmaj so although special effects , acting , etc are more or less on	just sort of meanders around and nothing happens (i do n't mean in terms of plot - no plot is fine , but no action ? xxmaj come on .) xxmaj in hindsight , i should have expected this - after all , how much can really happen between 4 teens and a bear ? xxmaj so although special effects , acting , etc are more or less on par
4	greetings again from the darkness . xxmaj writer / xxmaj director (and xxmaj wes xxmaj anderson collaborator) xxmaj noah xxmaj baumbach presents a semi - autobiographical therapy session where he unleashes the anguish and turmoil that has carried over from his childhood . xxmaj the result is an amazing insight into what many people go through in a desperate attempt to try and make their family work . \n\n xxmaj	again from the darkness . xxmaj writer / xxmaj director (and xxmaj wes xxmaj anderson collaborator) xxmaj noah xxmaj baumbach presents a semi - autobiographical therapy session where he unleashes the anguish and turmoil that has carried over from his childhood . xxmaj the result is an amazing insight into what many people go through in a desperate attempt to try and make their family work . \n\n xxmaj the

Then we have a convenience method to directly grab a `Learner` from it, using the `AWD_LSTM` architecture like before. We use accuracy and perplexity as metrics (the latter is the exponential of the loss), and we set a default weight decay of 0.1. `to_fp16` puts the `Learner` in mixed precision, which is going to help speed up training on GPUs that have Tensor Cores:

```
learn = language_model_learner(
    dls_lm, AWD_LSTM, metrics=[accuracy, Perplexity()],
    path=path, wd=0.1).to_fp16()
```

By default, a pretrained Learner is in a frozen state, meaning that only the head of the model will train while the body stays frozen. We show you what is behind the fine_tune method here and use a fit_one_cycle method to fit the model:

```
learn.fit_one_cycle(1, 1e-2)
```

epoch	train_loss	valid_loss	accuracy	perplexity	time
0	4.120048	3.912788	0.299565	50.038246	11:39

This model takes a while to train, so it's a good opportunity to talk about saving intermediary results.

You can easily save the state of your model like so:

```
learn.save('1epoch')
```

This will create a file in learn.path/models/ named *1epoch.pth*. If you want to load your model on another machine after creating your Learner the same way, or resume training later, you can load the content of this file with:

```
learn = learn.load('1epoch')
```

We can then fine-tune the model after unfreezing:

```
learn.unfreeze()
learn.fit_one_cycle(10, 1e-3)
```

epoch	train_loss	valid_loss	accuracy	perplexity	time
0	3.893486	3.772820	0.317104	43.502548	12:37
1	3.820479	3.717197	0.323790	41.148880	12:30
2	3.735622	3.659760	0.330321	38.851997	12:09
3	3.677086	3.624794	0.333960	37.516987	12:12
4	3.636646	3.601300	0.337017	36.645859	12:05
5	3.553636	3.584241	0.339355	36.026001	12:04
6	3.507634	3.571892	0.341353	35.583862	12:08
7	3.444101	3.565988	0.342194	35.374371	12:08
8	3.398597	3.566283	0.342647	35.384815	12:11
9	3.375563	3.568166	0.342528	35.451500	12:05

Once this is done, we save all of our model except the final layer that converts activations to probabilities of picking each token in our vocabulary. The model, not including the final layer, is called the *encoder*. We can save it with save_encoder:

```
learn.save_encoder('finetuned')
```

Who's That Pokémon? The Encoder

The encoder is the portion of the NLP model that maps input text to some tensors that we use to solve NLP tasks. The encoder itself is not specific to any task, and typically is used in conjunction with a "decoder" or "head" that is used to map the vectors onto some task-specific data structure.

Before using this to fine-tune a classifier on the reviews, we can use our model to generate random reviews—since it's trained to guess what the next word of the sentence is, we can use it to write new reviews:

```
TEXT = "I liked this movie because"
N_WORDS = 40
N_SENTENCES = 2
preds = [learn.predict(TEXT, N_WORDS, temperature=0.75)
         for _ in range(N_SENTENCES)]

print("\n".join(preds))
```

```
i liked this movie because of its story and characters . The story line was very
  > strong , very good for a sci - fi film . The main character , Alucard , was
  > very well developed and brought the whole story
i liked this movie because i like the idea of the premise of the movie , the (
  > very ) convenient virus ( which , when you have to kill a few people , the "
  > evil " machine has to be used to protect
```

With the language model fine-tuned on movie reviews, we can now modify it to *classify* them. The idea is that at this point, if the model is "smart enough" to predict the next word, it *must* be able to perform a simple positive/negative classification.

Training a Text Classifier

Using the same method as before, we can load the IMDb dataset again, but this time, we'll be using it for text classification. Note that we pass in the vocabulary as a parameter. This is to make sure that the text classifier understands the same set of words that the language model was trained on:

```
dls_clas = TextDataLoaders.from_folder(
    untar_data(URLs.IMDB), valid='test',
    text_vocab=dls_lm.vocab)
```

Then we can define our text classifier like before:

```
learn = text_classifier_learner(dls, AWD_LSTM, drop_mult=0.5, metrics=accuracy)
```

The difference is that before training it, we load the previous encoder:

```
learn = learn.load_encoder('finetuned')
```

The last step is to train with discriminative learning rates and *gradual unfreezing*. In computer vision, we often unfreeze the model all at once, but for NLP classifiers, we find that unfreezing a few layers at a time makes a real difference:

```
learn.fit_one_cycle(1, 2e-2)
```

epoch	train_loss	valid_loss	accuracy	time
0	0.347427	0.184480	0.929320	00:33

In just one epoch we get the same result as our training in the first section—not too bad! We can pass -2 to `freeze_to` to freeze all except the last two parameter groups:

```
learn.freeze_to(-2)
learn.fit_one_cycle(1, slice(1e-2/(2.6**4),1e-2))
```

epoch	train_loss	valid_loss	accuracy	time
0	0.247763	0.171683	0.934640	00:37

Then we can unfreeze a bit more, and continue training:

```
learn.freeze_to(-3)
learn.fit_one_cycle(1, slice(5e-3/(2.6**4),5e-3))
```

epoch	train_loss	valid_loss	accuracy	time
0	0.193377	0.156696	0.941200	00:45

Finally, we can unfreeze the entire model, and let it train all the layers to get a final boost in accuracy:

```
learn.unfreeze()
learn.fit_one_cycle(2, slice(1e-3/(2.6**4),1e-3))
```

epoch	train_loss	valid_loss	accuracy	time
0	0.172888	0.153770	0.943120	01:01
1	0.161492	0.155567	0.942640	00:57

Now, you have a text classification model that can accurately predict if a movie review has positive or negative sentiment based on the raw text content of the review alone. With an understanding of the `fastai` APIs, you should now be able to implement your own text classifier on a dataset of your choice.

While the IMDb dataset was fairly simple, many real-world NLP problems today can be formulated as text classification problems. Some of the things you can do with text classification include:

- Predicting the programming language of some source code
- Building a simple email spam classifier
- Improving the functionality of an automated content moderation bot for online chats or forums
- Categorizing documents based on their language[4]

One of the best parts about text classification is that there's a single, simple, interpretable metric to optimize—accuracy. So not only can you solve these tasks, but you can also know how well you're doing using statistics that many people are familiar with.

While the IMDb model we built just now does a wonderful job, it's perhaps not super impressive. We've had pretty good spam classifiers since the dawn of the dinosaurs, so binary predictions on text is not something you might associate with the glorious future we had previously sold you on. But it turns out that this idea of a language model is so powerful that it has become the poster child for NLP today.

To illustrate this, let's give a language model on its own, with no additional training or fine-tuning, a chance to flex its muscles.

Inference with Hugging Face

Now that we know how to train language models, we could conceptually train a very large one on a lot of data and get it to produce quite accurate-sounding text. Here, we'll use the Hugging Face library to get prediction samples from a language model trained using a procedure similar to the one we used in the previous section:

```
import torch
from transformers import GPT2Tokenizer, GPT2LMHeadModel

# Load pretrained model tokenizer (vocabulary)
tokenizer = GPT2Tokenizer.from_pretrained('gpt2')

# Encode a text inputs
text = "With great power comes great "
indexed_tokens = tokenizer.encode(text)

# Convert indexed tokens in a PyTorch tensor
tokens_tensor = torch.tensor([indexed_tokens])
```

---

4 To do this well, you need a powerful tokenizer that can recognize text encoding in many languages.

This code snippet initializes a *tokenizer*, which is a function that takes in strings as input and returns arrays of numbers that are easier for the model to interpret. We'll be covering tokenizers in much more detail in the next chapter, but for now, if you want a quick look into what our model sees, try printing tokens_tensor:

```
print(tokens_tensor)

tensor([[3152, 1049, 1176, 2058, 1049]])
```

Now, let's do the actual inference, which is, again, just a few lines of code thanks to the amazing Hugging Face transformers library:

```
# Load pretrained model (weights)
model = GPT2LMHeadModel.from_pretrained('gpt2')

# Set the model in evaluation mode to deactivate the DropOut modules
# This is IMPORTANT to have reproducible results during evaluation!
model.eval()

# Predict all tokens
with torch.no_grad():
    outputs = model(tokens_tensor)
    predictions = outputs[0]

# Get the predicted next subword
predicted_index = torch.argmax(predictions[0, -1, :]).item()
predicted_text = tokenizer.decode(indexed_tokens + [predicted_index])
print(predicted_text)

INFO:transformers.configuration_utils:Model config GPT2Config {
  "activation_function": "gelu_new",
  "architectures": [
    "GPT2LMHeadModel"
  ],
  "attn_pdrop": 0.1,
  "bos_token_id": 50256,
  "embd_pdrop": 0.1,
  "eos_token_id": 50256,
  "initializer_range": 0.02,
  "layer_norm_epsilon": 1e-05,
  "model_type": "gpt2",
  "n_ctx": 1024,
  "n_embd": 768,
  "n_head": 12,
  "n_layer": 12,
  "n_positions": 1024,
  "resid_pdrop": 0.1,
  "summary_activation": null,
  "summary_first_dropout": 0.1,
  "summary_proj_to_labels": true,
  "summary_type": "cls_index",
  "summary_use_proj": true,
  "task_specific_params": {
```

```
      "text-generation": {
        "do_sample": true,
        "max_length": 50
      }
    },
    "vocab_size": 50257
  }

  INFO:transformers.modeling_utils:Weights of GPT2LMHeadModel not initialized from
  > pretrained model: ['h.0.attn.masked_bias', 'h.1.attn.masked_bias',
  > 'h.2.attn.masked_bias', 'h.3.attn.masked_bias', 'h.4.attn.masked_bias',
  > 'h.5.attn.masked_bias', 'h.6.attn.masked_bias', 'h.7.attn.masked_bias',
  > 'h.8.attn.masked_bias', 'h.9.attn.masked_bias', 'h.10.attn.masked_bias',
  > 'h.11.attn.masked_bias', 'lm_head.weight']

  With great power comes great responsibility
```

Nice! It looks like whatever we just ran was able to re-create the wisdom of Uncle Ben[5] in just a few lines of code!

And to be clear, this wasn't just some simple lookup, database search, or something like that. This was an actual state-of-the-art neural network that after reading large amounts of text on the internet, was able to complete sentences based on the "knowledge" it gained. Pretty cool, huh?

But without context, this is all just a black box that you throw sentences into. So now, let's break down each line of code in the block we just ran to get a really good idea of what's going on.

Loading Models

First, we load a pretrained model. This is the single most important step for transfer learning. It downloads the model that we're going to use to make predictions from somewhere on the internet and loads it in the right format into an object in our code. All of that functionality is thankfully packed into this one line of code:

```
model = GPT2LMHeadModel.from_pretrained('gpt2')

INFO:transformers.configuration_utils:Model config GPT2Config {
  "activation_function": "gelu_new",
  "architectures": [
    "GPT2LMHeadModel"
  ],
  "attn_pdrop": 0.1,
  "bos_token_id": 50256,
  "embd_pdrop": 0.1,
```

---

5 A character from the *Spider-Man* comic book series, who once said, "With great power comes great responsibility," just like our language model did!

```
    "eos_token_id": 50256,
    "initializer_range": 0.02,
    "layer_norm_epsilon": 1e-05,
    "model_type": "gpt2",
    "n_ctx": 1024,
    "n_embd": 768,
    "n_head": 12,
    "n_layer": 12,
    "n_positions": 1024,
    "resid_pdrop": 0.1,
    "summary_activation": null,
    "summary_first_dropout": 0.1,
    "summary_proj_to_labels": true,
    "summary_type": "cls_index",
    "summary_use_proj": true,
    "task_specific_params": {
      "text-generation": {
        "do_sample": true,
        "max_length": 50
      }
    },
    "vocab_size": 50257
}

INFO:transformers.modeling_utils:Weights of GPT2LMHeadModel not initialized from
 > pretrained model: ['h.0.attn.masked_bias', 'h.1.attn.masked_bias',
 > 'h.2.attn.masked_bias', 'h.3.attn.masked_bias', 'h.4.attn.masked_bias',
 > 'h.5.attn.masked_bias', 'h.6.attn.masked_bias', 'h.7.attn.masked_bias',
 > 'h.8.attn.masked_bias', 'h.9.attn.masked_bias', 'h.10.attn.masked_bias',
 > 'h.11.attn.masked_bias', 'lm_head.weight']
```

Most deep learning libraries package this model-loading functionality neatly into a simple function. It's the last thing you'll have to worry about.

The specific model we're loading here is unimportant at this stage, but just so you know, it's called GPT-2, which was really revolutionary when it came out and basically broke the internet. You can read more about it in an article (*https://oreil.ly/aT5AG*) that Ajay wrote in 2019, but we'll talk about it in this book as well, in Chapter 9.

Loading Models

Loading models to a variable named model, regardless of the task or domain, is extremely common in deep learning, so keep that in mind when you're browsing notebooks or code samples online.

Next we run this little line of code, which tells our model that we're not training now and are instead going to make predictions (i.e., perform inference):

```
model.eval()
```

There are a few things that change internally in the model object when we call this line,[6] allowing us to generate predictions from the model. Again, this is not the most important line for what we're doing now, but make sure that you call this function whenever you would like to generate predictions. Running this line in a notebook will also print out all the layers of the model in the standard PyTorch format, so maybe scroll through that if you're feeling curious.

With the weights downloaded, the model loaded into memory, and the model object set into evaluation mode, it's time to crank out some output from our lean,[7] mean, text-generating machine.

Generating Predictions

We're going to group the next three lines together, since they work as a block:

```
with torch.no_grad():
    outputs = model(tokens_tensor)
    predictions = outputs[0]
```

The first line, with torch.no_grad():, tells PyTorch to run the lines in that indent block in the torch.no_grad() context, which means PyTorch won't calculate the gradients, or backward pass, for the model. If you're not familiar with backpropagation, or not entirely clear why gradients are calculated in the first place, refer to the resources we have in the introduction. Strictly speaking, we don't *need* to turn off gradient computation, but this saves time, memory, and compute, and makes the inference run faster.

In the torch.no_grad() context, we then run a forward pass. As always, PyTorch makes this extremely simple. Just call model as a function, with the tokens_tensor we prepared as the input.

But wait, wasn't model an object with the pretrained weights that we loaded earlier? How is it also a function?

---

6 Primarily, we disable the DropOut and BatchNorm layers, which are only useful during training.

7 OK, maybe this phrase is not applicable to GPT-2 specifically, but when we all have computers that are 300 times faster than what we have today, this adjective will be accurate.

Python Dunder Methods

In Python, you can actually do this! You have to define a __call__ method in your class, which is a special function called a *dunder method*. Python has a lot of these cool dunder functions, some of which you've likely encountered before, like __init__, which lets you set up a constructor for your class, and __len__, which lets you define a "length" property for your objects that you can access via the len() function. Python dunder methods allow you to define a lot of cool functionality for your custom classes, such as addition, equality, and more.

If you define a function called __call__() in your Python class, you can then treat instances of your class as functions, and the __call__() function will be invoked every time you do so. We'll soon talk about PyTorch nn.Module objects, which are the building blocks for neural nets. The nn.Module class implements the __call__ function by default. Therefore, every PyTorch model (and submodule) can also be called as a function, which can make your code very neat and tidy. This is why we can both define the model variable and call it as we would for a function at the same time.

If you're interested in learning more about Python dunder methods, check out this tutorial (*https://oreil.ly/LqU6v*) or read more online (there are plenty of great resources one search away).

Calling model(input_tensor), in general, will return a torch.tensor object with the predictions. But in this case, the Hugging Face library actually gives us a lot of other items as well. In this case, model(tokens_tensor) will return a tuple, where the first element is the predictions tensor. Let's quickly confirm all of this by checking a few lengths and shapes:

```
len(outputs)
outputs[0].shape
torch.Size([1, 5, 50257])
```

This checks out, because according to the Hugging Face transformers documentation, the predictions tensor is supposed to have shape (batch_size, sequence_length, config.vocab_size). Here, the batch size is 1, since we're only passing in one sentence. The sequence length should be 5, which makes sense if you take a look at the line where we define the input sentence, which had five words (space delimited substrings) in the string:

```
text = "With great power comes great "
```

The value of 50257 for the vocabulary size seems accurate, but this is something we could always double-check by going through the documentation for this model.

We can't emphasize enough the importance of this technique of checking the size, shape, and dimensions of torch.tensors. It's one of the most effective ways of debugging your model. Hopefully, as you start training more complex models and building your own architectures from scratch, this will come naturally. But until then, always remember to try to check the size with .size and reason through what's going on in your model.

Since it seems like outputs[0] is what we want, we'll assign it to the variable predic tions. Putting these together and wrapping them in the torch.no_grad() context gives us that mini-block of code that we had earlier:

```
with torch.no_grad():
    outputs = model(tokens_tensor)
    predictions = outputs[0]
```

predictions is a torch.tensor with values that describe the probability of each word. Remember, one of the dimensions of this torch.tensor is the size of the vocabulary (i.e., the number of possible words that the model could predict). What we want now is the word that is mostly likely to come next in our sentence. We grab this by using the argmax function, which gets the index of the largest value in the array:

```
predicted_index = torch.argmax(predictions[0, -1, :]).item()
```

To ensure that we're absolutely clear on what exactly we're doing, let's also quickly break down the way we index predictions. It's a three-dimensional tensor, so we specify three indices. The first, along the batch dimension, is 0. Since we're not running batch predictions, there's only one element in this axis, so it's what we pick. Along the sequence length dimension, we pick the last element. We do this because we want to predict the last word in the sentence we passed in. The last index is :, which means we want to grab everything. We need all the elements along the vocabulary dimension to calculate which one is most likely.

Finally, we decode the index we got into a word using the tokenizer.decode() function. This is just a simple lookup:

```
predicted_text = tokenizer.decode(indexed_tokens + [predicted_index])
print(predicted_text)
```

And there we have it! Re-creating wisdom in just a few lines of code.

Conclusion

In Chapter 8, we'll try putting these ideas together to develop a technique that utilizes both transformers and transfer learning to create an incredibly powerful set of models that can solve the tasks we just demonstrated, as well as many more.

There's a lot in this chapter that we haven't explained yet. We've intentionally left out a lot of details, such as what exactly a model is/does, how the tokenizer is implemented in code, and perhaps most importantly, how to use the pretrained model for transfer learning.

Don't worry, though: we'll eventually get to all that. The goal of this chapter was to help you understand some of the important components of an NLP pipeline by running code and seeing results in real time. To test your understanding of the material so far, try to use a different language model, swap out the prompt, and see if you can get the model to predict a popular quote, phrase, or idiom. Note that to do this, you might need to swap out the tokenizer as well.

Once you're able to perform these tasks, you should be ready to move on to the next chapter, in which we formally introduce some of the most popular NLP applications today and build a few together.

## CHAPTER 3

NLP Tasks and Applications

In Chapter 2, we gave you a gentle introduction to language models and fine-tuning. Now, let's explore more of what fine-tuning can actually be used *for*. It is good for more than just generating better domain-specific language models, as we alluded to in the previous chapter. Fine-tuning can be used to solve meaningful real-world tasks, which serve as the building blocks of complex real-world NLP applications.

In this chapter, we will officially introduce several of these "meaningful real-world tasks" and present several popular benchmarks, such as GLUE (*https://gluebench mark.com*) and SQuAD (*https://oreil.ly/o2ENK*), for measuring performance on these tasks. We will also highlight several standard publicly available datasets for you to use when solving these tasks on your own. And, most importantly, we will solve two of these tasks—named entity recognition (NER) and text classification—together to show just how all of this works.

We hope this chapter gives you a deeper, more applied and hands-on take to performing NLP and can serve as the launch pad for building your own real-world NLP applications.

Pretrained Language Models

As we mentioned in Chapter 1, NLP has come a long way over just the past few years. Instead of training NLP models from scratch, it is now possible (and advisable) to leverage pretrained language models to perform common NLP tasks such as NER. Only when you have highly custom NLP needs is it advisable to train your NLP model from scratch. But, before we proceed any further, let's define some of the terms we will use in this chapter. We have already covered some of these terms in the previous two chapters, but this will be a good refresher nonetheless to tie everything together.

Machine learning is an application of artificial intelligence that enables machines to improve their performance on a defined task by learning from data.

Natural language processing is the branch of machine learning that involves natural (aka "human") language, such as text and speech. Computer vision, which we will not cover in this book, is the branch of machine learning that involves visual data, such as images and video.

Machines can learn from labeled data or unlabeled data. The area of machine learning that involves labeled data (e.g., this is an image of a "cat" or a "dog") is known as *supervised learning*, and the area that involves unlabeled data (e.g., you have images of cats and dogs but none are labeled as such) is known as *unsupervised learning*.[1] The third major area of machine learning, known as *reinforcement learning*, involves software agents learning how to take action in an environment (either physical or digital) to maximize the rewards they receive.

In machine learning, the process of machines learning from data (also referred to as "training on data") to improve their performance on a specific task results in a model. Once the machines have learned/trained to a satisfactory level of performance on the task, the model stores the knowledge acquired from the training process in the form of model parameters (e.g., weights), which are used in the calculus and linear algebra performed in machine learning.

The model uses this stored knowledge (i.e., model parameters) to perform inference (i.e., generate predictions) on new or never-before-seen data. So long as the new data is similar to the data the machines had trained on, the performance on the new data should be similar to the performance the machines had achieved on the original training dataset.

Turning back to our original topic, we can use pretrained language models to perform common NLP tasks. When we refer to pretrained models, we refer to models that were previously trained on data. Instead of having machines train on data from scratch to perform NLP tasks, we start with pretrained language models that have already been trained on lots and lots of data to perform language modeling to good levels of performance. We then fine-tune the pretrained language models to perform specific NLP tasks beyond language modeling; this process of fine-tuning a language model to perform another NLP task is known as *transfer learning*, which we will turn to next. (Don't worry: we will discuss what these common NLP tasks are very soon, too.)

---

1 Ankur has an entire book on hands-on unsupervised learning (*https://oreil.ly/gjo83*) if you're curious.

Transfer Learning and Fine-Tuning

Using pretrained language models is the fastest way to perform common NLP tasks. In contrast, if you need to perform uncommon NLP tasks, you may need to train the model from scratch, including sourcing and annotating/labeling the data relevant for your task.

There will be times when your task is similar to but not exactly the same as the task the pretrained model was trained to perform. In these cases, it is possible to leverage some of the prior learning by the pretrained model instead of training a model entirely from scratch. You are effectively "transferring" learning from one model to another.

Transfer learning is possible because pretrained language models are neural networks. Neural networks are a class of models in machine learning in which machines learn to represent data in a manner that enables them to perform complex tasks such as data classification.

Neural networks typically involve learning a series of representations, with each subsequent representation making it easier for the machine to interpret the data from the prior representation. Each representation is learned by a layer in the neural network; the more layers a neural network has, the more representations are learned (see Figure 3-1). Modern neural networks typically have many layers—in other words, they are very deep. This is where the terms *deep learning* and *deep neural networks* come from.

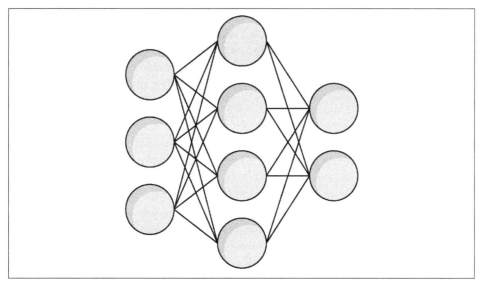

Figure 3-1. Artificial neural network

In transfer learning, we borrow the first several layers of a pretrained language model. These first several layers have already learned some useful representations of the data, making it easier for us to train the subsequent layers of the neural network for our specific task.

For example, these first several layers of the pretrained language model may have already discovered a good way to represent the various tokens in our text. Instead of having to learn these representations from scratch, we can just borrow and/or transfer the knowledge from the pretrained model and then train it some more (fine-tune it) on our specific task.

Transfer learning and fine-tuning are very common practices in NLP today and have helped accelerate the build of NLP applications in specific domains (e.g., finance, legal, etc.). If we had to train NLP models from scratch every time we switched from one domain to another (e.g., from analyzing finance documents to legal documents), building NLP applications would be a very slow and arduous process.

Instead, we could leverage a generic pretrained language model trained on lots of textual data crawled from the web and fine-tune it for finance or for legal and quickly build a domain-specific language model, similar to what we did for movie reviews in Chapter 2. Transfer learning is why NLP has blossomed in industry in recent years.

With this context in mind, let's introduce the common NLP tasks.

NLP Tasks

Hugging Face has an excellent overview of the common NLP tasks (*https://oreil.ly/ dpngk*), which we will present here now. These tasks include sequence classification, question answering, language modeling, text generation, named entity recognition, summarization, and translation. This list is by no means exhaustive, but it does highlight the most frequent use cases for NLP today in building applications and is a great place for us to start:

Sequence classification
    Sequence classification is as straightforward as it sounds; it involves classifying sequences into a given number of classes. When performed on text, sequence classification is also referred to as text classification, which we will perform together later in this chapter. An example of sequence classification is sentiment analysis, which we performed when we classified IMDb movie reviews as positive, negative, or neutral in Chapter 2. Another example is entailment, which involves labeling the relationship between two statements (known as the text and hypothesis, respectively) into one of three classes: positive entailment (hypothesis states something that is definitely correct about the situation or event in the text), neutral entailment (hypothesis states something that might be correct about the situation or event in the text), or negative entailment (hypothesis states

something that is definitely incorrect about the situation or event in the premise). Within the field of NLP, this is more specifically referred to as a natural language understanding (NLU) task given what the machine has to be able to infer from the data in order to perform this task well. The General Language Understanding Evaluation (GLUE) benchmark (*https://gluebenchmark.com*) is the most popular benchmark to measure progress on sequence classification tasks and natural language understanding, more generally. The authors of the original GLUE paper released an even harder benchmark to measure progress on NLU, known as SuperGLUE (*https://super.gluebenchmark.com*), which you should be aware of. You can find many more text classification datasets (*https://oreil.ly/rICba*) on Papers with Code.

Question answering

Question answering is the task of providing the correct answer from a sequence of text or audio given a question. Think of this as reading comprehension; the machine has to find the correct segment of text from a reading passage and present this as the answer to a question that is being asked. The most popular benchmark to measure progress on question answering is known as SQuAD 2.0 (*https://oreil.ly/xtIX9*). It is a collection of 100,000 answerable questions from the original SQuAD dataset (known as SQuAD 1.1) plus 50,000 unanswerable questions that look similar to answerable ones. The unanswerable questions were introduced to fool the machine, making the task more difficult. The machine has to decide whether the question is answerable or not, and, if it is, the machine has to provide the correct answer.

Language modeling

We have covered language modeling already, but, as a refresher, language modeling is the task of predicting the next sequence of words given a sequence of words. This particular type of language modeling is known as *causal language modeling* and is commonly used for *natural language generation* (NLG) in the field of NLP. Another type of language modeling is *masked language modeling*, in which the machine must predict the masked word or words in a sequence given the surrounding context. Given the nature of this task, there is no industry-setting performance benchmark, but there are plenty of datasets (*https://oreil.ly/Mg91w*) available.

Text generation

Text generation is similar to language modeling in that the task involves generating a coherent sequence of text that is a continuation of the given text, but it is more open-ended compared to language modeling. Think of text generation as longer sequence text prediction versus the shorter sequence text prediction involved in language modeling. Text generation gained mainstream popularity with the release of OpenAI's GPT-2 (*https://oreil.ly/oW7ya*) in 2019. There is no industry performance benchmark for this task, but here are some datasets (*https://oreil.ly/cdFp2*).

Named entity recognition

We introduced named entity recognition (NER) in Chapter 1; it is the task of classifying tokens of interest (think words) in a sequence of tokens (think sentence) into specific entity types, such as a person, an organization, or a location. The most popular dataset and benchmark for this task is CoNLL-2003 (*https://oreil.ly/56Rdp*), which is an NER challenge dating back to 2003. Back then, statistical NLP models were used to perform NER, but today the best-performing NER models are transformer-based. For more on NER, including datasets, visit the Papers with Code (*https://oreil.ly/56Rdp*) website. We will perform NER together later in this chapter.

Summarization

Summarization is the task of summarizing a document into a shorter text. The usefulness of this task should be fully apparent; this is a task all of us perform on a daily basis, synthesizing information from a long article into a shorter block/summary to hold as memory. The industry performance benchmark and dataset for this task is CNN/Daily Mail (*https://oreil.ly/67MBe*), and here are some public datasets (*https://oreil.ly/rSzCv*) that are available.

Translation

Translation (or *machine translation*, as it is commonly called) is the task of translating a text from one language to another. Think of Google Translate or the Translate app by Apple. The most popular metric to score the quality of machine translation is known as BLEU (*https://oreil.ly/fVx8m*). You can also find many datasets (*https://oreil.ly/Q2n0V*) for this task on Papers with Code.

To reiterate: this list is by no means exhaustive. These are just some of the frequent use cases for NLP today; other use cases include voicebots, chatbots, speech recognition, entity linking (which we explored in Chapter 1), and more. Nevertheless, this should give you a flavor of how NLP is being used in applications today.

Natural Language Dataset

Now that we've covered the common NLP tasks, let's perform two of them—named entity recognition and text classification—using pretrained language models. Before we do, we need a natural language dataset to work with.

We will use the AG News Classification Dataset in this chapter. AG is a collection of more than one million news articles, gathered from more than two thousand news sources. This dataset is provided by the academic community and is commonly used for research purposes (e.g., to benchmark performance of various NLP models over the years).[2]

We will use a specific version of this AG News Classification Dataset that was constructed by Xiang Zhang and is available on Kaggle.[3] This version of the dataset has better documentation and is readily available as a comma-separated values (CSV) file, whereas the original is not.

This Kaggle version of the dataset, which we will refer to as the AG News Topic Classification Dataset ("AG Dataset") from now on, is a labeled dataset. Each news article has a title and a description and is classified into one of four classes (1-World, 2-Sports, 3-Business, and 4-Sci/Tech). Each class contains 30,000 training samples and 1,900 testing samples, and the entire dataset has 120,000 training samples and 7,600 testing samples.

Explore the AG Dataset

Let's explore the training dataset in Google Colab.[4] Since we want to use GPUs to train our models, let's enable GPUs in Google Colab (or locally, if GPUs are available). In your Google Colab session, go to Edit → Notebook settings, select GPU under Hardware Accelerator, and click Save. Note that this restarts the runtime; all of your cell states get lost.

Next, we will load the data, convert all column names to lowercase and replace spaces with underscores, and add a new feature called "class_name" that maps the numerical labels to class names:

```
# Import libraries
import pandas as pd
import os

# Get current working directory
cwd = os.getcwd()

# Import AG Dataset
data = pd.read_csv(cwd+'/data/ag_dataset/train.csv')
data = pd.DataFrame(data=data)
data.columns = data.columns.str.replace(" ","_")
data.columns = data.columns.str.lower()
data["class_name"] = data["class_index"].map({1:"World", 2:"Sports",
                                              3:"Business", 4:"Sci_Tech"})
```

2 For more on the dataset, view the original source (*https://oreil.ly/QyXmB*).

3 For more on this dataset, visit the dataset page on Kaggle (*https://oreil.ly/VUW4C*).

4 To follow along, visit the Chapter 3 notebook in our GitHub repo (*https://github.com/nlpbook/nlpbook*).

Let's preview the data now:

```
# View data
data
```

	class_index	title	description	class_name
0	3	Wall St. Bears Claw Back Into the Black (Reuters)	Reuters - Short-sellers, Wall Street's dwindli...	Business
1	3	Carlyle Looks Toward Commercial Aerospace (Reu...	Reuters - Private investment firm Carlyle Grou...	Business
2	3	Oil and Economy Cloud Stocks' Outlook (Reuters)	Reuters - Soaring crude prices plus worries \ab...	Business
3	3	Iraq Halts Oil Exports from Main Southern Pipe...	Reuters - Authorities have halted oil export \f...	Business
4	3	Oil prices soar to all-time record, posing new...	AFP - Tearaway world oil prices, toppling reco...	Business
...	...	...	...	...
119995	1	Pakistan's Musharraf Says Won't Quit as Army C...	KARACHI (Reuters) - Pakistani President Perve...	World
119996	2	Renteria signing a top-shelf deal	Red Sox general manager Theo Epstein acknowled...	Sports
119997	2	Saban not going to Dolphins yet	The Miami Dolphins will put their courtship of...	Sports
119998	2	Today's NFL games	PITTSBURGH at NY GIANTS Time: 1:30 p.m. Line: ...	Sports
119999	2	Nets get Carter from Raptors	INDIANAPOLIS -- All-Star Vince Carter was trad...	Sports

```
120000 rows × 4 columns
```

As shown in the cell output, the training dataset has 120,000 observations and four features, as expected. The four features are class_index, title, description, and class_name.

Here are the number of observations per class (30,000 each, as expected):

```
# Count observations by class
data.class_name.value_counts()

Sports      30000
Sci_Tech    30000
World       30000
Business    30000
Name: class_name, dtype: int64
```

Next, let's view the titles and descriptions of the first 10 news articles to get a better sense of the data:

```
# View titles
for i in range(10):
    print("Title of Article",i)
    print(data.loc[i,"title"])
    print("\n")

Title of Article 0
Wall St. Bears Claw Back Into the Black (Reuters)


Title of Article 1
Carlyle Looks Toward Commercial Aerospace (Reuters)


Title of Article 2
Oil and Economy Cloud Stocks' Outlook (Reuters)


Title of Article 3
Iraq Halts Oil Exports from Main Southern Pipeline (Reuters)


Title of Article 4
Oil prices soar to all-time record, posing new menace to US economy (AFP)


Title of Article 5
Stocks End Up, But Near Year Lows (Reuters)


Title of Article 6
Money Funds Fell in Latest Week (AP)


Title of Article 7
Fed minutes show dissent over inflation (USATODAY.com)


Title of Article 8
Safety Net (Forbes.com)


Title of Article 9
Wall St. Bears Claw Back Into the Black

# View descriptions
for i in range(10):
    print("Description of Article",i)
    print(data.loc[i,"description"])
    print("\n")

Description of Article 0
Reuters - Short-sellers, Wall Street's dwindling\band of ultra-cynics, are
  > seeing green again.
```

Description of Article 1
Reuters - Private investment firm Carlyle Group,\which has a reputation for
 > making well-timed and occasionally\controversial plays in the defense
 > industry, has quietly placed\its bets on another part of the market.

Description of Article 2
Reuters - Soaring crude prices plus worries\about the economy and the outlook
 > for earnings are expected to\hang over the stock market next week during the
 > depth of the\summer doldrums.

Description of Article 3
Reuters - Authorities have halted oil export\flows from the main pipeline in
 > southern Iraq after\intelligence showed a rebel militia could
 > strike\infrastructure, an oil official said on Saturday.

Description of Article 4
AFP - Tearaway world oil prices, toppling records and straining wallets, present
 > a new economic menace barely three months before the US presidential
 > elections.

Description of Article 5
Reuters - Stocks ended slightly higher on Friday\but stayed near lows for the
 > year as oil prices surged past #36;46\a barrel, offsetting a positive
 > outlook from computer maker\Dell Inc. (DELL.O)

Description of Article 6
AP - Assets of the nation's retail money market mutual funds fell by #36;1.17
 > billion in the latest week to #36;849.98 trillion, the Investment Company
 > Institute said Thursday.

Description of Article 7
USATODAY.com - Retail sales bounced back a bit in July, and new claims for
 > jobless benefits fell last week, the government said Thursday, indicating the
 > economy is improving from a midsummer slump.

Description of Article 8
Forbes.com - After earning a PH.D. in Sociology, Danny Bazil Riley started to
 > work as the general manager at a commercial real estate firm at an annual
 > base salary of #36;70,000. Soon after, a financial planner stopped by his
 > desk to drop off brochures about insurance benefits available through his
 > employer. But, at 32, "buying insurance was the furthest thing from my mind,"
 > says Riley.

```
Description of Article 9
 NEW YORK (Reuters) - Short-sellers, Wall Street's dwindling band of ultra-
> cynics, are seeing green again.
```

Based on these titles and descriptions, you should now have a better feel for the data, including the somewhat noisy text in the descriptions (e.g., the description of article 8).

Let's preprocess the text some more to remove some of the noise in the data. This will remove and replace tokens that are superfluous (such as double spaces) and make reading the text (for humans) more difficult:

```
# Clean up text
cols = ["title","description"]
data[cols] = data[cols].applymap(lambda x: x.replace("\\"," "))
data[cols] = data[cols].applymap(lambda x: x.replace("#36;","$"))
data[cols] = data[cols].applymap(lambda x: x.replace("  "," "))
data[cols] = data[cols].applymap(lambda x: x.strip())

# Write data to CSV
data.to_csv(cwd+'/data/ag_dataset/prepared/train_prepared.csv', index=False)
```

Great! This is the dataset we will work with. Now, let's proceed with the our first NLP application, named entity recognition.

NLP Task #1: Named Entity Recognition

In Chapter 1, we briefly explored named entity recognition (NER), which parses notable entities in natural language and labels them with their appropriate class label such as "Person" or "Location." It is a form of text classification. NER models use the context around a given token of interest to predict the entity label. Once the entities are labeled correctly, we can use the extracted information to perform information retrieval (search documents based on people or places we care about), create structured data from unstructured documents (e.g., parse key binding legal terms from legal documents at scale), and more. Think of NER as adding rich metadata to every document, which then allows us to perform rich analysis downstream.

Perform Inference Using the Original spaCy Model

Let's first use a pretrained language model from spaCy to perform NER. spaCy offers four different pretrained models for NER: small, medium, large, and transformer-based. All four are trained on written text in the form of blogs, news, and comments, but differ in size. The larger the model and the more data it has trained on, the better the performance, generally speaking. In Chapter 1, we opted for the small model to perform the basic NLP tasks. Now, we will opt for the transformer-based model, spaCy's best model.

We will install spaCy on GPU by specifying `spacy[cuda110]`. You can specify other CUDA versions, too. For more, visit the spaCy documentation (*https://spacy.io/usage*). If you do not wish to use GPUs, install spaCy using `pip install -U spacy` (without the CUDA reference). If you run into issues, email us at *authors@appliednlpbook.com*.

If you haven't installed spaCy already, these commands will get you everything you need. If you're running them in a notebook, prefix each line with a ! character:

```
pip install -U spacy[cuda110,transformers,lookups]==3.0.3
pip install -U spacy-lookups-data==1.0.0
pip install cupy-cuda110==8.5.0
python -m spacy download en_core_web_trf
```

You may need to restart your runtime after installing spaCy and downloading the pretrained language model before you can successfully import the model in the next step.

```
# Import spacy and load language model
import spacy
spacy.require_gpu()
print(spacy.require_gpu())
nlp = spacy.load("en_core_web_trf")

True
```

If spaCy on GPU is successfully installed and activated, you will see "`GPU: True`". If you do not, troubleshoot your GPU installation or revert to CPU.

Now that we've installed spaCy and loaded the transformer-based model, let's print the metadata of the model, which highlights the underlying components and the associated accuracy metrics:

```
# View metadata of the model
import pprint
pp = pprint.PrettyPrinter(indent=4)
pp.pprint(nlp.meta)
```

Based on the metrics (which we will not print here, given the volume of text involved), we can see that the model has an NER component, which supports various entity types, including the following: CARDINAL, DATE, EVENT, FAC, GPE,

LANGUAGE, LAW, LOC, MONEY, NORP, ORDINAL, ORG, PERCENT, PERSON, PRODUCT, QUANTITY, TIME, and WORK OF ART.

Let's focus on three of the more common entity types: ORG (short for organization), PERSON, and GPE (i.e., geopolitical entity, such as country, city, and state). Let's review the accuracy metrics for these three. F is the F1 Score, P is the Precision, and R is the Recall.

As a refresher, precision is the percentage of true positives/the number of total positive predictions. Recall is the percentage of true positives/the number of total true positives. F1 is a blended metric and is calculated as $2 \times$ (Precision $\times$ Recall)/(Precision + Recall). The higher the F1, precision, and recall, the better:

```
'PERSON': {'f': 0.9546191248, 'p': 0.9481648422000001, 'r': 0.9611618799}

'ORG': {'f': 0.9012772751, 'p': 0.9046474359000001, 'r': 0.8979321315000001}

'GPE': {   'f': 0.9467271182, 'p': 0.9619925137, 'r': 0.9319386332}
```

From these metrics, we can see that the model is decently good at all of these entities but is worst at ORG, for which it has an F1 score of 90.

Now that we have loaded the spaCy model and reviewed some of its metadata, let's apply the spaCy model to our AG News data and generate the results of named entity recognition:

```
# Print NER results for Descriptions
for i in range(9):
    print("Article",i)
    print(data.loc[i,"description"])
    print("Text Start End Label")
    doc = nlp(data.loc[i,"description"])
    for token in doc.ents:
        print(token.text, token.start_char,
            token.end_char, token.label_)
    print("\n")
```

Here are the NER labels for the descriptions of the first nine articles, including the start and end positions of every tagged entity. Let's review the performance of the NER model:

```
Article 0: Reuters - Short-sellers, Wall Street's
dwindling band of ultra-cynics, are seeing green again.
Text Start End Label
Reuters 0 7 ORG
```

Great result.

```
Article 1: Reuters - Private investment firm Carlyle Group, which has
a reputation for making well-timed and occasionally controversial plays
in the defense industry, has quietly placed its bets on another part of
the market.
```

```
Text Start End Label
Reuters 0 7 ORG
Carlyle Group 34 47 ORG
```

Great result.

```
Article 2: Reuters - Soaring crude prices plus worries about the
economy and the outlook for earnings are expected to hang over the stock
market next week during the depth of the summer doldrums.
Text Start End Label
Reuters 0 7 ORG
next week 134 143 DATE
summer 168 174 DATE
```

Great result. Even the date entities were captured correctly.

```
Article 3: Reuters - Authorities have halted oil export flows from the
main pipeline in southern Iraq after intelligence showed a rebel militia
could strike infrastructure, an oil official said on Saturday.
Text Start End Label
Reuters 0 7 ORG
Iraq 86 90 GPE
Saturday 186 194 DATE
```

Great result.

```
Article 4: AFP - Tearaway world oil prices, toppling records and
straining wallets, present a new economic menace barely three months
before the US presidential elections.
Text Start End Label
AFP 0 3 ORG
barely three months 103 122 DATE
US 134 136 GPE
```

Great result.

```
Article 5: Reuters - Stocks ended slightly higher on Friday but stayed
near lows for the year as oil prices surged past $46 a barrel,
offsetting a positive outlook from computer maker Dell Inc. (DELL.O)
Text Start End Label
Reuters 0 7 ORG
Friday 42 48 DATE
the year 74 82 DATE
46 110 112 MONEY
Dell Inc. 173 182 ORG
```

Great result.

```
Article 6: AP - Assets of the nation's retail money market
mutual funds fell by $1.17 billion in the latest week to $849.98
trillion, the Investment Company Institute said Thursday.
Text Start End Label
1.17 billion 69 82 MONEY
the latest week 86 101 DATE
849.98 trillion 105 121 MONEY
```

```
the Investment Company Institute 123 155 ORG
Thursday 161 169 DATE
```

AP should have been recognized as an organization, but otherwise great result.

```
Article 7: USATODAY.com - Retail sales bounced back a bit in July, and
new claims for jobless benefits fell last week, the government said
Thursday, indicating the economy is improving from a midsummer slump.
Text Start End Label
July 50 54 DATE
last week 97 106 DATE
Thursday 128 136 DATE
midsummer 181 190 DATE
```

USATODAY.com should have been recognized as an organization, but otherwise great result.

```
Article 8: Forbes.com - After earning a PhD in Sociology, Danny
Bazil Riley started to work as the general manager at a commercial real
estate firm at an annual base salary of $70,000. Soon after, a financial
planner stopped by his desk to drop off brochures about insurance
benefits available through his employer. But, at 32, "buying insurance
was the furthest thing from my mind," says Riley.
Text Start End Label
Danny Bazil Riley 49 66 PERSON
annual 145 151 DATE
70,000 168 174 MONEY
32 315 317 DATE
Riley 380 385 PERSON
```

Forbes.com is an organization, and 32 is not a date.

All in all, the NER results from the pretrained spaCy model are excellent. This highlights why you should leverage pretrained models, where possible, for your work.

Custom NER

However, sometimes pretrained models are insufficient for the task at hand. This could be for several reasons. First, the corpus on which we want to apply a pretrained model may be materially different from the corpus on which the model was trained. For example, the transformer-based spaCy model we just used was trained on blogs, news, and comments on the web. If our corpus is materially different (e.g., a very technical corpus such as legal, finance, or health data), we may want to annotate a portion of our corpus and fine-tune the transformer-based spaCy model. By fine-tuning the model, the model will perform better on our specific corpus.

Second, the tasks that the transformer-based spaCy model was trained to perform may differ from the task we wish to perform. For example, the spaCy named entity recognition does not support stock tickers (TICKER) as an entity type. If we wish to add this TICKER entity type, we would have to annotate tickers in our data and fine-tune the transformer-based spaCy model.

To demonstrate how transfer learning and fine-tuning a model work, let's annotate a small portion of our data for the three core entity types (ORG, PERSON, and GPE) and add a new entity type (TICKER).

We will use an annotation platform called Prodigy to annotate our data. Prodigy, like spaCy, is the product of the software company Explosion (*https://explosion.ai*). Prodigy allows us to load our corpus into a beautiful browser-based UI to label our data however we wish. These labels then become available for us to fine-tune our spaCy model. Unfortunately, Prodigy is not available for free, but we do highly recommend it for purchase.

In the next section, we will install and use Prodigy to annotate a small portion of our AG News Dataset. Then, we will use these annotations to fine-tune our spaCy model from earlier. For those that do not wish to purchase a Prodigy license, feel free to skip the next section.

Annotate via Prodigy: NER

After purchasing a license for Prodigy, you will be able to download a Python *.whl* file (also known as a wheel). Unfortunately, this wheel cannot be installed on Google Colab, so we will need to install it locally on our own machine.

Before installing Prodigy, we recommend you create and activate a virtual environment on your local machine. If you have the Anaconda distribution of Python installed, you can create and activate a new virtual environment using the following commands on the command line. Even if you have set up your local environment using the README on our GitHub repo (*https://github.com/nlpbook/nlpbook*), you should create a separate virtual environment solely for Prodigy to avoid any conflicts with our main conda environment:

 It is generally preferable to create new virtual environments for every machine learning project you have. Having a separate environment for each project allows you to install the relevant libraries for your current project without having to uninstall libraries that you may need for other projects but that can cause code to fail for your current project. Think of a virtual environment as a blank canvas (i.e., new set of libraries) for you to do your work without having to worry about how changes to the current canvas conflict with canvases for your other projects.

```
$ conda create -n prodigy anaconda python=3.8
$ conda activate prodigy
```

Now, navigate to the directory with the Prodigy wheel and install the package. You may need to specify the wheel by its full filename if this doesn't work:

```
$ pip install prodigy*.whl
```

You will also need to install spaCy in this virtual environment and download the en_core_web_lg model if you haven't already:

As of March 2021, Prodigy does not support spaCy 3.x (hence no transformer-based pipelines). We expect Prodigy to introduce support for spaCy 3.x in the near future, but, for now, we will have to work with spaCy 2.x and the en_core_web_lg model.

```
$ pip install -U spacy[cuda110]==2.3.5
$ pip install -U spacy-lookups-data==1.0.0
$ pip install cupy-cuda110==8.5.0
$ python -m spacy download en_core_web_lg
```

Now, let's prepare a file to load into Prodigy. For NER, we need a CSV of text snippets with a column name of "text." We will use the descriptions from the AG News dataset as the text snippets and annotate these in Prodigy:

```
# Prepare text for annotation in Prodigy
train_prodigy_ner = data.copy()
train_prodigy_ner = train_prodigy_ner.description
train_prodigy_ner.rename("text",inplace=True)
train_prodigy_ner.to_csv(cwd +
                "data/ag_dataset/ner/raw/train_prodigy_ner.csv",
                index=False)
```

We can now load the data into Prodigy and begin annotating the data. We will annotate the data for the three main entities we care about (ORG, PERSON, and GPE) and a fourth new entity (TICKER).

To perform this annotation, we will use the Prodigy recipe called *ner.manual* (see Figure 3-2). This recipe allows us to mark entity spans in a text by highlighting them and selecting the respective labels.[5]

Figure 3-2. ner.manual recipe

---

5 For more on these Prodigy recipes, visit the Prodigy website (*https://oreil.ly/sKGFV*).

In the command line, we need to specify the name of the recipe (`ner.manual`), the name of the dataset to which we want to save the annotations to (e.g., `ag_data_ner_ticker`), a spaCy model (e.g., `en_core_web_lg` or `blank:en` if we want to start with a blank model), the text source (in our case, the path to the `train_prod igy_ner.csv`), and the entity labels we want available in the Prodigy UI to annotate the text:

```
$ python -m prodigy ner.manual <dataset> <spacy_model> <source> \
  --label ORG,PERSON,GPE,TICKER
```

If successful, you will see this message in the command line:

```
⚡ Starting the web server at http://localhost:8080 … Open the app in
your browser and start annotating!
```

Go ahead and copy the URL into your web browser. You should see an annotation UI, such as the one shown in Figure 3-3.

Figure 3-3. Prodigy NER annotation UI

We can now highlight spans and label the data with the correct entities, as seen in Figure 3-4. Click the big green checkmark box to proceed to the next example (or click "a" key on your keyboard). If you would like to skip an example because you are not sure of the answer, click the spacebar on your keyboard.

Figure 3-4. Prodigy NER annotation UI: annotating first example

Let's annotate a few hundred of these and then save them by clicking the floppy disk icon next to the word "prodigy" on the upper-left corner of the UI. A few hundred annotations should be good enough for a decent fine-tuned model, although, as always, the more annotations, the better the model's performance will be.

Once the annotations are ready, we can output the NER annotations in spaCy's JSON format using the *data-to-spaCy* Prodigy recipe (see Figure 3-5).

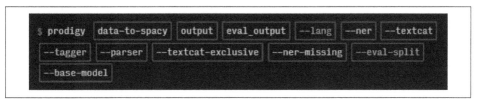

Figure 3-5. data-to-spaCy Prodigy recipe

For this recipe, we need to specify the output path (to train the model), an evaluation output path (to evaluate the model), the language ("en" in our case), and the NER dataset using the --ner tag:

```
$ python -m prodigy data-to-spacy <output> <eval_output> --lang en \
--ner ag_data_ner_ticker
```

This command outputs the annotations in JSON format, but, as of spaCy v3.0 (released in January 2021), spaCy's main data format is a binary format. Before we can train using spaCy, we need to convert the JSON format to binary. spaCy has a convert recipe for this (see Figure 3-6), which we will use now:

```
$ python -m spacy convert <path-to-json> <path-for-binary-output>
```

```
$ python -m spacy convert ./data.json
./output.spacy
```

Figure 3-6. Convert spaCy recipe

> We are converting to a binary format because we will use the annotations to fine-tune the transformer-based model in spaCy 3.x after we finish exporting from Prodigy.

Great! We are now ready to fine-tune our spaCy model with this annotated data.

Train the Custom NER Model Using spaCy

If you skipped the Prodigy section just now, do not worry. We have generated the train and eval annotations and made them available to you for this next section.

> At this point, deactivate the conda environment called "prodigy" and activate the main conda environment called "applied_nlp" if you are developing the spaCy model on your local machine.

We will train two separate NER models. First, we will train an NER model using transfer learning. To perform transfer learning, we will use a transformer model called RoBERTa (*https://oreil.ly/NuvuI*), a large, pretrained language model released by Facebook in 2019. Second, we will train an NER model without a transformer model and GPUs and rely just on a CPU-based training pipeline. This will help us compare the transformer-based GPU-enabled performance versus the standard CPU-based performance.

Let's go ahead and train the transformer-based model first. We will use the `train` command in spaCy, as shown in Figure 3-7.[6]

---

6 For more on the `train` command, visit the official spaCy documentation (*https://oreil.ly/w1uFU*).

Figure 3-7. spaCy train command

For this command, we will need to specify the `config` path, the output path, and the GPU tag to enable training on GPU. The requirement for the training configuration path is new to spaCy v3.0. The training `config` is the file that sets all the settings and hyperparameters for the model development:

```
$ python -m spacy train <config_path> --output <output_path> \
--gpu-id 0
```

Let's generate this config file for training first. Surprise! There is a spaCy recipe for creating config files from scratch (see Figure 3-8). For this command, we need to specify the lang (en), the pipeline component we need to modify (ner), the optimize tag ("efficiency" for faster inference/smaller model or "accuracy" for higher accuracy/ slower, larger model), whether GPUs will be used or not, and whether the command should overwrite the output file, if one exists.

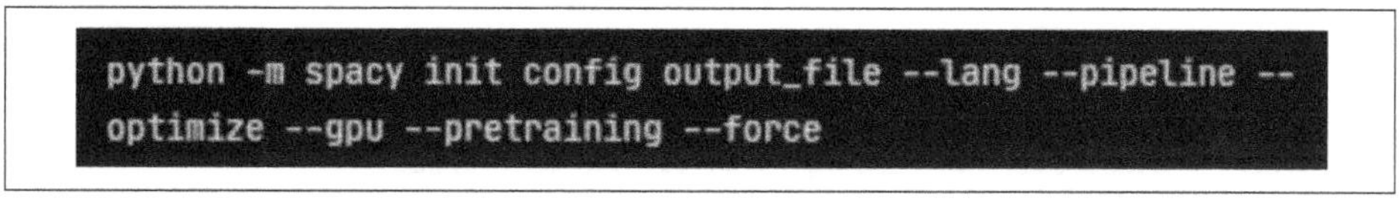

```
python -m spacy init config output_file --lang --pipeline --
optimize --gpu --pretraining --force
```

Figure 3-8. spaCy init config

```
$ python -m spacy init config <config_path> --lang --pipeline \
--optimize --gpu --force
```

Another option is to use the training configuration UI (*https://oreil.ly/gFMVb*) on spaCy's official website to generate the best practices version of the config file for NER. To kick off most projects, this is the best place to start because spaCy updates this configuration widget with the best practices it has discovered based on its model experimentation. This is what we will use. We will start a blank transformer-based template (with GPU enabled).

We need to auto-fill this base NER template from spaCy using another spaCy command called `init fill-config`, shown in Figure 3-9.

Figure 3-9. spaCy init fill-config

This command takes in two very simple parameters: an input path to the config file (which we downloaded from spaCy's website) and an output path. The command will generate the final output config file by auto-populating the remaining components of the base template generated from spaCy's widget:

```
$ python -m spacy init fill-config <config_path_original> \
<config_path_new>
```

Let's run this command now and then proceed to training. We will train for 30 epochs:

```
# Auto-fill base template
ner_path = "data/ag_dataset/ner/"

# The downloaded file from spaCy
config_file_path_input = cwd + ner_path + "config_spacy_template_gpu_blank.cfg"

# The output file we will use for training
config_file_path_output = cwd + ner_path + "config_final_gpu_blank.cfg"

python -m spacy init fill-config "$config_file_path_input" \
"$config_file_path_output"

# Train spaCy model on NER annotations
output_path = cwd + "/models/ag_dataset/ner/ner-gpu-blank"
train_path = cwd + "/data/ag_dataset/ner/annotations/binary/train"
dev_path = cwd + "/data/ag_dataset/ner/annotations/binary/eval"

python -m spacy train "$config_file_path_output" \
--output "$output_path" --paths.train "$train_path" \
--paths.dev "$dev_path" --training.max_epochs 30 --gpu-id 0 --verbose
```

Example 3-1 displays the results. As you can see, the model achieves an F1 score above 95 within 30 epochs.

Example 3-1. spaCy NER: transformer GPU-based

```
======================== Training pipeline =============================
[i] Pipeline: ['transformer', 'ner']
[i] Initial learn rate: 0.0
E     #        LOSS TRANS...  LOSS NER  ENTS_F  ENTS_P  ENTS_R  SCORE
---   -------  -------------  --------  ------  ------  ------  -----
  0        0         866.56   1087.32    3.31    1.75   29.99   0.03
  8      200      127924.74  63854.97   94.39   94.05   94.75   0.94
 17      400        2339.89   2798.22   94.13   93.78   94.48   0.94
 26      600         166.36   2400.21   95.40   95.00   95.81   0.95
```

Let's now train the second model, this time without transfer learning from a transformer-based model and no GPUs.

We will generate a config file first, and then we will train the model using this config file for 30 epochs. Notice that the GPU tag is missing, which is what we want. The absence of the GPU tag creates a config file that forgoes the transformer-based model. This second model does not use transfer learning from the RoBERTa model, whereas the first model we developed did:

```
# Generate config file
# The output file we will use for training
ner_path = "data/ag_dataset/ner"
config_file_path_output = cwd + new_path + "config_final_no_gpu_blank.cfg"

python -m spacy init config "$config_file_path_output" --lang en \
--pipeline ner --optimize efficiency --force

# Train spaCy model on NER annotations
output_path = cwd + "/models/ag_dataset/ner/ner-no-gpu-blank"
train_path = cwd + "/data/ag_dataset/ner/annotations/binary/train"
dev_path = cwd + "/data/ag_dataset/ner/annotations/binary/eval"

python -m spacy train "$config_file_path_output" \
--output "$output_path" --paths.train "$train_path" \
--paths.dev "$dev_path" --gpu-id 0 --training.max_epochs 30 --verbose
```

The results of the second model (as shown in Example 3-2) are not bad but clearly not as good as the results from the first model. This second model—which does not use transfer learning from a large, pretrained language model—achieves an F1 score that is near 90, well shy of the 95 F1 score of transformer-based models.

Example 3-2. spaCy NER: no transformer CPU-based

```
========================= Training pipeline =============================
[i] Pipeline: ['tok2vec', 'ner']
[i] Initial learn rate: 0.001
E    #         LOSS TOK2VEC  LOSS NER  ENTS_F  ENTS_P  ENTS_R  SCORE
---  -------   ------------  --------  ------  ------  ------  -----
  0       0          0.00      51.44    4.16    2.39   16.14   0.04
  0     200        719.12    2205.78   60.65   61.44   59.87   0.61
  1     400        105.93     871.47   70.72   69.26   72.24   0.71
  2     600        146.71     570.79   82.05   81.98   82.11   0.82
  3     800        195.22     349.08   86.29   86.22   86.36   0.86
  4    1000        302.78     276.36   88.16   87.59   88.75   0.88
  5    1200        190.30     193.66   87.47   87.31   87.63   0.87
  7    1400        229.27     116.89   87.44   86.58   88.32   0.87
 10    1600        184.20      82.39   88.55   91.75   85.56   0.89
 13    1800        216.00      82.64   87.67   87.60   87.74   0.88
 17    2000        256.72      87.17   88.04   88.56   87.53   0.88
 21    2200        179.27      60.26   89.19   89.91   88.48   0.89
 27    2400        244.17      60.08   87.50   86.75   88.27   0.88
```

Since the transformer-based model performs better than the non-transformer-based model (as expected), let's compare this fine-tuned transformer-based model (fine-tuned on the AG News Dataset) with the original transformer-based spaCy version (en_core_web_trf).

Custom NER Model Versus Original NER Model

It's not an apples-to-apples comparison to compare the fine-tuned transformer-based model with the original en_core_web_trf. This is because the fine-tuned model supports just four entity types (ORG, PERSON, GPE, and TICKER), while the original en_core_web_trf supports many more entity types (but does not support TICKER, which is the new entity type we just annotated for the AG News Dataset).

Nevertheless, we can compare the two models on a sample of article descriptions in the AG News dataset and see which model performs better. This will help us determine whether fine-tuning the RoBERTa model improved the NER performance on our dataset compared to the original spaCy model.

Before we compare the results of the two models, let's load our fine-tuned NER model and view its metadata:

```
# Load custom NER model
spacy.require_gpu()
custom_ner_model = spacy.load(cwd + \
    '/models/ag_dataset/ner/ner-gpu-blank/model-best')

# View metadata of the model
import pprint
```

```
pp = pprint.PrettyPrinter(indent=4)
pp.pprint(custom_ner_model.meta)
```

The fine-tuned NER model supports just four entity types, but the F1 scores are pretty good: 97 for GPE, 93 for ORG, 96 for PERSON, and 98 for TICKER. By comparison, the original spaCy model has F1 scores of 95 for GPE, 90 for ORG, and 95 for PERSON (and no F1 for TICKER, which the original spaCy model does not support). Note that the comparison is not apples to apples because the F1 scores were measured on different datasets, but this gives you a sense of relative performance.

Now, let's use a built-in spaCy visualizer for NER to compare the two models:

 We use the terms "original" and "base" interchangeably.

```
# Compare NER results on Descriptions: Original/Base vs. Custom
from spacy import displacy
import random

spacy.require_gpu()
base_model = spacy.load("en_core_web_trf")

options = {"ents": ["ORG","PERSON","GPE","TICKER"]}

for j in range(3):
    i = random.randint(0, len(data))
    print("Article",i)
    doc_base = base_model(data.loc[i,"description"])
    doc_custom = custom_ner_model(data.loc[i,"description"])
    print("Base Model NER:")
    displacy.render(doc_base, style="ent", options=options, jupyter=True)
    print("Custom Model NER:")
    displacy.render(doc_custom, style="ent", options=options, jupyter=True)
    print("\n")
```

As shown in Figure 3-10, the two models have similar NER results (which makes sense since the F1 scores are somewhat similar, albeit a bit higher for the fine-tuned model). For example, for article 55405, both the base model and the fine-tuned model capture "Apple" as an ORG. For article 4145, the base model misses "NewsFactor" as an ORG and "Cingular Wireless" as an ORG, both of which the fine-tuned model captures. The fine-tuned model misses "NYSE" as an ORG but captures "AWS" as TICKER. For article 106431, the results are identical, too.

While the fine-tuned model does seem to perform better than the base model overall, the fine-tuned model will not always outperform the base model for any given example. To see this, test the preceding code snippet to compare the results of the base model against the results of the fine-tuned model. You will surely find instances where the base model performs better.

Congratulations! We fine-tuned the RoBERTa model and added a new entity for stock tickers by annotating a small percentage of the AG News Dataset in Prodigy and training it using spaCy. We then compared the fine-tuned model against the original spaCy model and saw (generally) better performance from the fine-tuned model. We can also confirm that the fine-tuned model is now tagging stock tickers, as expected.

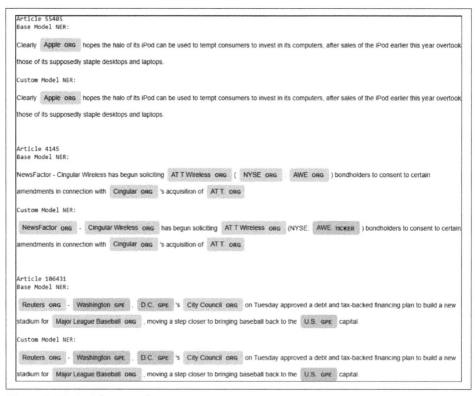

Figure 3-10. Article examples

This is a big accomplishment for two reasons. First, our work shows that fine-tuning a large, pretrained language model even on a small set of annotations (just a few hundred) improves performance. You don't need to train a model from scratch; you can leverage some prior learning from the pretrained language model and use that as a launch pad to improve performance on your specific task on your specific corpus. Transfer learning is a huge benefit to practitioners, dramatically reducing the time for any new model build. Second, we showed just how easy it is to develop your own NER model for your custom entity types (e.g., stock ticker). New model development is pretty painless; you can get up and running with new custom models fast.

In the next section, let's perform our second NLP task—text classification—applying some of the same techniques we used for our custom NER model. These techniques include annotating data and fine-tuning our large, pretrained language model to achieve good performance on this text classification task.

NLP Task #2: Text Classification

Now that we've finished performing NER, let's turn to a second NLP task: text classification. Text classification is a very common application of NLP; applications include news apps that classify news articles into topic-based categories, the spam/not spam feature of email apps, and the real news/fake news classification model on Facebook and other social platforms.

As a recap, all of the articles in the AG News `train` Dataset are already classified into one of four classes: Business, Sci_Tech, Sports, and World. We can skip annotations altogether and use these labels to train a text classification model using spaCy. But, in the real world, you will rarely have preannotated datasets like this. Instead, you will typically have to go through the exercise of annotating your data from scratch.

To show you how easy it is to annotate data and generate a text classification model by fine-tuning a large, pretrained language model, let's annotate several examples from scratch using Prodigy and then train a text classification model from the labels we generate.

Like before, you can skip this next section if you'd rather not purchase a Prodigy license, or if you would rather annotate the data in another annotation platform such as Labelbox (*https://labelbox.com*). We will export our annotations from Prodigy and make them available for you to train the text classification model so if you decide to skip the Prodigy annotations, do not worry.

Annotate via Prodigy: Text Classification

Like we did for NER, let's prepare a file to load into Prodigy for text classification. As before, we need a CSV of text snippets with a column name of "text." We will use the titles and descriptions (not just descriptions as we did for NER) from the AG News Dataset as the text snippets and annotate these in Prodigy.

Let's split the `train` dataset into two: one to use in Prodigy and one to use to evaluate the text classification model. We can call these "textcat_train" and "textcat_eval" sets, respectively. To perform this split, we will use the `train_test_split` function in Scikit-learn:[7]

```
# To train and evaluate text classification models in Prodigy
from sklearn.model_selection import train_test_split

# Prepare for text classification
textcat = data.copy()
textcat["text"] = textcat["title"] + str(" ") + textcat["description"]
textcat["label"] = textcat["class_name"]
textcat.drop(columns=["class_index","title","description","class_name"],
 inplace=True)
textcat_train, textcat_eval = train_test_split(textcat, test_size=0.2,
 random_state=2020, stratify=textcat.label)

textcat_train.to_csv(cwd +
 '/data/ag_dataset/textcat/raw/train_prodigy_textcat_train_with_labels.csv',
 index=False)

textcat_eval.to_csv(cwd +
 '/data/ag_dataset/textcat/raw/train_prodigy_textcat_eval.csv',
 index=False)

textcat_train = textcat_train.text
textcat_train.to_csv(cwd +
 '/data/ag_dataset/textcat/raw/train_prodigy_textcat_train_without_labels.csv',
 index=False)
```

We can now load the data into Prodigy and begin annotating the data. We will annotate the data using four mutually exclusive labels: Business, Sci_Tech, Sports, and World. To do this, we will use the Prodigy recipe called *textcat.manual* (Figure 3-11). This recipe allows us to manually annotate categories that apply to the text. We set the labels using the `--label` flag, and we use the `--exclusive` flag to designate the labels as mutually exclusive; in other words, an example may have only one correct class rather than multiple classes/labels.[8]

---

7 For more on the `train_test_split` function, visit the Scikit-learn documentation (*https://oreil.ly/YDl4A*).

8 For more on these Prodigy recipes, visit the Prodigy website (*https://oreil.ly/YUQ8x*).

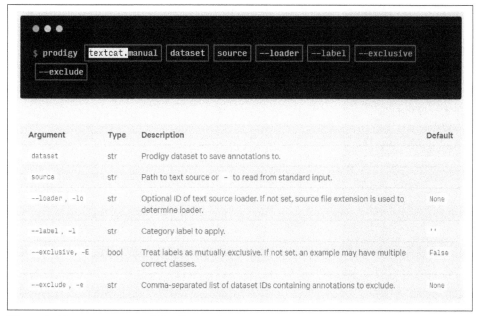

Figure 3-11. textcat.manual Prodigy recipe

In the command line, we need to specify the name of the recipe (textcat.manual), the name of the dataset to which we want to save the annotations (e.g., `ag_data_text cat`), the text source (in our case, the path to the *train_prodigy_text-cat_train_without_labels.csv*), the labels we want available in the Prodigy UI to annotate the text, and the `--exclusive` flag:

```
$ python -m prodigy textcat.manual <dataset> <source> \
    --label Business,Sci_Tech,Sports,World --exclusive
```

If successful, you will see this message in the command line:

```
✔ Starting the web server at <http://localhost:8080> … \
Open the app in your browser and start annotating!
```

Go ahead and copy the URL into your web browser. You should see an annotation UI, as shown in Figure 3-12. Make sure you see "choice" next to the "VIEW ID" in the upper-left corner; if not, you likely forgot to set the `--exclusive` tag.

We can now categorize each text into one of four categories. Click the big green checkmark box to proceed to the next example (or press the "a" key on your keyboard). If you would like to skip an example because you are not sure of the answer, press the spacebar on your keyboard.

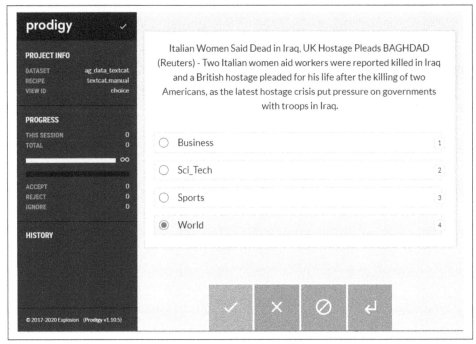

Figure 3-12. Prodigy Textcat annotation UI

Let's annotate a few hundred of these and then save them by clicking the floppy disk icon next to the word "prodigy" in the upper-left corner of the UI. A few hundred annotations should be good enough for a decent text classification model, although, as always, the more annotations, the better the model's performance will be.

Once the annotations are ready, we can output the annotations in spaCy's JSON format using the data-to-spaCy Prodigy recipe, which we also used earlier (Figure 3-13).

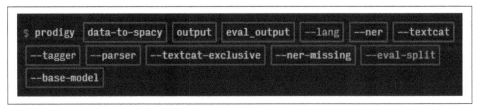

Figure 3-13. data-to-spaCy Prodigy recipe

For this recipe, we need to specify the output path (to train the model), the language ("en" in our case), the textcat dataset using the --textcat flag, and the --textcat-exclusive flag since we want to treat our classes as mutually exclusive. Note that we do *not* need to set an evaluation output path since we already have a labeled text cat_eval set, which we generated in the previous section using train_test_split:

```
$ python -m prodigy data-to-spacy <output> \
  --lang en --textcat ag_data_textcat --textcat-exclusive
```

Next, let's convert this training data from JSON format to a binary format for spaCy training:

```
$ python -m spacy convert <path-to-json> <path-for-binary-output>

# Convert from JSON to binary format for spaCy training
# Few Labels from Prodigy Annotations
json_path = "data/ag_dataset/textcat/annotations/jsons/"
bin_path = "data/ag_dataset/textcat/annotations/binary/"
input_path = cwd + json_path + "train_few_labels"
output_path = cwd + bin_path + "train_few_labels"
!python -m spacy convert "$input_path" "$output_path"
```

Finally, let's convert the *textcat_eval* set from a CSV format to a JSON format for use in spaCy. To perform this, we first need to load the CSV into Prodigy using the db-in recipe (see Figure 3-14). For this recipe, we need to designate the dataset name (e.g., *ag_data_textcat_eval*) and the file path (e.g., path to *train_prodigy_textcat_eval.csv*):

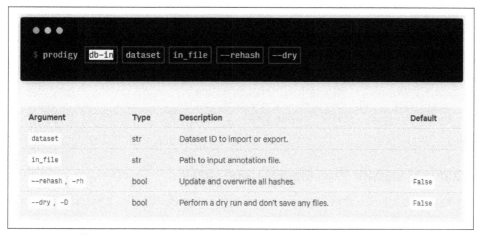

```
$ prodigy  db-in  dataset  in_file  --rehash  --dry
```

Argument	Type	Description	Default
dataset	str	Dataset ID to import or export.	
in_file	str	Path to input annotation file.	
--rehash , -rh	bool	Update and overwrite all hashes.	False
--dry , -D	bool	Perform a dry run and don't save any files.	False

Figure 3-14. db-in Prodigy recipe

```
$ python -m prodigy db-in dataset in_file
```

If successful, you should see the following message:

```
✓ Imported 24000 annotations to 'ag\_data\_textcat\_eval' \
in database SQLite Found and keeping existing "answer" \
in 0 examples
```

Now, we can use the data-to-spaCy recipe to export into spaCy's JSON format:

```
$ python -m prodigy data-to-spacy <output> \
  --lang en --textcat ag_data_textcat_eval --textcat-exclusive
```

This is the same as before, except we will need to change the output path and the -- textcat tag to ag_data_textcat_eval.

Now, let's also prepare the textcat_train_with_labels set because we will want to train a text classification model on the original labels as well to compare how well the Prodigy annotated model does versus one trained on many more labels.

We'll repeat the same steps that we used to prepare the eval set, but this time using the textcat_train_with_labels. We will call this dataset ag_data_text cat_train_with_labels:

```
$ python -m prodigy db-in dataset in_file
$ python -m prodigy data-to-spacy <output> \
  --lang en --textcat ag_data_textcat_train_with_labels --textcat-exclusive
```

Now, let's convert both of these JSONs to a binary format for spaCy training:

```
# Convert from JSON to binary format for spaCy training - Eval Set
input_path = cwd + "/data/ag_dataset/textcat/annotations/jsons/eval"
output_path = cwd + "/data/ag_dataset/textcat/annotations/binary/eval"
!python -m spacy convert "$input_path" "$output_path"

# Convert from JSON to binary format for spaCy training
# Full Set of Labels
json_path = "data/ag_dataset/textcat/annotations/jsons/"
bin_path = "data/ag_dataset/textcat/annotations/binary/"
input_path = cwd + json_path + "train_full_labels"
output_path = cwd + bin_path + "train_full_labels"
!python -m spacy convert "$input_path" "$output_path"
```

Great! We are now ready to train a text classification model with this annotated data.

Train Text Classification Models Using spaCy

If you skipped the Prodigy section just now, don't worry. We have generated the train annotations and made them available to you.

We will train two separate models. First, we will train a text classification model using the few hundred annotations we generated using Prodigy and evaluate it against the textcat_eval set we generated earlier. Then, we will train a second text classification model using the full set of labels in the textcat_train dataset from earlier and evaluate this, too, against the textcat_eval set.

To get started, let's first generate the config file for training. We will use a transformer-based model (RoBERTa) and perform transfer learning for our text classification models. We will designate this as a multilabel classification problem because we may have different labels for the same text; in other words, for the same text, different annotators may have labeled the data differently because they disagreed. This is a very common problem when annotating data. You will have internal disagreements/differing judgments among annotators. You could review all the disagreements and resolve them before training your model, or you could set up the model as a multilabel classification model, as we have chosen to do:

 We will refer to the Prodigy annotations version as the "few labels" model since we have only ~800 annotations in total. We will call the model trained on the 96,000 annotations the "full labels" model.

```
# Generate config file
# The output file we will use for training
config_file_path_output = cwd + "/data/ag_dataset/textcat/config_final.cfg"

python -m spacy init config "$config_file_path_output" --lang en \
--pipeline textcat_multilabel --optimize efficiency --gpu --force
```

If successful, you should see a message similar to Example 3-3. We have configured this model as a multilabel text classification model, optimized for efficiency, leveraging GPUs, and using the RoBERTa transformer model as its base model.

Example 3-3. spaCy textcat configuration

```
[i] Generated config template specific for your use case
- Language: en
- Pipeline: textcat_multilabel
- Optimize for: efficiency
- Hardware: GPU
- Transformer: roberta-base
[+] Auto-filled config with all values
[+] Saved config
```

Let's start by training the text classification model using our Prodigy annotations. As we did before in the NER training process, we will use the train command in spaCy (Figure 3-15):[9]

Figure 3-15. spaCy train command

```
# Train model on text classification annotations
# Few Labels from Prodigy
import spacy
```

---

9 For more on the train command, visit the official spaCy documentation (*https://oreil.ly/WM63M*).

```
annots_path = "data/ag_dataset/textcat/annotations/binary/"
output_path = cwd + "/models/ag_dataset/textcat/few_labels"
train_path = cwd + annots_path + "train_few_labels"
dev_path = cwd + annots_path + "eval"
```

Then launch the script via a separate command:

```
python -m spacy train "$config_file_path_output" \
--output "$output_path" --paths.train "$train_path" \
--paths.dev "$dev_path" --gpu-id 0 --training.max_epochs 30 --verbose
```

Example 3-4 displays the results of the training process.

Example 3-4. spaCy text classification model: Prodigy annotations

```
================== Initializing pipeline ====================
Set up nlp object from config
Loading corpus from path: /content/drive/My Drive/Applied_NLP-
Loading corpus from path: /content/drive/My Drive/Applied_NLP-
Pipeline: ['transformer', 'textcat_multilabel']
Created vocabulary
Finished initializing nlp object
Initialized pipeline components: ['transformer', 'textcat_mult
&#8730; Initialized pipeline


================== Training pipeline =========================
Loading corpus from path: /content/drive/My Drive/Applied_NLP-
Loading corpus from path: /content/drive/My Drive/Applied_NLP-
Removed existing output directory: /content/drive/My Drive/App
Removed existing output directory: /content/drive/My Drive/App
i Pipeline: ['transformer', 'textcat_multilabel']
i Initial learn rate: 0.0
E    #       LOSS TRANS...  LOSS TEXTC...  CATS_SCORE  SCORE
---  -------  -------------  -------------  ----------  ------
  0       0        0.00           0.75        50.00    0.50
  9     200        0.00         139.63        76.09    0.76
 18     400        0.00         114.52        79.24    0.79
 27     600        0.00          79.26        83.00    0.83
```

As you can see, the model gets to an F1 score of ~83 after 30 epochs. This is still remarkably good performance given that we trained the model on just a few hundred annotations.

Now, let's train the text classification model using the 96,000 original labels in the textcat_train set (remember 24,000 examples were set aside for the textcat_eval set using train_test_split). We should see a much higher F1 score since we will be training on a lot more labels now.

The spaCy `train` command remains the same as before except for the new output and train path:

```
# Train model on text classification annotations
# Full Set of Labels from AG Dataset
import spacy
annots_path = "data/ag_dataset/textcat/annotations/binary/"
output_path = cwd + "/models/ag_dataset/textcat/full_labels"
train_path = cwd + annots_path + "train_full_labels"
dev_path = cwd + annots_path + "eval"

python -m spacy train "$config_file_path_output" \
--output "$output_path" --paths.train "$train_path" \
--paths.dev "$dev_path" --gpu-id 0 --training.max_epochs 1 --verbose
```

Example 3-5 displays the results of the training process.

Example 3-5. spaCy text classification model: 96k original annotations

```
================== Initializing pipeline =======================
Set up nlp object from config
Loading corpus from path: /content/drive/My Drive/Applied_NLP-in
Loading corpus from path: /content/drive/My Drive/Applied_NLP-in
Pipeline: ['transformer', 'textcat_multilabel']
Created vocabulary
Finished initializing nlp object
Initialized pipeline components: ['transformer', 'textcat_multil
&#8730; Initialized pipeline

================== Training pipeline =========================
Loading corpus from path: /content/drive/My Drive/Applied_NLP-in
Loading corpus from path: /content/drive/My Drive/Applied_NLP-in
Removed existing output directory: /content/drive/My Drive/Appli
Removed existing output directory: /content/drive/My Drive/Appli
i Pipeline: ['transformer', 'textcat_multilabel']
i Initial learn rate: 0.0
```

E	#	LOSS TRANS...	LOSS TEXTC...	CATS_SCORE	SCORE
0	0	0.00	1.75	50.00	0.50
9	200	0.00	128.94	76.53	0.77
18	400	0.00	118.95	79.97	0.80
27	600	0.00	97.88	83.81	0.84
0	800	0.00	83.77	86.83	0.87
0	1000	0.00	92.94	89.22	0.89
0	1200	0.00	87.01	91.01	0.91
0	1400	0.00	81.47	92.29	0.92
0	1600	0.00	86.40	93.19	0.93
0	1800	0.00	70.29	93.87	0.94
0	2000	0.00	60.79	94.39	0.94
0	2200	0.00	63.48	94.78	0.95

As you can see, with the original 96k labels, the model gets an F1 score above 94 after just one epoch. This should be no surprise; with more data, the model performance improves dramatically.

Awesome! We have now just finished training our second NLP model.

Conclusion

In this chapter, we built models to solve two very popular and core NLP tasks—named entity recognition and text classification—using one of the most widely used and commercially relevant NLP libraries in the market today: spaCy. We also annotated our own data from scratch using Prodigy to develop these two models. You should now have a much better feel for how easy it is to get up and running with NLP models. Both of these models are ready to be used in production, and we will explore how to stand them up in a production pipeline in Chapter 11.

We cannot emphasize this enough: when possible, it is best to start with a large, pretrained language model and then fine-tune the model for your specific task on your specific corpus. By leveraging the prior learning of the pretrained model, you will need far fewer labels and considerably less time to achieve really great performance on tasks such as the ones we solved together in this chapter. In a nutshell, this ability to transfer learning from pretrained models to accelerate new model builds is what has made NLP such a hot topic of interest in the enterprise today.

Now that you have a better feel for state-of-the-art NLP and how to solve some real-world NLP tasks, let's go back to the basics and build some of the foundational knowledge you will need to perform NLP well. We will start with preprocessing and tokenization in the next chapter, followed by word embeddings, RNNs, and Transformers. Later in the book, we will return to these models when we discuss productionization of machine learning models.

## PART II

The Cogs in the Machine

With a high-level understanding of what NLP is all about, it's time to start diving into the details to understand how exactly modern NLP works from first principles.

In this section, we'll cover the following, in order:

- Tokenizers
- Embeddings
- Recurrent neural networks (RNNs)
- Transformers
- Transfer learning (part 2)

## CHAPTER 4

Tokenization

This is our first chapter in the section of NLP from the ground up. In the first three chapters, we walked you through the high-level components of an NLP pipeline. From here till Chapter 9, we'll be covering a lot of the underlying details to really understand how modern NLP systems work. The main components of this are:

- Tokenization
- Embeddings
- Architectures

Previously, all of these steps were abstracted away in the libraries we used (spaCy, transformers, and fastai). But now, we'll try to understand how these libraries actually work and how you can modify your code at a low level to build amazing NLP applications beyond the simple examples we presented in this book.

One thing to note: "low level" is a subjective term. While some may call PyTorch a low-level deep learning library, others may scoff at using that term for anything other than building a custom memory allocator in x86 assembly. It's a matter of perspective. What we mean by low level here is that after learning about these things, you'll have enough of an understanding to build useful applications with NLP in the real world and that you'll also be able to understand and follow the latest research in the field. We *won't* be discussing anything that's too far beyond the scope of NLP. For example, learning about how CUDA works is certainly both interesting and useful, and we'll do a bit of that in Appendix B. But CUDA itself as a tool is useful for many things outside NLP, so we'd consider that beyond the scope of this book. As much as possible, we'll try to keep the focus on things that actually improve the performance of your models in production.

Each of the items in the list that we just saw (i.e., tokenizers, embeddings, and models) can be thought of as an independent function. They take in some input and generate some output. Each of these functions then passes on its output to the next stage of the pipeline. To be more specific, we pass tokenized text into the embedding layer, and we pass embeddings into the model. You can treat these functions as black boxes if you would like and choose to focus on only one at a time. We'll look at each one in isolation, with tokenizers first.

A Minimal Tokenizer

As we start thinking about low-level parts of the deep learning stack, it's useful to understand components in terms of what their inputs and outputs are.

So what are the inputs and outputs here? The input is text. Usually, this is provided as a .txt file or something else that is read into a Python object. The output is a sequence of tokens. One of the main topics of this chapter will be a discussion of what exactly a "token" is and what it should be doing.

As always, one of the best ways to understand something is to look at the code. So here's essentially what a tokenizer is:

```
text = open('example.txt', 'r').read()
words = text.split(" ")
tokens = {v: k for k, v in enumerate(words)}

tokens

{'The': 0,
 'quick': 1,
 'brown': 2,
 'fox': 3,
 'jumps': 4,
 'over': 5,
 'the': 6,
 'lazy': 7,
 'dog.': 8}
```

A tokenizer reads in text and returns a mapping between words and indices. Essentially, it creates a dictionary (both figuratively and literally, since the preceding example creates a Python dictionary) that maps words to numbers. This is extremely useful, because we now have a representation of the source text that can be fed into an NLP model:

```
token_map = map(lambda t: tokens[t], words)
list(token_map)

[0, 1, 2, 3, 4, 5, 6, 7, 8]
```

This was, of course, a drastically oversimplified example. In practice, you'd never want to do tokenization this way. It's slow, for one thing, and does not account for a lot of intricacies across different languages. Furthermore, this simple tokenizer does not account for punctuation, grammar, or compound word structure (i.e., the fact that words ending in "-ing," "-ify," etc., are related) in any meaningful way. Nonetheless, it's a start.

Here's a more precise way of stating what a tokenizer *should* be: a tokenizer is a program that converts a sequence of characters into a sequence of tokens. Tokenizers as a general tool are very useful even outside NLP. Wherever there is a need to parse text, there is probably some form of a tokenizer. Let's take an example from the world of compilers, because it turns out that tokenization is a very old, fundamental, and useful thing to do.

 So useful, in fact, that there were popular tools like lex and flex invented in the '80s that generated the C code for a fast tokenizer given a simple description of the token you wanted to parse!

When building a compiler for a programming language, one of the first things to do is identify and mark keywords like if and for to pass on to the next stage. Here, the tokenizer reads in a file and builds a new representation of the source code where the raw ASCII/Unicode characters are replaced by tokens that represent these keywords, which can then be used to construct a data structure called a *parse tree*.

We're not building a compiler here, so the parse tree isn't entirely relevant, and in practice, we'll be using libraries instead of complex code-generation procedures. But we wanted to illustrate an example of how a tokenizer is a very useful and robust program to have, even outside of NLP.

The type of tokenizers we're interested in as deep learning practitioners, though, usually don't give us parse trees. What we want is a tokenizer that reads the text and generates a sequence of one-hot vectors.

That is the most important thing to understand about tokenizers from our top-down perspective. The input is raw text, and the output is a sequence of vectors. To be even more specific, the vectors, in our case, are simply one-hot encoded PyTorch tensors that we pass into an nn.Embedding layer. Once we get to that stage, where we can pass something to an embedding layer (which we'll discuss in the next chapter), we're done with tokenization.

Now that we understand the input and outputs, let's jump straight into the implementation, after which we'll look at some of the new ideas in this space, and examine them in more low-level detail.

In our opinion, there are two tools for tokenization that are superior to most of the others–spaCy's tokenizer and the Hugging Face tokenizers library.

spaCy's tokenizer is more widely used, is older, and is somewhat more reliable. It has its own unique tokenization algorithm that tends to work well for common NLP tasks. The `tokenizers` library is a slightly more modern package that focuses on implementing the newest algorithms from the newest research.

 Some models like BERT expect certain specific tokens, so you *cannot* use any tokenizer you like on these models. To work around this, recent versions of spaCy include wrappers around the Hugging Face `transformers` library, which allows you to combine the rest of your spaCy workflow with transformers. But behind the scenes, this will still use the BERT, not spaCy, tokenizer.

We've already used spaCy in Chapters 1 and 3, and will revisit it when we deploys model in Part III. So in this chapter, we'll focus on the Hugging Face `tokenizers` library.

Hugging Face Tokenizers

`tokenizers` is Hugging Face's official tokenization tool written in the Rust programming language (which happens to be Ajay's favorite programming language at the time of writing), with bindings to Python and JavaScript. While `tokenizers` could be used as a general-purpose tokenizer, it being Hugging Face, it's designed to be used specifically for deep learning and NLP, with a specific focus on fast subword tokenizer (which we'll look at in detail once we try out the code first).

Tokenization, unlike other parts of the deep learning pipeline, is typically done on the CPU. But that doesn't mean it has to be slow! Hugging Face's library makes good use of the multiple cores you might have on your machine, and can tokenize large datasets at the gigabyte scale (which is fairly large for nonacademic NLP) in under a minute.

The `tokenizers` library further subdivides the task of tokenizations into smaller, more manageable steps. Here's Hugging Face's description of the components of the tokenization process in its library:

Normalizer
    Executes all the initial transformations over the initial input string. For example, when you need to lowercase some text, maybe strip it, or even apply one of the common Unicode normalization processes, you will add a Normalizer.

PreTokenizer
    In charge of splitting the initial input string. That's the component that decides where and how to pre-segment the `origin` string. The simplest example would be like we saw before, to split on spaces.

Model

Handles all the subtoken discovery and generation. This part is trainable and really dependent of your input data.

Post-Processor

Provides advanced construction features to be compatible with some of the Transformer-based SOTA models. For instance, for BERT it would wrap the tokenized sentence around [CLS] and [SEP] tokens.

Decode

In charge of mapping back a tokenized input to the original string. The decoder is usually chosen according to the `PreTokenizer` we used previously.

Trainer

Provides training capabilities to each model.

Each of those logical modules has multiple options/implementations in the library:

Normalizer

Lowercase, Unicode (NFD, NFKD, NFC, NFKC), Bert, Strip...

PreTokenizer

ByteLevel, WhitespaceSplit, CharDelimiterSplit, Metaspace, ...

Model

WordLevel, BPE, WordPiece, ...

Post-Processor

`BertProcessor`, ...

Decoder

WordLevel, BPE, WordPiece, ...

You have some amount of freedom in choosing these, but more often than not, you'll be restricted to the components supported by the pretrained model you're using. In practice, you'll want to use whatever is suggested on the documentation (*https://oreil.ly/UAEX3*) for your model, so we suggest going through it if/when you encounter bugs.

Installing the library is as simple as running the following:

```
pip install tokenizers
```

But of course, we have already included this in our *requirements.txt* and *environment.yml* files on the GitHub repo:

```
import tokenizers
```

Subword Tokenization

If you continue looking through the documentation for `tokenizers`, you'll notice that there are a lot of different algorithms that are implemented in the library. But tokenization seems like a fairly straightforward task, right? What gives?

Well, it turns out that there are plenty of ways you can decide to form a "token" from a string of text.

For example, consider the strings `"cat"` and `"cats"`. One valid subtokenization of `"cats"` would be [`cat, ##s`], where the double-hashtag represents a prefix subtoken of the initial input. The advantage of this approach is that you get the semantic information that word-based tokenizers provide without incurring the cost of a very large vocabulary. These training algorithms might extract subtokens such as `"##ing"` and `"##ed"` over an English corpus.

This approach has pros and cons in terms of computation cost. On the one hand, you'll have fewer words in your vocabulary, meaning a smaller embedding matrix (discussed in Chapter 5). But on the other hand, one word will now have multiple tokens, so you'll be able to fit fewer words into a model that accepts a fixed number of tokens.

As illustrated in Figure 4-1, the simplest character-based tokenizers will generally never produce unknown tokens but will also break up a word into many small pieces, which may cause some loss of information. On the other hand, you can fully and accurately represent words with word-level tokenization, but then you'll need a very large vocabulary, or you risk having many unidentified tokens.

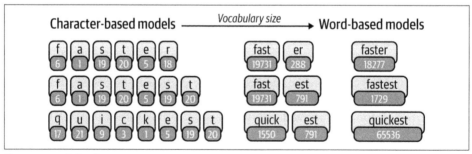

Figure 4-1. Subtokenization

So, the goal here is twofold:

- Increase the amount of information per token.
- Decrease the total number of tokens (vocabulary size).

Subword tokenizers achieve this effectively by finding a good balance between characters, subwords, and words.

 Subword tokenization algorithms (the newer ones, at least) are not set in stone. There is a "training" phase before we can actually tokenize the text. This is *not* the training of the language model itself, but rather a process we run to find the optimal balance between character-level and word-level tokenization.

The idea of using prefixes and suffixes is simple enough, and you could perhaps design a somewhat effective subword tokenizer by coding in rules for common subwords like "##ing" and "##ed". However, in practice, there are a number of difficulties with this approach:

- There are many different languages, each with its own rules. Building a good subword tokenizer would then mean understanding and implementing a new set of rules for each language.

- There is no guarantee that the rules you make are actually any good. As an extreme example, you might decide to make a subword token for "super##", but that might never show up in the text. So you've essentially wasted a spot in the dictionary. You could evaluate the number of tokens matched and tune your rules again, but at that point you might as well use a training algorithm.

- You as a human reading the text may not be able to capture intricacies in repeated language patterns. It's much simpler to have a computer read 40+ GB of text and figure out the repeating tokens than it is to actually read 40+ GB of text yourself!

So, the goal of the training procedure, then, is to identify recurring text in a corpus and "refactor" it into a token. If a particular pattern is not repeated often, it is not included as a token.

For example, if your text corpus has an even balance of the strings "car" and "cat" (along with many other words), then the tokens you might get would be ["ca##", "r", "t", ...]. But if your corpus has many more occurrences of "cat" than other words, then it might be beneficial to condense that into a single token, giving the tokens ["cat", "ca##", "r" ...]. Ideally, we want to avoid chunking entire words together into a single token like that, since it increases the vocabulary size, as shown in Figure 4-1. But when something is repeated often, like the word the, it is more efficient to chunk that information together into a single token.

Subword tokenization also reduces the impact of the issue where the model encounters a new word that it's never seen before. If your training corpus has the strings swim, play, and playing, a word-level tokenizer would identify the string swimming as an unknown word. However, `"swimming"` is simply a new word constructed on primitive subwords that the model *has* seen. So a subword tokenizer could identify it as [`"swim"`, `"##m##"`, `"##ing"`] and pass more relevant information to the model.

Let's take a look at how these ideas are implemented in the `tokenizers` library.

Building Your Own Tokenizer

The ready-to-use subword tokenizers are great, but sometimes, you really do need a tokenizer that picks out nuances specific to your text domain. The canonical examples are legal and medical text. These domains usually have a specific set of frequently used terms that are important enough to deserve their own token (think of molecule names or specific sections of legal documents).

> Yes, we said "train," because subword tokenizers need some criteria to decide how to split words, and learning is often the best solution.

If you want to train your own tokenizer, there are a few popular options. Here are some references to the state-of-the-art research in tokenizers:

Byte pair encoding (BPE)
    See R. Sennrich et al., "Neural Machine Translation of Rare Words with Subword Units," arXiv, 2015, *https://oreil.ly/dlFNw*.

WordPiece
    See M. Schuster and K. Nakajima, "Japanese and Korean Voice Search," International Conference on Acoustics, Speech and Signal Processing, IEEE (2012), *https://oreil.ly/fvGTh*.

SentencePiece
    See T. Kudo and J. Richardson, "SentencePiece: A Simple and Language Independent Subword Tokenizer and Detokenizer for Neural Text Processing," arXiv, 2018, *https://oreil.ly/YNFhP*.

Getting real-world medical data is actually quite hard due to regulations and a lack of privacy-preserving machine learning techniques. So for now, we'll use the WikiText-103 dataset, which is the set of Wikipedia articles we used in Chapter 2. Just know that if your text data represents the typical literary patterns on the internet, you won't have to train your own tokenizers from scratch most of the time.

First, we need to get the dataset (in case you didn't download it already):

```
wget https://s3.amazonaws.com/research.metamind.io/wikitext/
  wikitext-103-raw-v1.zip
unzip wikitext-103-raw-v1.zip
```

Using an established tokenizer is quite simple with Hugging Face's `tokenizers` library. Here, we first set up a byte-pair encoding (a form of subword tokenization) tokenizer in a single line of code:

```
from tokenizers import Tokenizer
from tokenizers.models import BPE

tokenizer = Tokenizer(BPE(unk_token="[UNK]"))
```

Next, we initialize a special `BpreTrainer` object. This is only required if you're training a new tokenizer from scratch:

```
from tokenizers.trainers import BpeTrainer

trainer = BpeTrainer(
    special_tokens=["[UNK]", "[CLS]", "[SEP]", "[PAD]", "[MASK]"])
```

Finally, we specify the files and train our BPE tokenizer:

```
files = [
    f"data/wikitext-103-raw/wiki.{split}.raw" for split in
    ["test", "train", "valid"]]

tokenizer.train(files, trainer)
```

How Tokenizers Are Made

Unlike training, tokenization is primarily a CPU-driven program. We typically don't use GPUs for standard tokenizers, even though there is scope for massive parallelization, for the same reason we don't use GPUs for PowerPoint or Excel—the gains are small, and writing efficient GPU code is very hard. However, there are some admirable new efforts from Rapids AI, which has built a modern CUDA-accelerated tokenizer for BERT.

From a practical standpoint, writing a GPU-accelerated tokenizer likely has a low return on investment. Hugging Face claims that their `tokenizers` library can tokenize a gigabyte of text in 20 seconds. If you're training on a 40 GB dataset (which is about the scale of GPT-2), tokenization would take 40 * 20 = 800 seconds, which is roughly 13.3 minutes. Compared to the days (or potentially weeks) it can take to actually train the model, that's small.

During inference, you likely aren't using text streams nearly as large as your training set, and the tokenization is much, much lower. Besides, if you *are* running inference on very large text samples, your bigger technical concern may be fitting the model and the data into memory and actually running a fast forward pass. In almost every scenario, a fast CPU tokenizer should be more than performant enough for your application.

But how were we able to get such efficient CPU tokenizers in the first place?

One of the main sources of speed in `spacy` and `tokenizers` is that they're both written in lower-level systems programming languages. `spacy` is written in C++, and `tokenizers` is written in Rust. These languages have a number of benefits when it comes to speed and memory usage, which is why they're used in performance-critical applications, even if they may be harder to read, write, and understand.

If you haven't already heard of C++, it's one of the oldest and most popular programming languages in the world. With C (a different but very similar language that is a subset of C++), it powers much of the world's technology infrastructure to this day.

Rust is a newer systems programming language built by Mozilla research that got its first stable release in 2015. It is designed to be syntactically similar to and perform similar tasks to C++, but incorporates many new ideas in programming language design that had been learned in the years since C++ was first released.

You can use these libraries written in other languages in your Python code because the developers also released a set of bindings to Python. This means that while it looks like you're running Python code, using Python functions, etc., what you're doing is calling into code that was written in an entirely different language!

The developers of these libraries go through all this trouble because of performance. Python as a language was designed for usability. Because of how it is designed and because it's a highly dynamic language, it's very easy to write Python code. But that comes at the cost of Python doing a lot of work behind the scenes that your computer may not appreciate.

The simplest example of this is the garbage collector. All variables we assign and use in our code take up memory. To ensure that we don't run out of memory, the OS needs to know when it can free up some of it. For example, if you load a file, read some information from it, and move on to another file to repeat the procedure, you could free the memory of the first file once you've processed it. In the past, all this memory allocating and freeing was performed manually by the programmer.

But later in the 20th century, we realized that this process was very tedious, and constantly thinking about memory can lead to a loss in programmer productivity. So, most modern high-level languages include some built-in mechanism for deciding when to free up memory. In Python, that implementation is a garbage collector, a small task that runs in the background and constantly monitors the state of variables to see if they are currently in use.

Conclusion

In this chapter, we looked at the first stage of a lower-level view of the NLP pipeline—tokenizers. Tokenizers are not the stage of the stack that most people should be optimizing because different tokenizers won't have a significant impact on your application's performance in the real world, but they are nonetheless a vital component. In practice, you should use `spacy` or `tokenizers` since they'll have the latest versions of the newest tokenizers from research implemented. If you have a custom dataset with a lot of domain-specific vocabulary (like in legal or medical applications) it makes sense to retrain an established tokenizer algorithm like WordPiece or SentencePiece.

We also explored some of the nuances of developing fast tokenizers. Specifically, we explored how the choice of programming language can have an impact on the performance of your tokenizer.

Now we have a working low-level understanding of tokenizers, and if you want you should be able to build your own from scratch (in practice, of course, it's not that useful). This allows us to take large text files and generate tokens that our model can use to solve complex NLP problems.

But we can't pass raw tokens into the model. Tokens are still essentially indices in dictionaries, which is not semantically useful for a deep learning model. Instead, we pass what are called "embeddings" of the tokens, which is what the next chapter is all about.

## CHAPTER 5

Embeddings: How Machines "Understand" Words

In the first stage of our journey through lower-level NLP, we figured out how to use tokenizers to massage our text data into a format that's more convenient for a neural net to read. The next piece of the puzzle is the embedding layer. If tokenizers are what our models will use to *read* text, embeddings are what they use to *understand* it.

Understanding Versus Reading Text

For a long time, machines have been able to represent characters (and by extension, words, sentences, etc.) digitally. The idea of using a binary encoding scheme for language and communication dates back to at least the invention of the telegraph in the 19th century.

One of the earliest forms of language encoding was Morse code. In this system, binary signals, such as switching a light on and off or sending a sequence of long and short pulses of audio, were used to represent different characters. If two people had a mode of binary communication and agreed upon a standard of what the binary sequences meant, they could reliably communicate in Morse code. This was one of the earliest and simplest methods of embedding natural human language into a binary format that machines could work with in some way. Notice how Morse code, illustrated in Figure 5-1, uses only dots and dashes—analogous to the 1s and 0s used in modern digital communication.

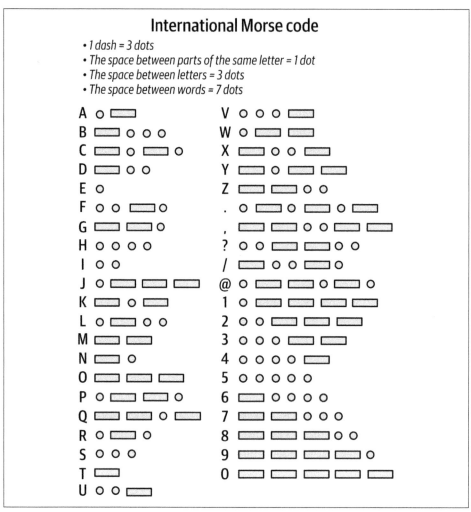

Figure 5-1. Morse code translation

Since that time, there have been many improvements in our ability to encode text/language. These include audio recordings; newer encoding algorithms like ASCII, which uses an integer number to represent text (shown in Figure 5-2); and Unicode, which lets us use characters from many different scripts.

Apart from the occasional practical issues of data integrity, corruption, etc., we have been able to reliably store, send, and access text data for a very long time. However, simply having a raw representation of text as characters can only take us so far.

ASCII TABLE

Decimal	Hexadecimal	Binary	Octal	Char
0	0	0	0	[NULL]
1	1	1	1	[START OF HEADING]
2	2	10	2	[START OF TEXT]
3	3	11	3	[END OF TEXT]
4	4	100	4	[END OF TRANSMISSION]
5	5	101	5	[ENQUIRY]
6	6	110	6	[ACKNOWLEDGE]
7	7	111	7	[BELL]
8	8	1000	10	[BACKSPACE]
9	9	1001	11	[HORIZONTAL TAB]
10	A	1010	12	[LINE FEED]
11	B	1011	13	[VERTICAL TAB]
12	C	1100	14	[FORM FEED]
13	D	1101	15	[CARRIAGE RETURN]
14	E	1110	16	[SHIFT OUT]
15	F	1111	17	[SHIFT IN]
16	10	10000	20	[DATA LINK ESCAPE]
17	11	10001	21	[DEVICE CONTROL 1]
18	12	10010	22	[DEVICE CONTROL 2]
19	13	10011	23	[DEVICE CONTROL 3]
20	14	10100	24	[DEVICE CONTROL 4]
21	15	10101	25	[NEGATIVE ACKNOWLEDGE]
22	16	10110	26	[SYNCHRONOUS IDLE]
23	17	10111	27	[ENG OF TRANS. BLOCK]
24	18	11000	30	[CANCEL]
25	19	11001	31	[END OF MEDIUM]
26	1A	11010	32	[SUBSTITUTE]
27	1B	11011	33	[ESCAPE]
28	1C	11100	34	[FILE SEPARATOR]
29	1D	11101	35	[GROUP SEPARATOR]
30	1E	11110	36	[RECORD SEPARATOR]
31	1F	11111	37	[UNIT SEPARATOR]
32	20	100000	40	[SPACE]
33	21	100001	41	!
34	22	100010	42	"
35	23	100011	43	#
36	24	100100	44	$
37	25	100101	45	%
38	26	100110	46	&
39	27	100111	47	'
40	28	101000	50	(
41	29	101001	51	)
42	2A	101010	52	*
43	2B	101011	53	+
44	2C	101100	54	,
45	2D	101101	55	-
46	2E	101110	56	.
47	2F	101111	57	/

Decimal	Hexadecimal	Binary	Octal	Char
48	30	110000	60	0
49	31	110001	61	1
50	32	110010	62	2
51	33	110011	63	3
52	34	110100	64	4
53	35	110101	65	5
54	36	110110	66	6
55	37	110111	67	7
56	38	111000	70	8
57	39	111001	71	9
58	3A	111010	72	:
59	3B	111011	73	;
60	3C	111100	74	<
61	3D	111101	75	=
62	3E	111110	76	>
63	3F	111111	77	?
64	40	1000000	100	@
65	41	1000001	101	A
66	42	1000010	102	B
67	43	1000011	103	C
68	44	1000100	104	D
69	45	1000101	105	E
70	46	1000110	106	F
71	47	1000111	107	G
72	48	1001000	110	H
73	49	1001001	111	I
74	4A	1001010	112	J
75	4B	1001011	113	K
76	4C	1001100	114	L
77	4D	1001101	115	M
78	4E	1001110	116	N
79	4F	1001111	117	O
80	50	1010000	120	P
81	51	1010001	121	Q
82	52	1010010	122	R
83	53	1010011	123	S
84	54	1010100	124	T
85	55	1010101	125	U
86	56	1010110	126	V
87	57	1010111	127	W
88	58	1011000	130	X
89	59	1011001	131	Y
90	5A	1011010	132	Z
91	5B	1011011	133	[
92	5C	1011100	134	\
93	5D	1011101	135	]
94	5E	1011110	136	^
95	5F	1011111	137	_

Decimal	Hexadecimal	Binary	Octal	Char
96	60	1100000	140	`
97	61	1100001	141	a
98	62	1100010	142	b
99	63	1100011	143	c
100	64	1100100	144	d
101	65	1100101	145	e
102	66	1100110	146	f
103	67	1100111	147	g
104	68	1101000	150	h
105	69	1101001	151	i
106	6A	1101010	152	j
107	6B	1101011	153	k
108	6C	1101100	154	l
109	6D	1101101	155	m
110	6E	1101110	156	n
111	6F	1101111	157	o
112	70	1110000	160	p
113	71	1110001	161	q
114	72	1110010	162	r
115	73	1110011	163	s
116	74	1110100	164	t
117	75	1110101	165	u
118	76	1110110	166	v
119	77	1110111	167	w
120	78	1111000	170	x
121	79	1111001	171	y
122	7A	1111010	172	z
123	7B	1111011	173	{
124	7C	1111100	174		
125	7D	1111101	175	}
126	7E	1111110	176	~
127	7F	1111111	177	[DEL]

Figure 5-2. The ASCII table (https://oreil.ly/acNAT)

For example, your hard drive will have no problem spelling out "supercalifragilisti-cexpialidocious" a million times with perfect accuracy. But for most of their history, computers lacked the ability to comprehend that "apple" can simultaneously be both a tech company with a trillion-dollar market cap and a juicy red fruit that keeps the doctor away.

When we humans see text, we see more than the raw information presented to us. The knowledge we've accumulated over time gives additional context about the things we read, which makes language and communication meaningful and efficient.

To be clear, it's perfectly OK for computers to not "understand" text to build useful things. Many older NLP systems used rule-based logic to some level of success:

```
    if(question == "What is your name"):
  print("""I'm Al, your AI assistant.
  I use whatever technology makes my investors happy.""")
```

But this type of hardcoded rule-based system is very brittle and does not generalize well, as anyone who lived through the iPhone 4s can attest to:

Me: Hey Siri, show me a sitcom.

Siri: Ok, calling mom…

How do we make computers understand words?

A computer is a machine that can only manipulate 1s and 0s. So when we say "understand," what we really mean is that we need a new way of encoding text into numbers that emphasizes the *meaning* of the text rather than the raw characters.

This is a conceptually difficult problem for humans to solve. How would you go about describing, say, the "Olympics" with just numbers? How would you convey the sense of excitement, intensity, and history that goes along with that word? Furthermore, the same word might mean different things to different people, so who would decide what numbers to use and how to use them? While ASCII, Unicode, etc., might not directly be a useful format for NLP, at least we can all agree on what the map between characters and numbers should be. How do we achieve that if the numbers are supposed to represent semantic meaning?

To clarify this idea of encoding text and language in numbers, let's think about a few tangible examples: we use social media followers to measure fame, IQ to measure intelligence, and wealth to measure success. Despite their flaws (*https://oreil.ly/ UYK9t*), we use these numbers all the time to quantify abstract concepts like intelligence and fame, which would otherwise be philosophical concepts with little practical value.

None of these measures are perfect, but they are concrete, and by extension, useful. We may not agree on how unhealthy french fries are and what "healthy" even means. But we *can* agree on how much trans fats they contain, and that trans fats are probably not good for you. It's not a perfect measure, but it is useful.

Furthermore, you can combine multiple numbers (numerical properties of the thing you're describing) to come up with a somewhat accurate and useful representation of all sorts of people, objects, places, things, and, more generally, words.

For example, you could say that person X has some specific number of followers, has some specific IQ, and earns some specific amount of money each year. The more quantifiable characteristics you add (like height, weight, place of birth, primary residence, etc.), the more accurate your description of this person will be. That's because the more numbers you add, the more *information* you have about person X.

In fact, let's strengthen that claim by saying that *any* word can be represented by a bunch of numbers that describes its properties.

This may get really weird really fast. Let's say we want to use 300 numbers. This means that we'll be using 300 different numerical properties to describe a significant portion of every word in the English language. We won't be able to perfectly encode all these words with just 300 numbers, of course. But that's not the point. We're trying to build a numerical representation that's *useful* for NLP, not accurate for communication.

For example, when describing food, one of those properties could be how some food item ranks on a scale of how spicy it is.[1] When describing humans, another property could be how much money they make.

But crucially, each word needs to have the *same* 300 properties. This can lead to a very disturbing decision-making process where we're forced to determine the flavor of humans and the net worth of fruits.

The way you could justify this goes something like this: let -1 represent super mild and let 1 represent super spicy on the spiciness scale. Similarly, let -1 represent "drowning in debt" and let 1 represent "richest human on earth" on the money scale. Now we can assign a score of 0 on the mild–spicy scale to every nonfood word, like "car" or "king," and 0 to every word that has no notion of income, like "chili pepper" or "jack fruit."

But the issue remains that it would take a lot of work to manually sit and code in these number properties for each and every single word in the dictionary. Also, deciding what 300 properties to ascribe to every word seems like something that would involve a lot of debate and result in some very unhappy people.

So instead, we can use machines to assign these number properties to words for us! "Wait a minute, I thought they *can't* do that by themselves. Isn't that why we have this chapter in the first place?" you ask.

You're right. As we mentioned before, computers on their own cannot infer the meaning of words just by looking at them. But by looking at words in the context in which they appear, maybe they can…

Word Vectors

To recap: we know that we can encode raw text accurately using established methods like ASCII and Unicode. However, we noted that having the raw text alone is not sufficient to create NLP models that dazzle investors. So, we need a way to map text to numbers that encode the meaning of the words rather than the raw information. We

---

1 This is not a made-up example. See the Scoville scale (*https://oreil.ly/C8rpE*).

know that there's no perfect way to do this, but we're hoping that we can do it in a way that's at least useful to solve the NLP tasks we talked about in Chapter 3.

We hypothesized that we can encode the meaning of a word into a collection of numbers that describes its various properties. What we need now is a way to map words to their number properties. We also need to perform this mapping using machines because it would take humans an incredibly long time to perform this task manually.

To make the problem more precise, we'll say that we want to store all these numerical properties of our words in vectors (which are simply 1D arrays). So the task, then, is to come up with an algorithm that maps words to vectors.

Arrays and Vectors

Technically speaking, arrays and vectors are *not* the same thing. Arrays are a data structure that allows us to arrange data in a particular way.

Vectors, on the other hand, are a specific kind of abstract mathematical object with a precise definition (a vector is an element of a linear vector space, and you could then define a vector space in terms of the properties of its elements).

If you want to venture into the deep depths of pure mathematics, this is probably important to keep in mind. But for all practical purposes that we care about, *vectors* and *1D arrays* are essentially the same thing. In this book, we'll use the terms interchangeably.

In fact, C++ even calls its dynamically sized array an std::vector, and we've managed to build a vast majority of the world's computing infrastructure with it, so I think we'll get by just fine.

If you remember your machine learning and data processing basics (which, hopefully you do if you've made it this far), you should remember the idea of a one-hot vector.

A *one-hot vector* is an array where one element is 1 and all the other elements are 0 (see Figure 5-3).

```
              Rome  Paris                      Word V
               ↓     ↓                           ↓
Rome   = [1,   0,   0,   0,   0,   0,   ...,   0]
Paris  = [0,   1,   0,   0,   0,   0,   ...,   0]
Italy  = [0,   0,   1,   0,   0,   0,   ...,   0]
France = [0,   0,   0,   1,   0,   0,   ...,   0]
```

Figure 5-3. One-hot vector

We're bringing this up because using large one-hot vectors is one of the easiest ways to map words to vectors.

The nth word in the dictionary will have a one-hot representation where the nth element is 1 and the rest are 0. For the rest of this chapter, we'll refer to this one-hot vector as o_n. Suppose "orange" is the 1152th word in our dictionary. The one-hot vector corresponding to orange will be o_{1152}. Let's tell that to the computer:

```
o = torch.zeros(20000)
o[1152] = 1
```

The dimensionality of the vector is the size of the dictionary. For example, a dictionary with 20,000 words means we'll have 20,000-dimensional one-hot word vectors. This is because each word in the dictionary takes up one position in the array, and the array can only have one non-zero element.

The components of that vector don't really carry semantic meaning. This is not what we were going for, but we do have *some* vector, and what we can do now is map the one-hot vector to *another* vector whose components actually carry some semantic meaning.

And luckily, we already have a pretty good tool for transforming vectors into other vectors—a matrix multiplication.

The matrix's job is to map some vector o_n to some other vector, which we'll call e_n. e_n is a new fancy vector that corresponds to the nth word in the dictionary. But unlike o_n, e_n's components have some meaning, like taste or how much it rhymes with sesquipedalian.

If we were to write it down in an equation, it would look like this:

$$e_n = E \cdot o_n$$

Or alternatively, in code:

```
E = torch.nn.Embedding(num_embeddings = 20000, embedding_dim = 300)
e = E(o)
```

What we're doing here is "embedding" the 20,000-dimensional one-hot vectors into a smaller vector with only 300 components. Unlike the one-hot vector, the embedding vector (e_n in equations and e in code) has components that can be any floating-point number: e.

Note that there is one somewhat important detail in the implementation of this embedding matrix multiplication—it's not actually a matrix multiplication. Well, yes, the formula you just read is correct, but this isn't the most efficient process. Remember that o_n is a one-hot vector, meaning that most of its elements are 0, like for the example in Figure 5-4. When you actually go through the matrix multiplication with all those 0s, you'll notice that you'll be multiplying by a lot of 0s. Not good.

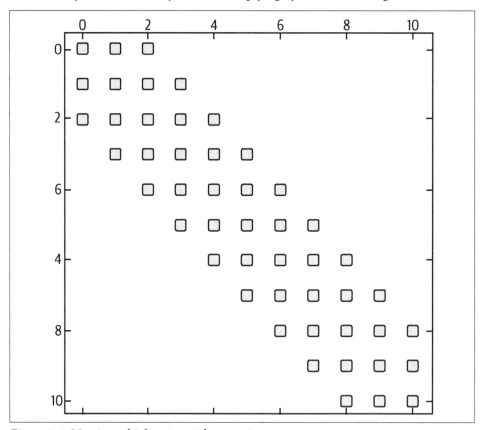

Figure 5-4. Matrix multiplication with many 0s

We're forcing our computers to do a lot of useless multiplications. Instead, we simply ignore all the multiplications that we know are going to be zero, and since the only number in the one-hot vector is a one, we just pick out the corresponding column from the embedding matrix, as shown in Figure 5-5.

This reduces the complicated matrix multiplication into a much simpler and computationally efficient array lookup. Just retrieve the column index from the embedding matrix, and you have your vector e_n.

However, there is one minor annoyance to resolve: how do you get the darn E matrix in the first place!?

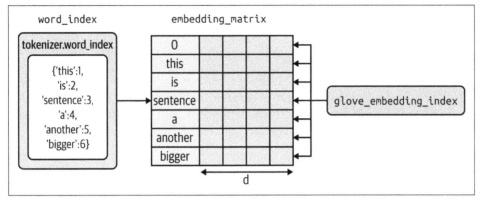

Figure 5-5. Picking out the column from the embedding matrix

Word2Vec

A few years ago, we generated this embedding matrix through an algorithm that goes through text, performs some analyses, and generates a single, static vector for each word in the vocabulary.

Some of these algorithms are Word2Vec, GloVe, and more recently, fastText. We have a more detailed explanation of these older algorithms for historical context in Chapter 8, but you should also look these up if you're interested. Jay Alammar's article (*https://oreil.ly/jWLHw*) is a good starting point. We'll be using them in "Embeddings in Practice" on page 117 just for evaluation purposes.

But these methods, as cool as they once were, are typically not used in the current state-of-the-art models. Here are the reasons why.

A new hope

Word2vec and GloVe are falling out of fashion because there are newer, sleeker systems that do the same thing. To be specific, when we refer to Word2Vec, we're essentially talking about the giant embedding matrix. If you download a Word2Vec model online, you're basically getting a function that takes in words and returns vectors. But newer, faster, better-documented solutions like Flair and fastText are probably better choices.

The English language strikes back

Another major downside of Word2Vec and probably the most important reason you should avoid it (or any other direct word/token → vector mapping, for that matter) is that Word2Vec doesn't consider context.

Consider the following two sentences:

> "I'm going to rob a bank."

> "Hey, that's a pretty cool river bank."

It's clear that the word "bank" has different meanings in each of these contexts. With Word2Vec, both versions of "bank" will have the same vector embedding, which means the model will understand both versions of "bank" as the same thing even though the two versions of "bank" are very different.

The solution to this is to generate embeddings that are not only a function of the word you're looking to get an embedding of, but also the rest of the sentence/paragraph/document (the so-called context of the word). We'll go into detail on how we do this when we discuss ELMo in Chapter 10. For now, just know that today richer contextual embeddings exist, and they are much better than context-free embeddings.

The Return of the Character-Level Models

We've been saying Word2Vec, but the name should really be "Token2Vec" because we're technically using tokens, not just words. In fact, Word2Vec is able to generate embeddings even when there are no fully formed words; in other words, Word2Vec can accommodate subword tokens.

To understand this problem more clearly, let's quickly recap subword tokenization.

We noticed that there tend to be patterns in the construction of words in the English language that we could potentially exploit. For example, the words "fast," "faster," and "fastest" all share the same root word but have different suffixes. But Word2Vec can't notice that since it only sees words as indices to an embedding matrix.

But newer tokenization methods like byte-pair encoding (seriously, read Chapter 4 if you haven't already!) are able to construct more artisanal, handcrafted vocabularies, with exotic tokens like "xxer" and "xxest" that are used to represent general suffixes. So what we need isn't a word → vector mapping, but a token → vector mapping.

With these token embeddings, we can let our models understand the words "fast," "faster," "fastest," "slow," "slower," and "slowest" (and other adjectives that can use those suffixes, but you get the idea) using four independent vectors instead of six. Not only is this more efficient, but linguistically, it's the right thing to do.

Additionally, Word2Vec can generate embeddings for words it has seen before. The way we try to deal with this issue is by creating a special unknown word token that is used whenever our model encounters something it's never seen before. But this limited vocabulary size can still become a major problem when dealing with domain-specific text data. Don't know about you, but we're fairly confident we don't want our models confusing transistors and microorganisms!

The subword models, on the other hand, have all the individual tokens built into the vocabulary. In other words, these subword models will try to pick up at least some parts of the word, and if not, they will have embeddings for the individual characters.

Unfortunately (or fortunately, depending on how you look at it), most of the new transformer networks have their own set of special tokens that do their own thing (we'll explore these details more in Chapter 7). Each of the big, new milestone models (e.g., BERT and GPT-2) have implemented their own tokenizer and embedding layer.

This means we typically do not need to download embedding matrices from the internet anymore. The original goal with Word2Vec was to have some reusability in terms of what you feed into the model. But, considering that we can now do transfer learning with the model itself, reusing embeddings isn't required.

So, what *should* we do then?

Embeddings in the Age of Transfer Learning

The keen-eyed among you will have noticed that we spent the last four sections telling you not to use Word2Vec. Again, I'd like to clarify that there are no hard-and-fast rules here. If Word2Vec works for your application, go for it.

That said, if you're using transfer learning with transformers (which is what you should be doing if you're reading this book), here's a good way to approach embeddings and vectors: first, perform the preprocessing steps from the previous chapter. Use whatever shiny new subword tokenizer you like (or the amazing spacy tokenizer, which will work fantastically well in most cases), and generate a rich numericalized subword vocabulary. For models like BERT, remember that you have to use a custom tokenizer. If you're using transfer learning (which you should!), the pretrained model you're using will have the embedding layer built in, which performs the lookup and gets vectors that correspond to the dataset that the model was pretrained on. Over the course of fine-tuning the model, you're going to update the embedding layer as well. This will give you the best of both worlds—an embedding matrix that is built upon the foundations of a large corpus of text while also capturing the subtleties of your particular dataset.

Now that you know what to do, let's do it! On to the code!

Embeddings in Practice

It's nice to reason about what works and all, but you should believe none of what we said without actual experimental evidence. So let's see how these embeddings stack up against each other in practice.

For those of you reading this from the print book, remember that the rest of this chapter is a 100% executable Jupyter Notebook. So as always, we'd highly encourage you to hop on to Colab or your favorite cloud computing service (or on your local machine, if that's how you roll) and run the code in real time, edit it, play around with hyperparameters, and have fun.

Preprocessing

Before doing anything at all, we need to import the libraries we'll be using, which are PyTorch and `torchtext`. We'll be importing a few submodules under certain specific names, since this is the convention with PyTorch:

```
import torch.nn.functional as F
import torch.nn as nn
from torch import optim
import torch

from torchtext import *
import torchtext
```

We'll also set up a CUDA device, which is just a way of telling PyTorch to use the GPU for faster computation. If you're using Colab, make sure that you've selected the GPU runtime type to ensure the greatest possible speed:

```
dev = torch.device("cuda") if torch.cuda.is_available() else torch.device("cpu")
```

Cool! The main thing we'll need is a dataset (duh!). For this notebook, we've chosen the IMDb dataset, which contains 50,000 movie reviews, each labeled with "positive" or "negative." Follow the comments to understand what's going on.

If you aren't able to figure all of this out at first glance, don't worry. Our goal here is to understand word vectors, not text preprocessing and PyTorch setup functions. We're following the "do whatever works well enough to allow for rapid experimentation" principle here, so we're going to skip using any fancy subword tokenizers, and instead we will use the tried-and-tested `spacy` tokenizer with `torchtext`.

The main line you should be interested in is:

```
TEXT.build_vocab(train, vectors='glove.6B.100d')
```

This is what's responsible for getting the vectors and building the vocabulary. Try using different arguments for the `vectors` parameter and see how your model performs. In general, you'll see higher performance with higher-dimensional vectors, since they have more space to represent the "meaning" of the words, as we discussed earlier in the chapter. But with larger vectors come larger compute requirements, so we'll leave it to you to find a happy medium.

Here are some values you can try (from the `torchtext` documentation):

```
'charngram.100d',
'fasttext.en.300d',
'fasttext.simple.300d',
'glove.42B.300d',
'glove.6B.100d',
'glove.6B.200d',
'glove.6B.300d',
'glove.6B.50d',
'glove.840B.300d',
'glove.twitter.27B.100d',
'glove.twitter.27B.200d',
'glove.twitter.27B.25d',
'glove.twitter.27B.50d'
```

Hopefully, the meaning of each of these values is fairly easy to interpret. This is something you'll have to get used to in NLP/deep learning. The models, datasets, etc., that you download online often have somewhat cryptic names like the ones here, sometimes with no documentation explaining what exactly each one is. Understanding that the d stands for dimension is an example of that. Here, the number before the dimension is an indication of the vocabulary size that the embeddings were trained on (for example, 42B indicates 42 billion different words):

 This next block of code involves downloading both the dataset *and* the embedding matrix, so it can take a while to run. Be patient!

```
# Set up fields
TEXT = data.Field(lower=True, include_lengths=True, \
batch_first=False, tokenize='spacy')
LABEL = data.LabelField()

# Make splits for data
train, test = datasets.IMDB.splits(TEXT, LABEL)

# Build the vocabulary
TEXT.build_vocab(train, vectors='glove.6B.100d') \
# use 'glove.42B.300d' for greater accuracy or \
'glove.6B.100d' for greater speed
LABEL.build_vocab(train)

# Make iterator for splits
train_iter, test_iter = data.BucketIterator.splits((train, test), \
batch_sizes=(128,1024), device=dev, sort_within_batch=True, repeat=False)
```

After running this code block, you should now have the IMDb dataset downloaded, tokenized, and vectorized. We're now ready to start building a model to process the IMDb word vectors.

Model

Remember, our goal here is to try different word embeddings and see their effect on performance on a simple dataset. Instead of overcomplicating, we're going to stick to a few simple, default models that come built-in with PyTorch (remember the rapid experimentation principle!). We won't be using any crazy new architectures or training techniques from modern research.

But note that *since* we're not using any fancy stuff, our model will perform pretty badly relative to what's out there today. You should almost never use the code here for your projects or in production, since there are far better performing NLP models and techniques today.

At a high level, this is what our model consists of the following:

Pretrained embedding layer that performs an array lookup with the GloVe vectors that we already downloaded
> This is what we're interested in.

Standard RNN module
> nn.RNN() implements a simple recurrent neural network in PyTorch. You can find the implementation in the PyTorch docs (*https://oreil.ly/wuDAW*).

Classification head that consists of two fully connected layers
> The final layer outputs a single number, which we will pass through a sigmoid to get a prediction:

 We're now going to define the RNN classifier model. This might be your first time looking at a PyTorch model (implemented as an nn.module). If so, refer to "PyTorch" on page 201 or to some of the excellent resources online.

```
class RNN_classifier(nn.Module):
    def __init__(self, embedding_size = 100, hidden_size = 512, num_layers = 3):
        super().__init__()

        # Set up an embedding layer with the right dimensions, \
        and copy the weights from the pretrained glove embeddings
        vocab = TEXT.vocab
        self.embed = nn.Embedding(len(vocab), embedding_size).cuda()
        self.embed.weight.data.copy_(vocab.vectors)

        # Set up a standard PyTorch RNN sections with the right \
        dimensions and a variable number of layers
        self.rnn = nn.RNN(embedding_size, hidden_size, num_layers)

        # Add a two layer classification head with the right dimensions. \
        The final layer must output a single number
```

```
        self.classificationLayer1 = nn.Linear(hidden_size,10)
        self.classificationLayer2 = nn.Linear(10,1)


    def forward(self, input, lengths=None):

        embed_input = self.embed(input)
        packed_emb = nn.utils.rnn.pack_padded_sequence(embed_input, \
        lengths, batch_first=False)

        output, hidden = self.rnn(packed_emb)
        hidden = hidden[-1]
        x = hidden.squeeze(0)
        x = self.classificationLayer1(x)
        x = self.classificationLayer2(x)

        logits = x.view(-1)
        return logits
```

We just set up the model as a Python class. Now, we need to create an actual instance of the RNN_classifier to use it. Here, you can tweak the hidden_size and num_lay ers to change the dimensionality of the hidden state and the number of layers, respectively.

Generally, the larger the values you use for both of these parameters, the better results you'll get. However, they involve more computation, so your code will run slower:

```
model = RNN_classifier(hidden_size=256, num_layers=1)
model.to(dev)
```

As a quick test, let's run through one batch of our training data and check the shape of the output. Checking the dimensions at various stages of computation is generally a good way to debug PyTorch code.

We should get an output tensor of 128, which is our batch size. The 128 number corresponds to 128 predictions, one for each example in our batch:

```
for batch in train_iter:
    (x,x_len) = batch.text
    pred = model(x,x_len)
    print(pred.shape)
    break
```

Training

On to the training phase. First, set up a few hyperparameters:

```
loss_func = F.binary_cross_entropy_with_logits
opt = optim.Adam(model.parameters(), lr=1e-4)
epochs = 6
```

To make our lives easier later on and to monitor training effectively, we'll define a quick function that runs through the test sets and computes the model accuracy:

```
def get_metrics(model, test_data):
    model.eval()
    correct, total = 0, 0
    with torch.no_grad():
        for batch_idx, batch_data in enumerate(test_data):
            text, text_lengths = batch_data.text
            logits = model(text, text_lengths)
            predicted_labels = (torch.sigmoid(logits) > 0.5).long()
            total += batch_data.label.size(0)
            correct += (predicted_labels == batch_data.label.long()).sum()
        return correct.float()/total
```

Final step: the training loop. This is where we run through the training data and update our model's parameters. After running this block, you'll see a progress bar and the accuracy printed at the end of each epoch:

```
from tqdm import tqdm_notebook as tqdm

for epoch in tqdm(range(epochs)):
    model.train()
    for batch in tqdm(train_iter):
        (x,x_lengths)=batch.text
        pred = model(x,x_lengths)

        actual=batch.label.float()
        loss = loss_func(pred,actual)

        loss.backward()
        opt.step()
        opt.zero_grad()

    if (epoch==5):
        for g in opt.param_groups:
            g['lr'] = 3e-3

    print("Accuracy: " + str(get_metrics(model, test_iter).cpu().numpy()))
```

Hopefully you're getting >70% accuracy. Note that this can vary due to random factors like initialization, so if your model isn't working that well, consider changing a few hyperparameters and run the code again.

Validation

Great! We're done! We now have an RNN-based text classifier that's about 75% accurate at predicting whether a movie review is positive or negative.

Let's see how our model performs on some real data. To make predictions quickly, let's construct a function that does all the hard work for us, so that we can focus on the fun stuff:

```python
import spacy
nlp = spacy.load('en')

def predict_sentiment(model, sentence):
    # based on:
    # https://github.com/bentrevett/pytorch-sentiment-analysis/blob/
    # master/2%20-%20Upgraded%20Sentiment%20Analysis.ipynb
    model.eval()
    tokenized = [tok.text for tok in nlp.tokenizer(sentence)]
    indexed = [TEXT.vocab.stoi[t] for t in tokenized]
    length = [len(indexed)]

    tensor = torch.LongTensor(indexed).to(dev)
    tensor = tensor.unsqueeze(1)
    length_tensor = torch.LongTensor(length)
    prediction = torch.sigmoid(model(tensor, length_tensor))
    return prediction.item()
```

Let's try predicting the score of a review the model has never seen before. The following is a review of *Spider-Man: Far From Home* on Rotten Tomatoes. The original score was 3/4, which equates to 75% positive.

What does our RNN say?

```python
review = """I like that Far From Home is trying something new and that its
humor  feels more real than the ironic cracks in most superhero movies.
I just wish its good pieces all came together more satisfyingly."""

print('Probability positive:')
predict_sentiment(model, review)
```

Hmm…not too bad. Not too bad at all.

Now, it's time to go back to the beginning and try out some different embeddings. Have fun!

Embedding Things That Aren't Words

Now that you're (hopefully) comfortable with using word embeddings, let's move on to another tangential use of embeddings. This should help you build intuition for how embeddings can be powerful inputs to a neural network.

In the notebook, you just saw that the models we're building, regardless of whether it's some sort of RNN, LSTM, or transformer, take in sequences of word vectors and perform operations that manipulate them. Depending on the specifics of the model, these manipulations could be used for classification, regression, text generation, etc.

What they do with this sequence is entirely up to you and your application. This is a key point to remember.

We haven't discussed exactly how these networks work from a low-level perspective yet, but we don't need to. For now, we can understand that RNNs/LSTMs/transformers process sequences of vectors, and we can implement that idea in code. That should be enough.

But wouldn't it be cool if we could also run the same exact models on entirely different kinds of data?

After all, these NLP models take in vector sequences, but that doesn't mean the vectors have to represent words. They can be absolutely anything. As long as you can create a mapping from x to a vector representation of x, you can create a model that works on x.

Was that too many xs? Let us articulate:

- Want a model that can remove background noise from speech recordings? Find a way to embed raw audio waveforms into vectors, feed that into an NLP model, and *boom*, you're now the owner of the most subscribed-to ASMR YouTube channel.

- Want a model that can predict stock movements? Find a way to embed stock pricing information into vectors, feed that into an NLP model, and *boom*, you're a millionaire![2]

- Want a model that can play Fortnite? Find a way to embed useful game metadata like HP, ammo, etc., into a vector, feed it into an NLP model, and *boom*, you're now livestreaming with Ninja!

OK, the last one might have been a bit of a stretch,[3] but you get the idea.

This, of course, begs the million-dollar question: how do we map these seemingly disparate items into vectors?

That depends. As the expert in your field/project, how you choose to create vector embeddings of your data for uncommon formats that haven't been worked on before is entirely up to you.[4]

---

2 Please don't actually do this in practice. There are a lot of ways it can go wrong, and there are much better models, algorithms, and techniques to deal with stocks. We are by no means expert traders. This was just an example.

3 Or is it… (*https://oreil.ly/mOVWN*)

4 We encourage you to look up the literature, though. Often, you'd be surprised at the sort of things people build with neural nets.

But just so that this doesn't seem like a bunch of Master Shifu wisdom without substance, let's go over an example—engineering embeddings for music data. This fantastic example was again provided by Jay Alammar.[5]

A sonnet in the MIDI protocol

The MIDI protocol, if you haven't heard of it, is a way of representing music digitally. We don't mean the raw audio as waveform data; that's been done for ages. MIDI stores the actual information about the notes that are played by different instruments of a song (but no vocals). It does this through a series of commands such as note on and note off.

But the protocol allows for much more than that since just note on and note off commands would result in music that sounds monotonous and would be inefficient in terms of storage/memory utilization.

MIDI also adds a set velocity command, which allows you to control "how hard" the note is played. But remember, MIDI doesn't store any sort of audio information, it only encodes the semantics of the musical notes. You can think of it as a digital representation of sheet music.

And just like sheet music, you can play MIDI tracks on a variety of instruments and do things like switch the piano part with a heavily distorted guitar.

Hopefully this gives you a fair idea of how MIDI works at a high level. But, if you're unfamiliar with music arrangement or if this still seems a little foreign, try out an online MIDI editor or search for "Synthesia" on YouTube.

We understand if you're still skeptical about MIDI's ability to encode music realistically. That's fair. After all, MIDI isn't perfect, and there are many subtleties in how instruments are played that can't be captured in simple rule-based logic.

However, MIDI is still a powerful encoding format for digital music and, more importantly, one that we can use to generate vectors that we pass to neural nets.

Making Vectorized Music

With MIDI in hand, we're now one step closer to retrofitting our NLP neural net (we really need to come up with a better name for this) to do cool things with music data. We know that music can (more or less) be represented as a sequence of MIDI commands. Somehow, we need to transform those MIDI commands into vectors.

---

5 If you haven't gotten the idea yet, check him out! He has a lot of well-written, clear blog posts on his site (*http://jalammar.github.io*).

Well, this shouldn't come as a surprise by now, but there are no hard-and-fast rules in machine learning, and one of the simplest solutions here is to just concatenate all the MIDI commands into a giant one-hot vector (an example of which can be seen in Example 5-1).

Example 5-1. OpenAI's MIDI embedding vector

```
bach piano_strings start tempo90 piano:v72:G1 piano:v72:G2 piano:v72:B4 piano:v72:D4
violin:v80:G4 piano:v72:G4 piano:v72:B5 piano:v72:D5 wait:12 piano:v0:B5 wait:5
piano:v72:D5 wait:12 piano:v0:D5 wait:4 piano:v0:G1 piano:v0:G2 piano:v0:B4
piano:v0:D4 violin:v0:G4 piano:v0:G4 wait:1 piano:v72:G5 wait:12 piano:v0:G5
wait:5 piano:v72:D5 wait:12 piano:v0:D5 wait:5 piano:v72:B5 wait:12
```

In fact, this is more or less what OpenAI used in 2019 to create MuseNet, the transformer-based composing AI that stunned a small, nerdy group of people on Twitter that were dying to hear Bon Jovi play Chopin (see Figure 5-6).[6]

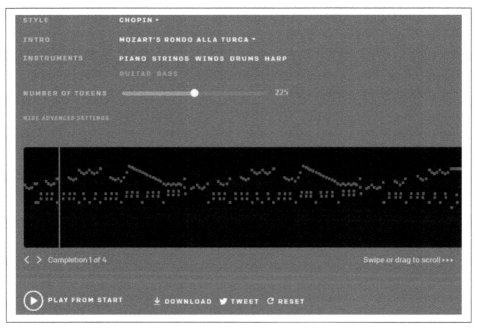

Figure 5-6. Example from OpenAI's MuseNet

---

6 To see what they did, see their blog post (*https://openai.com/blog/musenet*). It has an interesting section on the different embedding techniques they tried, which is relevant to what we've discussed in this chapter.

Some General Tips for Making Custom Embeddings

With the example of making embeddings for MIDI tracks from scratch, you should have a fair idea of how to create embeddings for the task you're working on.

But we should emphasize that the golden rule if you're trying to create your own custom embeddings is—don't. For most NLP tasks, you'll almost never want to use handmade embeddings. This simply takes too much manual effort and does not improve model performance a lot. This is a job best left to the learning process.

In cases where a straightforward embedding scheme is not readily available (as was the case with MIDI), we'd still recommend crafting a clever way to preprocess your data into nicely formatted text and then let subword tokenization and learned embeddings deal with the rest.

If you do find yourself in a situation where you *really* need to make vectors out of your data, be careful how much metadata you supply. You don't want to make your vectors too big, as that would make computation more intensive. But at the same time, concatenating extra information on your vectors almost never hurts.

To get a sense of what's enough in terms of how much you should concatenate, let's quickly think about another example: images. We're going to try image classification with transformers (it's not as crazy as it sounds).

First, we need a way to feed raw pixel values into the transformer. To do this, let's stack up the RGB intensities into a 3D vector, as shown in Figure 5-7.

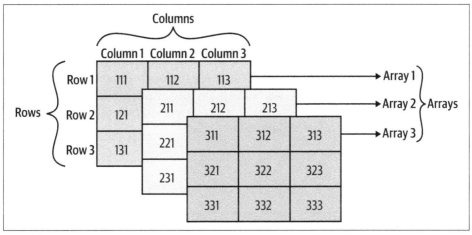

Figure 5-7. Stacking RGB values into an array

We could then "read" the pixels from left to right, row by row. This would create a sequence of 3D vectors, which is a suitable format to feed into a transformer.

If you think about it, you as a living, breathing human being would probably find it difficult to classify images if I laid out the pixels into a giant strip. You'd need *some* way of knowing where pixels belong relative to each other in space.

A reasonable piece of metadata to add to our 3D pixel vectors, in this case, would be position. We'd literally just concatenate the row and column numbers (in other words, the *x* and *y* coordinates) of the pixel onto that pixel's embedding vector (as shown in Figure 5-8).

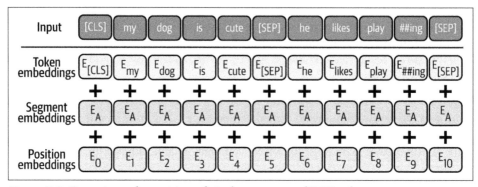

Figure 5-8. Concat x and y position of pixel onto array of RGB values

This helps the transformer understand exactly where each pixel is located, which is super useful when classifying images.

But on the other hand, let's go over some types of metadata that you probably wouldn't want to concatenate onto your pixel vectors.

A nice example of this would be values of the pixel in another color space like HSL or CMYK (see Figure 5-9). These might be useful, but, considering that a neural net could technically learn the RGB → HSL mapping internally if required, this doesn't make a lot of sense. Here HSL isn't adding any extra useful information that the model couldn't have figured out in the first place, and would just add unnecessary complexity and computational requirements.

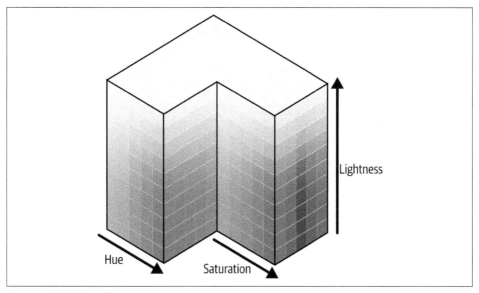

Figure 5-9. HSL color space

Conclusion

In this chapter, we looked at the concept of embeddings—vectors or 1D arrays that use numbers to represent semantic properties. Embeddings have historically been generated with algorithms like Word2Vec, but with the advent of transfer learning, copying model weights allows you to copy embeddings as well, with no extra effort. We also looked at an example that used embeddings with MIDI data and learned that the same architecture can be used for multiple tasks.

With the advent of contextual embeddings, using the embeddings we presented in this chapter is no longer enough. So why settle for static vectors that don't accurately capture the meanings of words when we know we can do better? In Chapter 9, we'll revisit the idea of embeddings in the context of ELMo, BERT, and others, which are the modern alternatives that you *should* be using instead.

At this point, we have now covered enough of the pipeline to read in raw text from a file and generate a sequence of semantic vectors that can be fed into any model of your choosing. What model you might want to choose is what we'll cover next.

## CHAPTER 6

Recurrent Neural Networks and Other Sequence Models

One of the big themes of this book so far has been transformers. In fact, almost every model we have trained so far has been some member or relative of the transformer family. Even the tokenizers we built and used were constructed with specific transformer architectures in mind.

But transformers aren't the only model in town.

Transformers themselves are relatively recent—the original paper by Vaswani et al.[1] was first published on arXiv in June 2017 (eons ago in the deep learning community but not too long ago in the span of human history). Before then, people weren't really using transformers. So what was the alternative?

Recurrent neural networks (RNNs) were the name of the game back in the day. With all of our talk about how transformers and transfer learning have revolutionized the field, we might have given you the (false) impression that NLP wasn't really a thing until BERT came out. This is most certainly not the case.

RNNs and their variants were the convolutional neural networks (CNNs) of NLP. In 2015, if you wanted to learn deep learning, most courses introduced CNNs as the "solution" for vision and RNNs as the "solution" for NLP. Perhaps the most salient example of 2015 RNN hype was Andrej Karpathy's blog post, "The Unreasonable Effectiveness of Recurrent Neural Networks" (*https://oreil.ly/QVCAW*), which shows how RNNs can be used to do a lot of interesting things and actually work.

---

1 A. Vaswani et al., "Attention Is All You Need," arXiv, June 12, 2017, *https://oreil.ly/f7uk1*.

RNNs and their variants, unlike transformers, are not new. The very first LSTM network designs (along with a fair bit of drama surrounding who actually created them) trace back to at least the 1980s. They grew in popularity, just as deep learning did, in the 2010s, and became the dominant architecture for deep learning–based NLP. Their most popular use case was translation and speech-to-text systems. Today, RNNs are not as popular for NLP, but popularity in the research community does not always equate to practicality in the real world.

A good example of this is the self-driving system in comma.ai products, which uses a GRU (another RNN variant). Some of the most revolutionary work from DeepMind, including AlphaStar, used LSTM networks. Because of the rapid transition to transformer networks that happened at roughly the same time as the transfer learning revolution, some researchers have questioned whether RNNs can be just as effective (*https://oreil.ly/TXAbw*) when used properly.

One of the biggest selling points of transformers, thanks in no small part to the work done by OpenAI on GPT, is scale. Transformers parallelize better, steadily improve accuracy as dataset size increases, and present a solid platform for transfer learning.

However, as we've seen in Chapter 2, *initially* training transformers can sometimes be finicky, and the attention mechanism is still a very memory-hungry operation. In the real world, having perfect large datasets is also not too common.

RNNs, then, present an interesting middle ground that might be worth considering. They can be (but not always are) easier to train, are smaller overall, and consume less memory. If you're deploying to a low-resource edge device, that is very appealing.

RNNs for General Sequence Modeling

As we mentioned before, the architectures we're talking about here (including transformers) are not just for text. More generally, they are designed for *sequences*. In NLP, we decide to tokenize text and construct a sequence of tokens, but in the end, the computer sees only numbers.

RNNs, just like transformers, can be used for all sorts of sequence modeling tasks, like time series forecasting, reinforcement learning, and audio. However, it turns out that RNNs work especially well for a particular kind of sequence: sequences that are *Markovian*.

Markovian means that the next item in the sequence depends only on what the current item is. For example, in some games like chess, you could, in principle, walk into the middle of a game, look at the state of the board, and decide what move to make.[2]

---

[2] If you're a perfect machine, that is. In practice, knowing your opponent's previous moves likely helps you understand their psychology.

All the information you need to know is encapsulated in the positions of the pieces of the board at the time you look at it. This is not the case with natural language, where there can be complex long-term dependencies across sentences, paragraphs, etc. The attention mechanism in transformers excels at capturing long-range dependencies, but in a Markovian sequence, that is not very useful.

We won't be talking too much about Markovian sequences in this book, but if it sounds interesting, you might want to look into the field of reinforcement learning.

Now, we'll walk you through the workings of the RNN architecture and compare it to more advanced variants like the LSTM and GRU.

Recurrent Neural Networks

We begin with vanilla RNNs, which planted the seeds for deep learning in NLP. RNNs are like every other neural network: they use the general idea of putting together a lot of matrix multiplications and nonlinear activation functions to do interesting things.

There are many ways in which RNNs are very similar to transformers:

- They both "operate" on sequences of word vectors.
- Both can be used for most NLP tasks.
- Both can take advantage of attention mechanisms.
- Both can use similar transfer learning techniques.

But there are a few important differences between RNNs and transformers:

- Transformers take in sequences of fixed-length, but RNNs can handle sequences that are as long or as short as you want.
- Transformers "process" multiple words in parallel, while RNNs work with one word at a time.

In fact, if you remember, you already used an RNN in the last chapter. That tells you that the process for actually training and using an RNN isn't very different from that for a transformer. There are fundamental differences in the architecture, but you can reuse most/all of your data pipeline, training loop, and other surrounding infrastructure that isn't directly related to the architecture of your model.

Most deep learning frameworks you're likely to use will have some API to build an RNN without too much effort. The simplest way to do this in PyTorch is:

```
import torch

model = torch.nn.RNN(300, 512)
```

This initializes an RNN that takes 3D word vectors as input and internally uses a 512-dimensional vector as its hidden representation. You can now use this just like you would use any other PyTorch nn.Module—create a dataloader and an optimizer, then train. But before we actually do that, let's look at the RNN docs to see some of the configuration options:

`input_size`
> The number of expected features in the input x

`hidden_size`
> The number of features in the hidden state h

`num_layers`
> Number of recurrent layers. E.g., setting `num_layers=2` would mean stacking two RNNs together to form a *stacked RNN*, with the second RNN taking in outputs of the first RNN and computing the final results. Default: 1

`nonlinearity`
> The nonlinearity to use. Can be either `tanh` or `reluv`. Default: `tanh`

`bias`
> If `False`, then the layer does not use bias weights b_ih and b_hh. Default: `True`

`batch_first`
> If `True`, then the input and output tensors are provided as (`batch,seq,feature`). Default: `False`

`dropout`
> If nonzero, introduces a *Dropout* layer on the outputs of each RNN layer except the last layer, with dropout probability equal to `dropout`. Default: 0

`bidirectional`
> If `True`, becomes a bidirectional RNN. Default: `False`

Most of these hyperparameters are not new and are analogous to the corresponding parameters in transformers. The one interesting parameter is `bidirectional`, which we'll get to in a bit.

What RNNs *actually do*, though, is not that complicated. An RNN is essentially a neural network with a `for` loop. In simplest form, you could implement it like this:

```
for word in words:
    state = f(word, state)
```

In English, this means that an RNN has a loop that iterates through the sequence. For each word in the sequence, it passes the current word and the previous state to an "RNN cell" that performs some computation to generate the next state. This is repeated until you reach the end of the sequence. The result is a final state that you can feed into a feed-forward layer, whose functionality depends on the task you're solving.

 In RNN literature, you'll often hear the word "cell" being thrown around. A cell represents a unit of computation that is applied at each time step or word.

We have left the meaning of the word "state" here intentionally vague because different variants of the RNN architecture (LSTM, GRU, etc.) implement state differently. But at their core, this is what all RNN architectures do—read in the sequence one word at a time and update some state as they do so.

A common visual depiction of RNNs you might see is a block with an arrow that loops back to itself (shown in Figure 6-1). This captures the idea that RNNs loop through the sequence and pass the previous state back as input into the cell to get the next state.

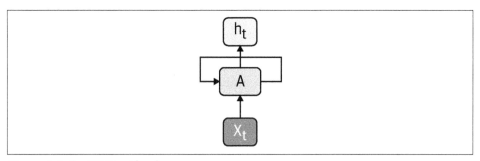

Figure 6-1. An RNN with a loop

The loop here can then be unrolled, to get something that looks more like the transformer diagrams we've been looking at. The unrolled version, shown in Figure 6-2, depicts how you would pass a sentence into the RNN more clearly.

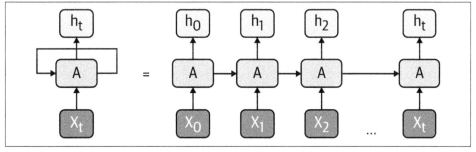

Figure 6-2. An unrolled RNN

For a vanilla RNN, the cell is implemented in two simple matrix multiplications: one to transform the word vector and another to transform the hidden state. We'll explain that more clearly in a bit, but to get a firm understanding of cells and how to use them in a loop, let's implement an RNN in PyTorch.

RNNs in PyTorch from Scratch

We've talked about this briefly before, but `fastai`'s functionality is split into modules. Most of the NLP functionality is in the `text` submodule. In typical `fastai` style,[3] we import all the things we need from that module. The `fastai` library automatically handles a lot of imports for us behind the scenes, so you don't need to worry about importing things like PyTorch yourself.

 As you might have guessed from the name, `transformers` (the Hugging Face library, not the family of architectures) is mostly focused on implementing state-of-the-art transformers and exposing an API to interact with them. It is not really a general-purpose NLP or deep learning framework. As a consequence, `transformers` doesn't really have a great way to train nontransformer models, and there's no reason it should! Implementing things that are not transformers is not a goal of that library. So for this chapter, we'll be using `fastai` to train and evaluate our RNN models. We'll focus on the core architecture and let the library deal with setting up the dataloaders, optimizer, and training loop. Remember, the choice of deep learning framework is not as important as how you use it.[4]

The `RNN` class discussed previously drives the core functionality of the model we're going to build, but there are a few things we need to add around it. First, there's an embedding layer (which we explored in detail in Chapter 5). Then, we pass the word vectors to our PyTorch RNN model.

---

3 Again, we highly recommend checking out the `fastai` library and courses!

4 ...if you're ignoring performance, that is. Of course, it's better to use one that's well optimized and fast. But you get the idea. For more information on deep learning frameworks and other tools, check out Chapter 9.

As you should with all other `fastai` code in this book, make sure you're using `fastai` version 2 when running this code. It is not backward-compatible with version 1. You can check your library version with the following code snippets:

```
import fastai
fastai.__version__

'2.0.16'

from fastai.text.all import *
```

The output of the RNN module will be the final hidden state in the network. This essentially encodes information about what the processed sentence means. There are variants of RNN models that use the hidden state for every item in the sequence, but we'll keep it simple for now.

We'll be trying a simple text classification problem: positive/negative sentiment analysis on the IMDb dataset. While admittedly a little too basic and boring at this point, we want to focus on actually seeing if we can use that last hidden state of our RNN to do useful things.

While PyTorch *does* provide a built-in `RNN` class, let's try to build something similar ourselves. It's instructive and not too hard to do. Later, we can swap out our module for the real `torch.nn.RNN`, because reinventing the wheel is not very useful in practice.

We'll build our RNN modularly. There are two parts to our RNN implementation:

Loop
> The loop takes in a sequence, loops over it while updating the hidden state, and returns the final hidden state.

Cell
> The cell takes a single word vector and the previous hidden state and returns the next hidden state.

The cool part is that since almost every recurrent architecture follows this framework, we'll also get to see how we can easily swap out cells to get better performance.

First, the vanilla RNN cell. The mathematical formulation for the simple RNN cell computation is:

$$h_{t+1} = \tanh\left(W_{ih}x_t + b_{ih} + W_{hh}h_t + b_{hh}\right)$$

The subscript *ih* means "input to hidden," and *hh* means "hidden to input" (i.e., W_{ih} takes a vector that's the size of an input and transforms it to a vector that's the size of the hidden vector). You might recognize the $W_{ih}x_t + b_{ih}$ and $W_{hh}h_t + b_{hh}$ terms.

These are simply the usual, feed-forward layers, so that's how we'll implement it. This abstraction simplifies the equation a bit:

$$h_{t+1} = \tanh\big(\text{Linear}(x_t) + \text{Linear}(h_t)\big)$$

The RNN cell, then, simply takes the word vector and hidden state vector, passes both of them through separate linear layers, adds them up, and then passes them through a *tanh* function. The result is a vector that is the next hidden state and is what our for ward function should return.

We implement our RNNCell just like you implement every other PyTorch layer—by extending nn.Module:

```
class RNNCell(nn.Module):

    def __init__(self, input_size, hidden_size):
        super(RNNCell, self).__init__()

        self.input_size = input_size
        self.hidden_size = hidden_size
        self.ih = nn.Linear(input_size, hidden_size)
        self.hh = nn.Linear(hidden_size, hidden_size)

    def forward(self, x, h = None):
        if h is None:
            h = torch.zeros(x.size(0), self.hidden_size)
        h = torch.tanh(self.ih(x) + self.hh(h))
        return h
```

See how simple that was! Apart from setting things up, all the computation essentially boils down to one line of code:

```
torch.tanh(self.ih(x) + self.hh(h))
```

Now we need to make our RNN itself. This is also fairly straightforward. All we have to do is initialize our cell and run it in a loop:

```
class RNN(nn.Module):

    def __init__(self, input_size, hidden_size):
        super(RNN, self).__init__()
        self.cell = RNNCell(input_size, hidden_size)

    def forward(self, x, h = None):

        print(x.shape)
        for i in range(x.shape[1]):
            h = self.cell(x[:,i], h)

        return h
```

Now we have a working RNN! But it's still not 100% ready to be used for IMDb classification. What we built just now is a general-purpose RNN that takes in a sequence of word vectors and outputs a single hidden state vector. There are a few final pieces we need to add to get a model that can classify text. Our model will have three components:

1. An embedding layer
2. The RNN section, which runs cells in a loop
3. Fully connected layers to transform the final hidden state into whatever size we want

We've already seen and implemented embedding layers and fully connected layers in previous chapters, so we can use the PyTorch versions of those. But we'll use the RNN class we just built for the RNN portion. To keep things simple (i.e., reduce one hyperparameter you have to set), we'll use our embedding layer to create embeddings that are the same size as the hidden state size. For the final stage, we'll use two fully connected layers to take in the hidden state and return a single value, which we interpret as the binary classification result:

```
class TextClassifier(nn.Module):

    def __init__(self, vocab_size, hidden_size):
        super(TextClassifier, self).__init__()
        self.emb = nn.Embedding(vocab_size, hidden_size)
        self.rnn = RNN(hidden_size, hidden_size)
        self.fc1 = nn.Linear(hidden_size, 10)
        self.fc2 = nn.Linear(10, 1)

    def forward(self, x):

        x = self.emb(x)
        x = self.rnn(x)
        x = self.fc1(x)
        out = self.fc2(x)

        return out
```

That's it for the architecture. Now let's train. Just like we did in Chapter 4, we need to create a `DataLoaders` object and a `Learner`. In the following code snippet, `fastai` handles downloading the dataset, reading in the files, and tokenization:

```
path = untar_data(URLs.IMDB)
dls = TextDataLoaders.from_folder(path, valid='test', bs=256)
```

To remind you of what the IMDb dataset looks like, let's look at a quick sample from the training dataset. `fastai` has a really handy function called `show_batch` that you call as a method from your `DataLoaders` object:

```
dls.show_batch(max_n=5)
```

	text	category
0	xxbos xxmaj match 1 : xxmaj tag xxmaj team xxmaj table xxmaj match xxmaj bubba xxmaj ray and xxmaj spike xxmaj dudley vs xxmaj eddie xxmaj guerrero and xxmaj chris xxmaj benoit xxmaj bubba xxmaj ray and xxmaj spike xxmaj dudley started things off with a xxmaj tag xxmaj team xxmaj table xxmaj match against xxmaj eddie xxmaj guerrero and xxmaj chris xxmaj benoit . xxmaj according to the rules of the match , both opponents have to go through tables in order to get the win . xxmaj benoit and xxmaj guerrero heated up early on by taking turns hammering first xxmaj spike and then xxmaj bubba xxmaj ray . a xxmaj german xxunk by xxmaj benoit to xxmaj bubba took the wind out of the xxmaj dudley brother . xxmaj spike tried to help his brother , but the referee restrained him while xxmaj benoit and xxmaj guerrero	pos
1	xxpad xxpad	pos
2	xxpad xxpad	pos
3	xxpad xxpad	neg

	text	category
4	xxpad xxpad	pos

To create the `Learner`, we use a built-in function that creates one from a `DataLoaders` and a specified model class (`TextClassifier` in our case):

```
learn = Learner(dls, TextClassifier(len(dls.vocab[0]), 100),
                loss_func=CrossEntropyLossFlat(),
                metrics=accuracy)
```

And that's pretty much it! `fastai` abstracts away the other details that we don't care about at the moment (such as the loss function and optimizer). All that's left is the training step:

```
learn.fit(10)
```

OK, so not exactly a stellar model, but it does work. Let's look at some ways we can improve it. In this chapter, we'll be focusing on strictly architectural improvements, which means we will only edit/change the `RNNCell`, `RNN`, and `TextClassifier` classes. We will continue using the same training loop, dataset, etc. This means that you *could* get better performance if you spend time on the tokenizer, optimizer, and some hyperparameter tuning, but that's not the focus of this chapter.

You might be wondering why we chose to use three `nn.Module` subclasses instead of just putting everything in one to make the code shorter. Well, for one, separating the functionality into modules is a good engineering practice. But more importantly, now that they are all individual modules, you can customize the functionality more effectively. If you want to make a multilayer RNN, you just have to edit the `RNN` class. If you want to swap the cell for a more advanced one, just replace `RNNCell` with something else. Want to add more fully connected layers at the end? Or perhaps modify the network to perform multiclass classification? All you have to do is customize the fully connected layers in `TextClassifier`.

As a matter of fact, this is how RNNs are implemented in PyTorch. For each of the recurrent network types that PyTorch supports natively (RNN, LSTM, and GRU), there is a corresponding class for the cell and the module itself. When implementing your own text classifiers, language models, etc., you'll want to use the default PyTorch modules directly, rather than building it yourself. Let's take a look at the PyTorch version of RNN:

```
import torch
??torch.nn.RNN
```

It's very similar to the RNN module that we built, but adds some useful features like dropout, multiple layers, and the ability to select an activation function. You could try implementing these things yourself if you want to for fun, but it's more trouble than it's worth for a real production system. So from now on, we'll use `torch.nn.RNN` instead of our custom RNN. They are similar enough that the PyTorch version is a drop-in replacement in `TextClassifier`:

```
class TextClassifier(nn.Module):

    def __init__(self, vocab_size, hidden_size):
        super(TextClassifier, self).__init__()
        self.emb = nn.Embedding(vocab_size, hidden_size)
        self.rnn = nn.RNN(hidden_size, hidden_size, batch_first=True)
        self.fc1 = nn.Linear(hidden_size, 10)
        self.fc2 = nn.Linear(10, 2)

    def forward(self, x):

        x = self.emb(x)
        _, x = self.rnn(x)
        x = self.fc1(x)
        out = self.fc2(x)

        return out

learn = Learner(dls, TextClassifier(len(dls.vocab[0]), 100),
                loss_func=CrossEntropyLossFlat(),
                metrics=accuracy)
learn.fit(10)
```

epoch	train_loss	valid_loss	accuracy	time
0	0.695069	0.692872	0.513840	00:04
1	0.692819	0.685738	0.547360	00:04
2	0.694167	0.697343	0.463360	00:04
3	0.693335	0.690784	0.531040	00:04
4	0.693080	0.688063	0.545880	00:04
5	0.692383	0.692549	0.511240	00:05
6	0.689648	0.679611	0.571080	00:04
7	0.686122	0.688807	0.531920	00:04
8	0.677578	0.693136	0.532440	00:05
9	0.687349	0.686864	0.552560	00:04

Fifty-five percent accuracy is not great, and is a nice illustration of why we needed better architectures. But thankfully, even within the framework recurrent sequence models, there are better alternatives.

Bidirectional RNN

The idea of a bidirectional RNN is similar to the bidirectional transformer used in BERT, but in this case, the directionality is more apparent. Instead of just traversing the sentence from left to right, a bidirectional RNN has two "paths" for the hidden state that are computed simultaneously. In effect, you'll end up with a sequence of left-to-right hidden states and a separate sequence of right-to-left hidden states.

The TL;DR of bidirectional RNNs is that it adds some more computation but generally improves performance without much tweaking. You should almost always use the bidirectional variant of your RNN model as long as it is computationally feasible.

There is one important consideration—in practice, a lot of the problems you might want to use an RNN for in this day and age (versus a transformer) don't really have a bidirectional structure. For example, in text generation, your model can't "see" the end of the sequence, since the end of the sequence is what we're generating! Where it is perhaps most useful is in the simpler NLP tasks with larger inputs, like document classification or summarization, where a transformer might work better but is computationally impractical to use.

For the IMDb text classification problem, we *do* have access to the entire sequence at once, so we can use a bidirectional RNN by simply setting bidirectional=True. This will give us two hidden states instead of just one, so we concatenate them and pass it on to the fully connected layer:

```
class TextClassifier(nn.Module):

    def __init__(self, vocab_size, hidden_size):
        super(TextClassifier, self).__init__()
        self.emb = nn.Embedding(vocab_size, hidden_size)
        self.rnn = nn.RNN(hidden_size, hidden_size,
                          bidirectional=True, batch_first=True)
        self.fc1 = nn.Linear(hidden_size * 2, 10)
        self.fc2 = nn.Linear(10, 2)

    def forward(self, x):

        x = self.emb(x)
        _, x = self.rnn(x)
        x = torch.cat((x[0], x[1]), dim=-1)
        x = self.fc1(x)
        out = self.fc2(x)

        return out
```

```
learn = Learner(dls, TextClassifier(len(dls.vocab[0]), 100),
                loss_func=CrossEntropyLossFlat(),
                metrics=accuracy)
learn.fit(10)
```

epoch	train_loss	valid_loss	accuracy	time
0	0.682959	0.663150	0.606560	00:08
1	0.676049	0.679050	0.566600	00:08
2	0.659499	0.711453	0.541720	00:08
3	0.671983	0.681267	0.562640	00:08
4	0.639950	0.636450	0.643600	00:08
5	0.623661	0.645424	0.624920	00:08
6	0.625853	0.648754	0.628800	00:07
7	0.590960	0.616835	0.664600	00:08
8	0.599594	0.628637	0.665120	00:08
9	0.549145	0.599172	0.683880	00:08

Wow! The simple act of reading backwards gave our model a *huge* boost in accuracy. Note that with transformers, there is no concept of directionality to begin with, since they read all the words you throw at them in parallel. But with recurrent models, making them bidirectional is a simple and effective way to improve performance while incurring some computational cost.

But there's more we can do with RNNs than just text classification.

Sequence to Sequence Using RNNs

As long as you can build a model that uses the hidden state you get from the RNN in some way, you can build an NLP model for most common tasks. PyTorch's nn.RNN also returns the hidden state of the last layer for each time step, so now you have a sequence of hidden states to use—just as we did when training transformers. You can use these hidden states however you like.

For example, if you want to build an RNN to do machine translation, you can split the task into an encoder and decoder phase—just like we did for transformers.[5] The encoder creates a hidden state, and the decoder uses it to generate text in another language (visualized in Figure 6-3).

---

5 In fact, this is where the transformer terminology comes from, since RNNs are older.

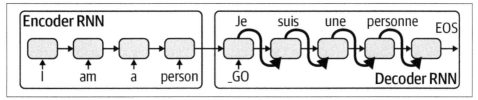

Figure 6-3. RNN for neural machine translation

It turns out that a lot of the tasks we mentioned in Chapter 3 can be solved with RNNs as well as transformers. So you if you have the budget, it may be worth experimenting with both. RNNs, generally speaking, are easier to train if you start from scratch. But in practice, there are many more large pretrained transformer models available today than there are RNNs.

There's more we can do to the improve the architecture of RNNs than change how the state vectors flow between cells, though. We can also change the architecture of the *individual* cells. The LSTM cell is perhaps the most famous improvement.

Long Short-Term Memory

A big improvement to the RNN architecture (along with some drama surrounding who actually created it) came in the form of the LSTM network. Fundamentally, there's not too much new here. As we mentioned, almost all RNNs are just a cell block that updates a hidden state in a loop. The LSTM architecture uses a more complex cell block.

Instead of representing the hidden state as a single vector, the LSTM block uses two vectors with some machinery to manage when it updates these states. Figure 6-4 gives you a sense of what's going on.

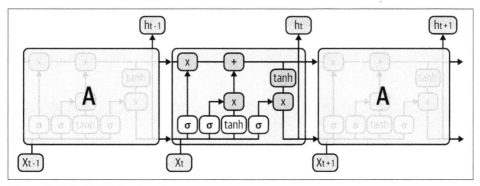

Figure 6-4. An LSTM network

We won't be covering the specifics of the LSTM block here, since there are plenty of fantastic tutorials online.[6] Rather, we'll focus on using it in our existing text classifier.

PyTorch has a built-in class for LSTM: nn.LSTM. This takes similar parameters to nn.RNN and works in pretty much the same way functionally. All we have to do is swap out nn.RNN with nn.LSTM:

```
class TextClassifier(nn.Module):

    def __init__(self, vocab_size, hidden_size):
        super(TextClassifier, self).__init__()
        self.emb = nn.Embedding(vocab_size, hidden_size)
        self.rnn = nn.LSTM(hidden_size, hidden_size, batch_first=True)
        self.fc1 = nn.Linear(hidden_size, 10)
        self.fc2 = nn.Linear(10, 2)

    def forward(self, x):

        x = self.emb(x)
        x, _ = self.rnn(x)[1]
        x = self.fc1(x)
        out = self.fc2(x)

        return out
```

Thanks to the elegant design of the fastai library, we don't need to change the code for anything else to train our LSTM-based text classifier. We just have to re-initialize the learner with the updated TextClassifier and train again:

```
learn = Learner(dls, TextClassifier(len(dls.vocab[0]), 100),
                loss_func=CrossEntropyLossFlat(),
                metrics=accuracy)
learn.fit(10)
```

epoch	train_loss	valid_loss	accuracy	time
0	0.692424	0.686630	0.541640	00:06
1	0.655113	0.609996	0.681640	00:05
2	0.626896	0.749849	0.528720	00:06
3	0.592931	0.597747	0.694080	00:05
4	0.528877	0.511302	0.762520	00:06
5	0.539924	0.553975	0.720920	00:05
6	0.475588	0.478583	0.784360	00:06
7	0.412415	0.451568	0.798320	00:06
8	0.397446	0.446312	0.802120	00:05

---

6 In particular, we recommend Chris Olah's blog post (*https://oreil.ly/S1kba*) on the topic.

epoch	train_loss	valid_loss	accuracy	time
9	0.356494	0.406632	0.821800	00:06

That was much better! LSTMs usually are. At the time of writing, the best RNN (in terms of NLP SOTA leaderboards in published research) is a variant of this architecture, called the AWD-LSTM. But that performance comes at a cost. As you can see from the implementation, LSTM networks are more conceptually and computationally inefficient than vanilla RNNs, and a lot of research has gone into making cheaper variants of them over the years. The one that lasted was the gated recurrent unit (GRU).

Gated Recurrent Units

The GRU cell tries to solve the same problem that the LSTM cell tries to solve (learning long-term dependencies) using a method that is similar but simpler both computationally and conceptually. But in the end, GRU is just another cell and follows the same formula as every other RNN. So we can now swap out our LSTM for a GRU without much hassle:

```
class TextClassifier(nn.Module):

    def __init__(self, vocab_size, hidden_size):
        super(TextClassifier, self).__init__()
        self.emb = nn.Embedding(vocab_size, hidden_size)
        self.rnn = nn.GRU(hidden_size, hidden_size, batch_first=True)
        self.fc1 = nn.Linear(hidden_size, 10)
        self.fc2 = nn.Linear(10, 2)

    def forward(self, x):

        x = self.emb(x)
        _, x = self.rnn(x)
        x = self.fc1(x)
        out = self.fc2(x)

        return out
```

Again, the training loop remains unchanged:

```
learn = Learner(dls, TextClassifier(len(dls.vocab[0]), 100),
                loss_func=CrossEntropyLossFlat(),
                metrics=accuracy)
learn.fit(10)
```

epoch	train_loss	valid_loss	accuracy	time
0	0.689930	0.676298	0.577360	00:05
1	0.604351	0.529154	0.740560	00:05

epoch	train_loss	valid_loss	accuracy	time
2	0.503720	0.482746	0.781160	00:05
3	0.445455	0.418563	0.814600	00:05
4	0.372754	0.401952	0.833400	00:05
5	0.326986	0.349531	0.851880	00:05
6	0.292445	0.340987	0.854440	00:05
7	0.245959	0.350378	0.859120	00:05
8	0.260215	0.346354	0.854800	00:05
9	0.201884	0.315813	0.879160	00:05

In this case, the GRU performed better than the LSTM, but this is not always the case. The benefit of GRUs is that they do less work in each cell, which means they are more efficient. This is particularly useful in edge device deployment, where CPU resources are scarce, and LSTMs are known to be CPU-hungry. Comma AI, the self-driving car startup, uses a GRU-based network for their in-car compute module.

Conclusion

There are many other RNN variants, such as AWD-LSTMs, QRNNs, SHA-RNNs, and other three-to-seven–letter acronyms that expand to polysyllabic words that can make you sound really smart.[7] But most of these are similar in spirit—they use some sort of cell that processes a single element of the sequence and repeats that computation multiple times in a loop.

 If you look hard enough, you'll also find many more exotic variants that do other things. Are these really RNNs if they don't have a loop structure? That's up to you! Deep learning is a highly experimental field, and we don't have super-rigorous definitions for things. But most models that call themselves RNNs can be expressed as repeating a computation in a loop to update a hidden state. As we saw earlier with LSTMs and GRUs, what differs is usually the cell block.

One question for the next architecture improvement in RNNs is: have we come up with the best possible cell blocks, or are there more interesting ones yet to be made? We believe that this remains an open question. But one thing that's clear is that a large portion of the field of NLP has moved on from the idea of using a loop with a cell block.

---

7 The people who made them certainly are!

In our opinion, the verdict is still out on RNNs. While many may claim that the age of the recurrent neural network is over and that transformers will forever be the future, there are still some concerns with that architecture—for extremely long sequences (like documents), the Transformer architecture's n^2 memory complexity is not fun to deal with. For now, RNNs present a satisfactory middle ground in terms of performance and computational cost.

In the next chapter, we'll turn our attention to the latest and greatest in NLP today—the Transformer architecture.

## CHAPTER 7

Transformers

In the previous chapter, we covered RNNs, the modeling architecture in vogue in NLP until the Transformer architecture gained prominence.

Transformers are the workhorse of modern NLP. The original architecture, first proposed in 2017, has taken the (deep learning) world by storm. Since then, NLP literature has been inundated with all sorts of new architectures that are broadly classified into either *Sesame Street* characters or words that end with "-former."[1]

In this chapter, we'll look at that very architecture—the transformer—in detail. We'll analyze the core innovations and explore a hot new category of neural network layers: the attention mechanism.

Building a Transformer from Scratch

In Chapters 2 and 3, we explored how to use transformers in practice and how to leverage pretrained transformers to solve complex NLP problems. Now we're going to take a deep dive into the architecture itself and learn how transformers work from first principles.

What does "first principles" mean? Well, for starters, it means we're not allowed to use the Hugging Face Transformers library. We've raved about it plenty in this book already, so it's about time we take a break from that and see how things actually work under the hood. For this chapter, we're going to be using raw PyTorch instead.

---

1 An inside joke for the people following the names of new NLP research papers.

When deploying models in production, especially on edge devices, you may have to go to an even lower level of abstraction. The tooling around edge device inference, as we mentioned in Chapter 2, is not great at the moment. Currently, it's not uncommon to have models exported and transpiled into complex C++-based formats.[2] ONNX seems to be a promising new project that we would love to see more of in the near future. But at present, running inference on dedicated servers where you can choose your own software stack seems to be the way to go. A major benefit of this approach is that you can use PyTorch without having to worry too much about compiling C++ libraries and transpiling between 102 different formats. So for now, PyTorch is about as "low level" as we'll go.

PyTorch, being a fully fledged deep learning library that most researchers use, naturally has an implementation of the extremely popular transformer architecture, just like a Hugging Face library does. This version, though, exposed as an nn.Module, is much more DIY and is meant to be used with the other familiar PyTorch tools like dataloaders, optimizers, etc.

As we've mentioned before, one of the best ways to see what *any* deep learning–related class/function does is by looking at the type signature and the dimensionality of the inputs and outputs. So let's do that:

```
import torch
model = torch.nn.Transformer()
model.encoder.layers[0]

TransformerEncoderLayer(
  (self_attn): MultiheadAttention(
    (out_proj): Linear(in_features=512, out_features=512, bias=True)
  )
  (linear1): Linear(in_features=512, out_features=2048, bias=True)
  (dropout): Dropout(p=0.1, inplace=False)
  (linear2): Linear(in_features=2048, out_features=512, bias=True)
  (norm1): LayerNorm((512,), eps=1e-05, elementwise_affine=True)
  (norm2): LayerNorm((512,), eps=1e-05, elementwise_affine=True)
  (dropout1): Dropout(p=0.1, inplace=False)
  (dropout2): Dropout(p=0.1, inplace=False)
)
```

---

2 Again, see Chapter 2 for details on what these tools do.

In Jupyter Notebooks, you can enter ?? followed by a variable name to get more information about its type, methods, documentation, and more. It's a really useful tool to use for debugging. For PyTorch `nn.Module` objects, you get a full description of the model's layers. We aren't using it here due to size constraints, but you can try this out yourself in a Jupyter Notebook.

At the outset, there doesn't seem to be too much to take away from this. It's a fairly standard PyTorch `nn.Module` with the standard `forward()` function defined for us. In principle, we could just plug it into our training pipeline and carry on. In fact, this is essentially what we did in Chapter 2. But let's try to understand the exact components of this module.

Of particular interest is the `MultiheadAttention` layer. Most of the other layers, like `Dropout`, `Linear`, and `LayerNorm`, are things you'd expect to see in nontransformer models as well. This particular implementation of the transformer by PyTorch (with no additional configuration parameters), exactly matches the specification of the architecture in the original paper (shown in Figure 7-1) which, coincidentally, is titled "Attention Is All You Need."[3]

In short, it's safe to say that the most important component of this `Transformer` class is the `MultiheadAttention` layer. So it makes sense to take some time to understand what that is and how it works.

Attention Mechanisms

An attention mechanism is a layer in a deep neural network. Its job, while still open to interpretation, is to learn long-range, "global" features. An attention mechanism acts as what we like to call an "information router" that decides what components of the input sequence of embedding vectors contribute to a single output vector. This idea will become more clear as we actually work through the details.

We're just as excited to talk about attention as the other couple thousand people that attended NeurIPS[4] within the last year, but before we do, we should mention that an important theme to pay attention to[5] is the computational complexity of the

---

3 A revolutionary new architecture isn't the only thing this paper brought to the deep learning community. Since its publication, we'd argue that this paper normalized the idea of having catchy and attractive titles that help market your paper.

4 A popular AI conference.

5 Yes, the pun was intentional, and no, it's not going to stop. Living with attention puns is a reality you must be able to navigate if you have any hope of comprehending NLP literature.

operations involved. Think about how many dot products/matrix multiplications you see and the size of the tensors involved.

Computational Complexity

In computer science, there's a known method to measure the speed or efficiency of an algorithm by looking at what's known as its "computational complexity." In this method, you don't measure how fast a given algorithm runs by taking speed/timing measurements, but instead use theoretical principles to predict how the algorithm *scales*.

You might be familiar with the so-called "Big Oh" notation used to write down complexity. In practice, this is not very useful for deep learning, as real-world performance is often dictated by a concoction of interdependent performance considerations like programming language, CPU/GPU architecture, degree of parallelism, etc.

Dot Product Attention

OK, strictly speaking, we don't think we've seen this type of attention actually being applied in real networks. Scaled dot product attention is usually just talked about as a component of the next thing we'll discuss: Multi-Head Self-Attention.

The most important question you need to ask in the world of exotic attention mechanisms is this: how, exactly, do you measure the similarity between things? This core idea, shrouded in a veil of linear algebra and bucket-loads of GPUs, is what drives the fundamental behavior of neural nets in NLP today.

And the scaled dot product uses probably one of the simplest and most intuitive methods of measuring similarity—the dot product.

You should be familiar with this, but let's do a quick recap. The dot product is an operation that takes two vectors, multiplies them element-wise, and then adds up the results. This measures similarity because if the two vectors that we're "dot-producting" have similar components, the product of their elements will be large, and vice versa (in the sense that vectors with dissimilar components will have a small dot product).

But the real question is, what exactly are we taking the dot product of? To answer this question, let's focus on how these attention mechanisms are implemented in transformers (see Figure 7-1).

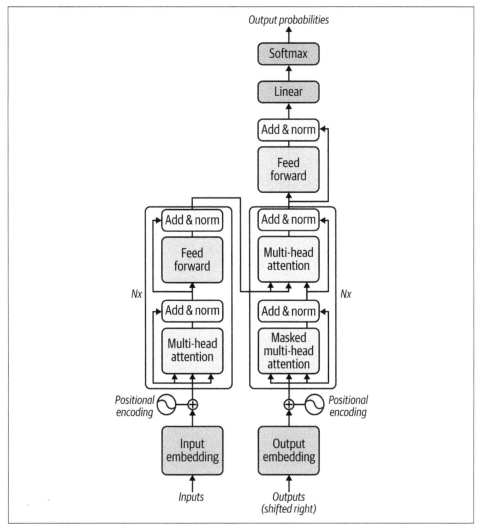

Figure 7-1. A single layer of a transformer

A typical transformer takes in sequences of word vectors as input, and at each layer, transforms (and no, we don't think that's how they got their name) them into another sequence of vectors, which we call the *hidden representation/state*.

So at each hidden layer in the network, we have sequences of vectors that we want to "attend" over. See Figure 7-2.

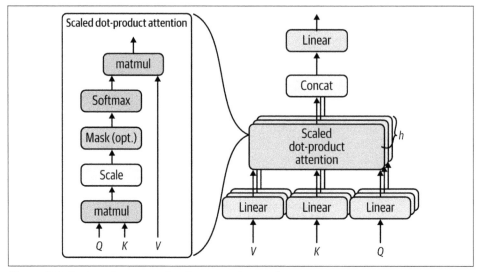

Figure 7-2. Dot product attention in a transformer layer

Now, here's the important bit, so pay attention (pun very much intended).

What we're going to do is transform each one of these hidden state vectors into three separate, completely independent vectors—the query, the key, and the value.

We do this transformation via a simple matrix multiply, and the dimensions of these vectors are up to us. The only restriction is that the query and key vectors need to have the same dimensions (since we're going to take the dot product between them):

$$k_i = W^K h_i, \quad q_i = W^Q h_i, \quad v_i = W^V h_i$$

We then compute the attention weights by taking the dot product of the query vector at each time step as with all of the key vectors, and softmax the result. To do this over all time steps simultaneously, it's more efficient to pack these vectors into a matrix that performs the multiplications in parallel. The final calculation would look something like this:

$$z_i = \text{softmax}\left(q_i K^T\right) V$$

That's not all we can do, though. Since each of the query vectors are independent, we can parallelize across time (something that wasn't possible with RNNs, since the computation would be dependent on z_{i-1}):

$$Z = \text{softmax}\left(Q K^T\right) V$$

But why? That's the question we were asking ourselves when reading the transformer paper. Splitting into three vectors seems a little arbitrary and complicated. Like, why not two or four?

Based on just the naming, it seems like the intuition here is rooted in databases. Think about how this would work in regular old Python dictionaries, no neural nets involved.

You have a large sequence of key-value pairs. That's the dictionary structure. It could look something like this:

```
sentence = {
  "word_1": "Squirtle"
  "word_2": "is"
  "word_3": "the"
  "word_4": "greatest"
  "word_5": "Pokemon"
  "word_6": "ever"
}
```

Now I know what you're thinking—"Puh-lease! We all know Squirtle doesn't stand a sliver of a chance against Charizard."

Well, we beg to differ. Deal with it.

When you want to get a value from the dictionary, you'd use a query that looks something like this:

```
a = sentence['word_3']
```

And what Python would do, behind the scenes, is compare your query word_3 against all the possible keys in the sentence dictionary. It would then return the value and store it in a variable.

What we're doing with dot product attention is similar. The query vector represents, in some abstract sense, what the current word is looking for. The key associated with each word kind of represents what each word has to offer. The value vector contains the information that the query vector was looking for. But we know that sounds super abstract, so let us show you an example.

Consider the following sentence:

```
Mario is short, but he can jump super high.
```

Now say our transformer is currently working on the word "he," and it's trying to propagate it to the next layer in the network. The query vector here might be something that's looking for a name or a person to clarify what exactly the pronoun "he" is referring to. So, the transformer takes the query vector for "he" and computes dot products of this query vector with the key vectors of every other word in the sentence. Each of these dot products generates a sort of alignment score that measures how much the query and key match.

As it does it, the key vector corresponding to "Mario" is likely to light up, and will generate the largest alignment score. This indicates to the network that there's something interesting going on there, and the network should pay attention (see what we did there?).

But the job isn't done yet. Once the transformer calculates all the alignment scores between "he" and the other words in the sentence, it passes these scores through a softmax, to generate a nice distribution. You can interpret the scores more naturally: 0 would tell you that there's little connection between the words, and a 1 would tell you that there's a near-perfect alignment.

Remember that each word also has an associated value vector, which, in our picture, is supposed to represent the actually meaningful content of the word, just like in the case of values in Python dictionaries. Unlike Python dictionaries, however, each query doesn't return a single result. Instead, the transformer takes the normalized alignment scores that we calculated for each word and uses them to perform a weighted sum over *all* the value vectors. The reason for this is somewhat simple—say the sentence we were working with was now "Mario and Luigi are short, but they can jump very high." Here, the query for "they" is not just looking for a single word, but every possible person that fits into this group.

Creating a distribution of alignment scores now lets us pick up different parts of the sentence in different amounts! Oversimplifying a bit, you can imagine that the normalized alignment scores for the words "Mario" and "Luigi" are 0.5 and 0 for all other words.

The transformer has now attended (seriously, is that even a word?) over the sentence, and has created a vector for a particular word ("he" and "they," in our example) that encapsulates how the relevant parts of the sentence relate to this word in the grand scheme of things.

You'd now repeat this process for every word in the sentence, thereby getting another sequence of vectors to pass on to deeper layers in the network.

When we're computing the so-called "self-attention" in the encoder parts of the transformer, the following hidden states are used to calculate:

$$k_i, q_i, v_i$$

These all come from the sequence in that layer of the encoder. The same is true for self-attention in the decoder.

There's another one, though—the attention layer used in the decoder that uses the decoder hidden representation for the queries, and the encoder hidden representation for the keys and values. This allows the decoder to attend over all previous encoder hidden representations, which is useful in tasks like machine translation. You wouldn't want your French translator to starts spewing out gibberish without actually reading the whole sentence in English first.

You can visualize the self-attention layer in Figure 7-2 and the entire layer put together in Figure 7-1. Stack a few of these layers on top of one another, and *boom!* You've (almost) got yourself a transformer.

Scaled Dot Product Attention

There's a minor problem with this, though. Although dot products are really fast, cool, and all that, when the size of the vectors are large, the dot product can get pretty big.

To see what we mean, consider two random vectors. Instead of just talking about it, though, let us show you some actual computations from NumPy:

```
import numpy as np

small_dots = [
    np.dot(np.random.randn(10),
           np.random.randn(10))
    for i in range(100)]
np.mean(np.absolute(small_dots))
```

```
2.7733341538409992
```

What we just did there was generate two random arrays of size 10 and take the dot product of them. Just to be sure, we repeated this 100 times and calculated the average magnitude of the dot product to make sure that we're not getting a random outlier.

And so the value was around 2.74. How's that useful? Well, let's try the same thing with arrays of size 10,000:

```
large_dots = [np.dot(np.random.randn(10000),
                     np.random.randn(10000))
              for i in range(100)]
np.mean(np.absolute(large_dots))
```

```
85.0101478977957
```

OK. That's a lot bigger. But think about it—since we're using dot products to measure alignment, something is clearly wrong here. In both cases, we generated purely random vectors, so ideally, their alignment scores should be similar.

But since the components are chosen from a standard normal distribution with mean 0 and variance 1, an n-dimensional vector will have a variance of n (you get this by adding up the variances of the components, and if you're going to be pedantic, it's the trace of the covariance matrix of the vector, but that's way too long a name).

To correct for this and ensure that vectors of any dimensionality have roughly the same alignment scores, we'll scale our previous attention mechanism similar to how you'd normalize to unit variance in statistics.

The new, corrected attention mechanism would be:

$$Z = \text{softmax}\left(\frac{QK^T}{\sqrt{d_k}}\right)V$$

Multi-Head Self-Attention

Here's something you might find interesting: the two attention mechanisms that we just discussed, and the one we're about to show you now, all came from the same paper—"Attention Is All You Need" (aka the transformer paper). Pretty cool, huh?

Anyway, the next thing we can do is try to split up our attention mechanism into many smaller attention mechanisms (with an "s"). Why would we want to do this? A good way to illustrate the rationale is through a popular attention test video (*https:// oreil.ly/jrrmP*).

Now you've probably seen that video before (if you haven't, surprise!), and you know why it's so hard to spot the gorilla on your first pass—it's easier and more natural to pay attention to one thing at a time. In this case, that's basketball passes, since that's what the video asks you to look for. If instead, you were asked to look for a gorilla, it probably would have been easier to find the gorilla.

Attention mechanisms kind of work in the same way. There's a lot of stuff to pay attention to and keep track of in language, like pronouns, as we discussed earlier ("Mario is short, but he can jump super high"), but also other things, like where the main characters are going in physical space ("Mario went to the flower store and then to the gym, where he did 50 squats").

Having one set of queries, keys, and values do all that work might be a bit too much, and they might miss out on the occasional gorilla, just like you probably did.

Multi-head attention mechanisms try to fix this issue by independently applying the attention mechanism multiple times on the same sequence in a single pass. In terms of the gorilla video, this would be like having your buddy watch the video with you. One of you could pay attention to the passes, while the other could look for gorillas, thereby increasing the overall attention capabilities.

Crucially, the query key and value matrices need to be different, otherwise redoing the whole attention thing multiple times would just be a waste of computation (asking your friend to look for passes while you also look for passes).

To create variety in the queries, keys, and values, the transformer network simply uses multiple separate weight matrices to transform the input into multiple queries, keys, and values:

$$Q_1 = W_1^Q x, \quad K_1 = W_1^K x, \quad V_1 = W_1^V x$$

$$Q_2 = W_2^Q x, \quad K_2 = W_2^K x, \quad V_2 = W_2^V x$$

. . .

$$Q_n = W_n^Q x, \quad K_n = W_n^K x, \quad V_n = W_n^V x$$

Here, n is the parameter you set, and it's called the number of heads. It represents how many different attention computations are being done on the same sequence. You can think of it as the number of people you invite over to watch that gorilla video with you.

Are you tired of that analogy yet? Don't worry, we're almost done with it.

Each one of these "heads" performs the scaled dot product attention calculation independently (and, crucially, in parallel):

$$head_1 = \text{softmax}\left(\frac{Q_1 K_1^T}{\sqrt{d_k}}\right) V_1$$

$$head_2 = \text{softmax}\left(\frac{Q_2 K_2^T}{\sqrt{d_k}}\right) V_2$$

. . .

$$head_n = \text{softmax}\left(\frac{Q_n K_n^T}{\sqrt{d_k}}\right) V_n$$

At the end of all this number-crunching, we're going to be left n different output vectors per spot in the sequence, corresponding to the outputs from each of the attention heads. But since the next layer needs a sequence of vectors (and a sequence of n vectors), the transformer concatenates the output from the multiple attention heads and passes it through another learned linear transform to make the dimensions work right:

$$z = W^O[\text{head}_1; \text{head}_2; \ldots; \text{head}_n]$$

A sequence of these new concatenated and transformed z vectors is what gets passed on to the next layer of the transformer.

That's definitely a lot of linear algebra to take in at once, so go through it slowly again to make sure you actually get it. In particular, visualizing Multi-Head Self-Attention is probably the best way to understand how it works. Jay Alammar has an excellent set of articles on this (*https://oreil.ly/A7jmk*), and we highly encourage you to take a look at the visualizations presented there.

Adaptive Attention Span

OK, we're finally moving on to some (relatively) newer and cooler stuff. In 2019, some cool people at Facebook AI Research asked a really cool question—what if we could get transformers to learn what to pay attention to?

But isn't that what transformers already do? Isn't this the entire point of the attention mechanism?

Well, yes. But there's also another very important thing we haven't talked about—computational cost. You see, adding an attention mechanism isn't cheap. If you have n words in a batch/sentence, it would take n^2 dot products (per layer) to compute each of the attention weights across all the tokens in the sequence. This is because you have to take the dot product of each of the n query vectors with each of the n keys.

As you can tell, this can blow up pretty fast. If you had, say, 50 tokens/words in your batch/sentence, then there are at least $50^2 = 2,500$ dot products to compute. But simply by increasing the number of tokens by two, to 52, you'd now have more than $52^2 = 2704$ dot products to compute. That's about 200 more dot products just for adding two extra tokens per batch, and that's not even factoring in multi-headed attention!

Of course, one could question if we really need to compute attention over every single token every single time. It seems a little excessive. Especially in character-level or subword-level models, where some of the attention heads might simply be looking at the last few tokens to try and fit characters or subwords together into words. But then again, other heads might actually be looking over the entire sequence, so we can't just make every head look at only the last few tokens.

The way we (or in this case, the Facebook team; we are just reaping the benefits of their work) strike a balance is by having some heads attend over a larger set of tokens, and have some heads attend over only the last few tokens.

There's one term we'll introduce here: *attention span*. This simply refers to how many previous tokens the model is attending to. So if a head has an attention span of 5, this means that head runs an attention mechanism over the last 5 tokens from the current position in the sequence.

So how do we decide the attention span for each of the heads? Typically, this would involve experiments, plots, some hand-waving, and a fair bit of guesswork. But what makes adaptive attention span so cool is that each head can learn its own attention span through the training process!

This idea is really cool because it takes something that would have been a hyperparameter, the number of tokens to attend over, and makes it a simple parameter that can be automatically tuned through backprop.

Here's the main issue at hand: the number of tokens that each head looks at, also called the *attention space*, is an integer, and therefore can't be differentiated. Being nondifferentiable means that you can't really learn that parameter through training. So instead, the research team had to come up with a clever way to get a differentiable version of the attention span.

They did this by creating something called a *masking function*, which takes in the distance between tokens and outputs a value between 0 and 1. In the paper, they define the masking function like this:

$$m_z(x) = \min\left[\max\left[\frac{1}{R}(R + z - x), 0\right], 1\right]$$

Which we guess looks a little weird. But the plot is actually pretty clear and simple, as shown in Figure 7-3.

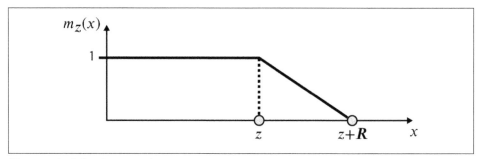

Figure 7-3. Adaptive attention span

So the intuition here is that if the distance x between two tokens is large enough, the value of $m_z(x)$ will be zero, which means we don't do the attention computation between those two tokens.

Since this $m_z(x)$ function is smooth, we can get its gradient and tune the value of z for each attention head. With a larger z, the attention head would look across more tokens, and vice versa. R is a hyperparameter that controls the smoothness of that ramp section you see on the plot.

But most importantly, the adaptive attention span transformer has some pretty cool results. It achieves state-of-the-art performance on the enwik8 dataset using considerably less memory and FLOPs than other transformers.

Persistent Memory/All-Attention

This modification to the self-attention mechanism is a little interesting, because it focuses on something that deep learning research rarely does—simplicity.

The all-attention layer, introduced in a paper by FAIR (yes, those same people again) doesn't significantly improve performance or decrease computational cost. Instead, it takes a multistep process in the original Transformer architecture and reformulates it into a single step that involves just the attention mechanism, nothing else.

In the original implementation, the transformer uses a position-wise feed-forward network in each layer. What this means is that after running the attention mechanism, the transformer passes each of the vectors in the sequence through a tiny vanilla neural net before passing it on to the attention mechanism in the next layer.

And here's the juicy bit—the persistent memory paper says that most of the parameters from the transformer are used in these feed-forward networks, not the attention and self-attention mechanisms.

So their idea was to get rid of the position-wise feed-forward network entirely. Not necessarily to reduce the number of parameters (because they end up adding back in a lot more parameters eventually), but just because.

They showed that if you stare at the computation of the position-wise feed-forward networks, it actually looks similar to the computation that an attention mechanism is doing. Let's take a look and see what the authors mean:

$$\text{FeedForward}(x_t) = U \cdot \text{ReLU}(Vx_t + b) + c$$

$$\text{Attention}(x_t) = \text{softmax}\left(\frac{QK^T}{\sqrt{d_k}}\right)V$$

where U, V in the feed-forward network are weight matrices.

Don't really see the connection between the two? Yeah, neither do we. But take a look at what happens when we remove the bias terms and swap out the ReLU for a softmax:

$$\text{FeedForward}(x_t) = U \cdot \text{softmax}(Vx_t)$$

Now if you look carefully at that last step, you'll notice that what we're doing is a matrix-vector product between U (the matrix) and Vx_t (the vector). And you remember the details of how that works—this is basically taking a weighted sum of the columns of the U matrix:

$$\text{FeedForward}(x_t) = U \cdot \text{softmax}(Vx_t) = \sum_{i=0}^{d_f} a_{ti} u_i$$

where the attention weights a_{ti} are computed from the Vx_t product and u_i is the ith column of U.

Looking at the computations in this way, x_t, V, U are analogous to the queries, keys, and values in scaled dot product attention.

So what's the point of all this math, you ask? Well, actually not much. Sorry.

The main conclusion of the paper is that since the computation that the feed-forward networks are doing is very similar (in fact, almost equivalent if you ignore the bias terms and activation function), we can probably swap them out and make the Transformer architecture simpler.

In our opinion, it would have been equally valid to just say, "Hey look, so we got rid of those feed-forward network things after the attention mechanism and just used a bunch of attention instead. It worked pretty well." But hey, it is what it is.

If you're beginning to question the meaning of life after spending the last five minutes of your precious free time breaking your head over a bunch of equations that we just told you do pretty much nothing new, fear not. Because this paper did have another really cool idea: persistent memory.

Considering that replacing the feed-forward networks with attention would reduce the number of parameters in the model, the authors benevolently decided to not let their GPU memory get too bored, so they found some new ways to crank up the temperature on their Nvidia home heaters.

Now of course, if you wanted to add more parameters to your model, you could always do something simple, like increasing the number of layers, increasing the context size, etc. But instead, this FAIR team decided to do something very clever. They decided to give the model an independent memory bank.

We'll be specific. When we say "memory bank," we mean a large collection of key-value vector pairs. You can have as many of these key-value vector pairs as you want, and they are completely independent from the actual training data.

Once you have this large bank of vectors, you can choose to run the attention mechanism over these vectors as well, not just the sequence from the text data. These vectors are then updated over the course of training, and used in the attention mechanism at inference time as well.

The key-value vectors then act as a sort of indexed knowledge base. If a transformer language model is trying to predict the next word of the sentence "World War II ended in," it would have a query for the next position that corresponds to asking for the year that the Second World War ended. However, this information is nowhere to be found anywhere else in the sentence, so the model just kind of has to guess.

But with a dedicated memory bank, the transformer can store all sorts of little tidbits like that, and when the query vector hits the right key in the memory bank, it can access the right information in it.

A few technical details for those of you who care: the positional embeddings for the memory vectors are zero, and the keys and values are stacked into a matrix and concatenated onto the sequence for running the attention mechanism.

The idea of a dedicated memory unit in a neural net isn't exactly new. But it's the idea of using a persistent memory bank as a way to inject more parameters into a relatively simple neural net architecture that makes this attention mechanism interesting.

Product-Key Memory

Let's dive down the memory-augmented attention rabbit hole a bit further, since it seems to be a thing that's getting more popular, at least in the deep learning literature.

This next attention mechanism + memory unit that we're going to look at doesn't seem that cool if you look at it on its own. But it's actually used in XLM and CTRL, two state-of-the-art transformers that came out after this layer was introduced.

By the time this paper was published, memory in transformers was already a thing. So the goal of this project was to make memory more efficient.

It starts off with a very similar premise to the previous memory mechanism we talked about. We have a memory bank that consists of a large collection of key-value pairs, where the keys and values are both vectors.

In persistent memory, we attend over the entire memory bank, which can quickly blow up if the memory bank gets too big (which wasn't a super-big deal last time since the authors were mostly trying to use memory to substitute for parameters lost in the feed-forward networks). Here, the authors propose a different solution.

Instead of attending over a huge memory bank, most of which will be pretty useless for each query, why not just pick a few keys and use the corresponding value? Specifically, they suggest finding the top k keys that maximize the dot product with the query, and using a weighted sum of the k corresponding values to get a result from the memory bank, as shown in Figure 7-4.

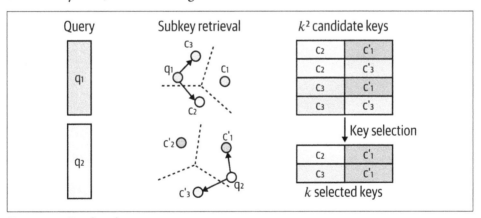

Figure 7-4. Product-key memory

This seems neat, but it gets even cooler. Consider the case when you have a large number of keys; you then have to compute a lot of dot products, because you need to dot-product the query with each key to get the similarity scores before picking the top keys.

To make the top-k key search more efficient, we can split each of the keys into half, so that instead of having, say, a key as a vector/array with 10 elements, you can have 2 keys with 5 elements each.

Now if you pull out your old undergrad combinatorics textbook, you'll see that if you have n half-keys, and consider a full key to be the concatenation of two half-keys, then in total, you can make up to n^2 keys. An example with 3 subkeys is shown in Figure 7-5. What this means is that for a memory bank of n^2 value vectors, all we need is n half-keys!

Subkey set 1		Product keys	
c_1		c_1	c'_1
c_2		c_1	c'_2
c_3		c_1	c'_3
		c_2	c'_1
		c_2	c'_2
Subkey set 2		c_2	c'_3
c'_1		c_3	c'_1
c'_2		c_3	c'_2
c'_3		c_3	c'_3

Figure 7-5. Generating product keys from subkeys

Using the power of half-keys, Figure 7-6 shows how we'd now access values in the memory bank.

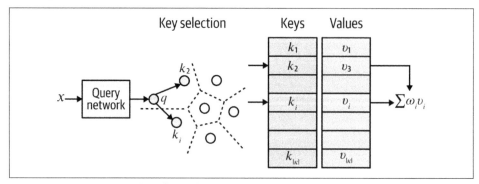

Figure 7-6. Retrieving values from the memory bank

Now, let's break down what that diagram is saying. First, you split the query vector into two parts. With the first half of the query vector, you dot product it with all the first-half parts of the half-keys, and pick the top k subkeys. Do the same for the bottom-half subkeys.

Now, since you picked k subkeys for the first half, and k subkeys for the bottom half, you'll end up with k^2 full-keys to pick from.

Now, instead of having a huge number of keys to search through, we just have k^2. So we compute the dot product between the query and these k^2 keys, but this time we use the full query and keys. Here, we're assuming that k^2 is much smaller than the full memory bank size, so this is actually still much more efficient than searching through every single one of the full-keys.

From there on out, it's just the standard scaled dot-product attention computation. Attend over those k memory units that you just selected, and you've got yourself a super-efficient memory module to plug into your transformer.

But is all this effort worth it? How well does this half-key memory method work in practice? Well, according to the paper, they were able to beat a 24-layer BERT using just 12 layers + memory. So we'll leave it up to you to decide.

Here, we provided you a small set of variants on the traditional attention mechanism that we found interesting. But this list is by no means complete, and the interest around attention mechanisms is at an all-time high. The Google Trends results for terms like "attention mechanism" and "transformers" look much more like stock prices during a bull run than the search frequency of scientific literature.

As the transformer architecture exploded in popularity, the entirety of the deep learning research community decided to go bullish on it, and since the release of the original transformer in 2017, the field has seen an influx of new variants on the Transformer architecture that promise to be more efficient, scale better, have a lower memory cost, etc. Today, there are more transformer-like architectures than we can possibly hope to include in one book, and new ideas keep pouring in on a weekly basis.

Hopefully this gives you the impression that transformers are not one single monolithic model that will be etched into stone walls like the fundamental equations of physics. Today, there are more variants than we can count, and it seems like there will soon be more variants than we can possible hope to name. Linformer, Longformer, Reformer, Performer, and Perceiver are just a few of the many new variants of the original Transformer architecture that are rapidly eating up the English language vocabulary.

Navigating this architectural landscape is hard. Many times, research papers pitch their ideas as the best thing since sliced bread for doing one particular thing, but may completely ignore others. For example, big research labs often have a very high computational budget, and focus on developing new architectures that may consume an obscenely high amount of compute resources to top a benchmark leaderboard by a fraction of a percent. Thankfully, many researchers now understand and appreciate that not everyone can fit a supercomputing cluster in their two-bedroom studio apartment, and there is an increasing interest in creating small, lightweight models.

But apart from this, transformers are increasingly being used in other domains, where they might not seem like a great fit initially. One of these is computer vision.

Transformers for Computer Vision

While transformers are ubiquitous in modern NLP, that's not the only place you'll find them.

As the accessibility of compute and GPU resources has been decreasing, we are now starting to see transformers being used more seriously in computer vision tasks as well. The two most prominent examples of this in recent memory are the *vision transformer* (ViT) and *detection with transformers* (DETR).

The most common architecture in computer vision is the convolutional neural network (CNN). These use convolutional layers to transform images, similar to an attention layer. However, convolutional layers only learn local features, and do not necessarily produce same-sized outputs. CNNs, unlike RNNs, are already well-parallelized, and many engineers at Nvidia have spent years building optimized algorithms to perform convolution extremely quickly on GPUs. So why would anyone bother trying out transformers here?

In truth, the verdict on transformers for vision is still not in. We've seen some promising results, but the n^2 memory complexity is too hard to ignore, especially when we already have a well-parallelized, fast architecture that has been working well for years. Convolutions likely won't go away anytime soon, but vision transformers may still be worth looking at. One benefit is that after training a transformer-based vision network with self-attention, you can use the attention weights as an interpretability tool, as we discussed earlier.

The attention visualization is actually much more intuitive in computer vision—high attention weights means that the network is "focusing" on that region when making a prediction. For example, say we build a network that takes in images and generates captions. Here, we'd have an image encoder, and a text decoder. Then, we can use the encoder-decoder attention weights to create a heatmap over the original image that may look something like Figure 7-7.

Figure 7-7. Using attention weights to create a visual heatmap

Conclusion

So there you have it—a deep dive into the transformer architecture. At this stage in the book, we hope that you are starting to get some idea of what deep learning researchers and engineers today are thinking about. You might also start to come up with ideas of your own. Usually, these start simple—something along the lines of "Gee, this attention mechanism doesn't fit on my GPU. I wonder if I can generate a smaller set of matrices in some way." We highly encourage you to try these out! Often, these simple ideas, after iteration and testing, are what lead people to create breakthrough research ideas and revolutionary new products.

Here's a quick summary of the key ideas in this chapter:

- Transformers were first proposed in the 2017 paper "Attention Is All You Need" by Vaswani et al.

- Transformers remove the recurrent portion of the RNN architecture and use only an attention mechanism, allowing them to be parallelized across sentences.

- Attention mechanisms are a type of layer in a neural network that allows them to collect and combine "global features" (information from every point in a large input sequence).

- Attention mechanisms come in many flavors and are used across many domains and architectures, not just transformers.

- The standard attention mechanism used in the Transformer architecture is called *Multi-Head Self-Attention* (MHSA). It transforms the input into a small key space and repeats the dot product attention multiple times.

- Attention mechanisms are very powerful but are also computationally expensive. The standard MHSA has an n^2 memory cost, which means that if you have 10 words in your sentence, you need to store `10*10` = `100` attention weights.

- The attention weights between x and y can be interpreted as "how much are x and y related?" in an abstract sense (useful in pronoun resolution).

- Attention weights can be a useful visualization tool.

- There is significant research being conducted in assessing how to build a new, more computationally efficient attention mechanism. So far, there is no clear best approach, and most practitioners still use MHSA for simplicity.

While this chapter is now coming to an end, the story of transformers is not. Next, we'll look at the sequence of events that fed the explosive growth of NLP in the last several years. Transformers played a huge role here, and new models like BERT, RoBERTa, and GPT-3 will show you how we can take this simple idea of an attention mechanism, scale it up, and create incredibly powerful NLP models.

## CHAPTER 8

BERTology: Putting It All Together

Together, we've come a long way since we started with fiddling with spacy in Chapter 1. We started with solving the most common NLP problems using the microwave-meal equivalent of deep learning libraries, and then we proceeded to the low-level details, including tokenization and embeddings. Along the way, we covered recurrent networks, including RNNs, LSTMs, and GRUs, as well as the Transformer architecture and attention mechanisms.

This chapter, in many ways, is the grand finale. We will tie all the pieces together and trace back the steps that led to the so-called ImageNet moment in 2018, which has since led to a flurry of excitement regarding the potential commercial applications of these advances in NLP. We will touch on some of these possibilities, too. Let's get started.

ImageNet

It's worth taking a moment to clarify what we mean by "ImageNet moment." Image-Net is a computer vision dataset that was originally published in 2009. It became a benchmark for the progress in image classification, a core computer vision task, and spawned an annual computer vision competition to see which research team could best identify objects in the dataset's images with the lowest error rate.

The high visibility of the competition helped spur significant advances in the field of computer vision starting in 2010. From 2009 through 2017, the winning accuracy jumped from 71.8% to 97.3%, surpassing human ability (achieving superhuman ability) and capturing the world's imagination as to what machine learning could do.

Looking back, 2012 was the breakthrough year for computer vision and the so-called original ImageNet moment. In 2012, a team from the University of Toronto, led by

Geoffrey Hinton, Ilya Sutskever, and Alex Krizhevsky, beat the rest of the field by a 10.8% margin.[1]

This performance shocked the AI research community and began to convince more commercially minded enterprises to pay more attention to computer vision. Over the next few years, enterprises used pretrained ImageNet models to solve a wide array of computer vision tasks, including tasks the models were not trained for explicitly. In other words, ImageNet was when computer vision broke through a performance and ease-of-application barrier that helped draw the attention of the rest of the world.

The Power of Pretrained Models

In much the same way that 2012 was the breakout year for computer vision, 2018 was the breakout year for NLP. This was the year the world started to pay much more serious attention to what NLP could accomplish in the enterprise, and since then there has been very active interest in NLP for commercial applications. Let's retrace the events that led to this breakout moment for NLP, its so-called ImageNet moment.

Prior to 2018, the mainstream view was that NLP models had to be trained mostly from scratch in order to solve specific NLP tasks. There was little to reuse from other language models to help develop a model for your specific task. The only thing that was of value to transfer from other language models was pretrained word embeddings, which could help your model get started but provided limited value.

This presented a major problem for solving specific NLP tasks in enterprise because, to train a model mostly from scratch, you needed a lot of annotated data for your specific task at hand. Without this large volume of annotated data, you would not be able to train a model from scratch to sufficiently good levels of performance. But, getting such a large volume of annotated data was a nonstarter for many companies, limiting the applicability of NLP in the enterprise.

This train-from-scratch paradigm in NLP contrasted sharply with the leverage-pretrained-models paradigm in computer vision, which became dogma by late 2017. In computer vision, it was considered foolish to train computer vision models from scratch. Instead, applied machine learning engineers would leverage the first several layers of large, pretrained computer vision models, which had already learned some of the basic elements of computer vision such as identifying edges and shapes, to develop computer vision models for their specific task.

Transferring some of the "knowledge" from these pretrained models to new models required less annotated data than would otherwise be necessary and improved the adoption of computer vision in the enterprise. Unfortunately, as of the end of 2017,

---

1 For more, read this thorough piece on ImageNet by Quartz (*https://oreil.ly/0f3IH*).

such a transfer of knowledge from pretrained models was not possible in NLP, requiring teams to gather a lot of annotated data to train their specific models from scratch.

The Path to NLP's ImageNet Moment

In 2018, the mainstream view changed dramatically as NLP researchers showed that pretrained language models could be used to achieve state-of-the-art results on a wide range of NLP tasks; you did not need to train language models from scratch to solve specific NLP problems. This led to a watershed moment for NLP because now applied machine learning teams could leverage pretrained language models to solve a wide array of NLP tasks, just like computer vision engineers were leveraging pretrained ImageNet models to solve a wide array of computer vision tasks. By reusing several layers of pretrained language models, applied NLP scientists and engineers needed much less annotated data to solve specific NLP problems. Previously intractable problems in NLP became ripe for solving.[2]

To understand what led to this breakthrough moment in NLP, let's retrace the progress in NLP over the last several years. This will help us tie together the major concepts across this book, deepening your understanding of the field.

Pretrained Word Embeddings

One of the first steps in NLP is tokenization, which we covered in Chapter 5. Tokenization breaks down text into discrete units (e.g., words, punctuation, etc.), after which we can apply NLP algorithms to learn the structure of the text, including how to represent each token.

Learning how to represent each token is generally the second step in NLP. This process is called *learning word embeddings* (i.e., word vectors), which we covered in Chapter 6. Word embeddings are vital in NLP because they capture the relationship between words. Unless a model learns the relationship between words, it cannot perform more complex NLP tasks, such as text classification, well.

Prior to 2013, NLP researchers had to train their own word embeddings from scratch for much of the work they did. Starting in 2013, pretrained word embeddings began to rise in prominence, allowing NLP researchers to leverage them for model development, speeding up their training process.

---

2 For more on NLP's ImageNet moment, read Sebastian Ruder's excellent piece on the topic (*https://ruder.io/nlp-imagenet*).

The Limitations of One-Hot Encoding

Before we dive into these pretrained word embeddings, let's visit why simple one-hot vector encoding of words would not be an optimal approach at generating meaningful word vectors. If we had to apply one-hot encoding for every word in a large corpus, the dimensionality of the encoding matrix would be equal to the number of unique words, which would be quite massive and impractical to work with.

For example, if our corpus had a vocabulary of 400,000 unique words, our one-hot encoding matrix would have 400,000 dimensions, which is very large. This matrix would be a sparse matrix (mostly zero) and would suffer from the curse of dimensionality (e.g., we would need a lot of data to train a model that generalizes well because this matrix is both large and sparse, making parameter estimation more difficult).

Aside from the high dimensionality, a one-hot encoding matrix would not capture any of the semantic properties of words. For example, "queen" and "king" would have vectors that are orthogonal, implying that they are completely different when they are in fact related.

In contrast, word embeddings trained with algorithms such as Word2Vec, GloVe, and fastText store contextual information in a much lower dimensional space. For the same vocabulary of 400,000 unique words, we could store the contextual information for each word using just a few hundred dimensions, far less than the 400,000 dimensions required from one-hot encoding.

Moreover, the word embeddings trained by Word2Vec, GloVe, and fastText store semantic information for each word, unlike one-hot encoding. Words such as "queen" and "king" have vectors that are closer together in space, implying that there is some semantic relationship/similarity between the two. By capturing this semantic property, word embeddings trained by Word2Vec, GloVe, and fastText capture more of the structure in language compared to one-hot encodings, which is how these word embeddings helped materially advance the field of NLP starting in 2013. This was the year pretrained word embeddings that capture semantic information began to become widely available to the researchers in the NLP community.

Word2Vec

> A word is characterized by the company it keeps.
>
> —John Rupert Firth

In 2013, pretrained word embeddings became popular with the rise of Word2Vec, the first of the major word embedding algorithms. As you may recall from Chapter 6, Word2Vec is a highly efficient algorithm that is used to learn word associations from a large corpus of text. Each distinct word is represented with a vector (hence

Word2Vec, which is short for "word to vector"). You can think of Word2Vec and other word embedding algorithms as unsupervised feature extractors for words.

Word2Vec learns how to represent each word with a vector based on the surrounding context of each word; in other words, the words around the target word help define the vector representation for the target word. There are two approaches to do this: continuous bag of words (CBOW), which uses a neural network to predict which word is most likely given its context, and skip-gram, which predicts the surrounding words given a target word (the opposite of CBOW).[3]

The magic of Word2Vec is that semantically similar words have vectors (e.g., numerical representations) that are similar because the words appear in similar contexts. In other words, in a high-dimensional space, words that have similar meaning, such as "queen" and "king," have similar representations (i.e., vectors) and, therefore, are located closer together.[4]

Instead of having to learn word embeddings from scratch, ML engineers could use the pretrained word embeddings trained by Word2Vec in their model development, leveraging some of the "learning" done beforehand. This emergence of pretrained word embeddings helped ML engineers because they did not have to start model development entirely from scratch.

Despite its successes, Word2Vec has shortcomings. First, it relies on a relatively small window-based model to learn the word embedding for a particular word. It does not consider the word in the context of the entire document. Second, it does not consider subword information, which means that it cannot efficiently learn, for example, how a noun and an adjective that are derived from the same subword are related. For instance, "intelligent" and "intelligence" share the subword "intelligen" and are related as a result, sharing similar semantic information.

Third, Word2Vec cannot handle Out of Vocabulary (OOV) words; it can only vectorize words that it has seen in training. Finally, Word2Vec cannot disambiguate the context-specific semantic properties of words. For example, with Word2Vec, the word "bank" has the same word vector regardless of whether it appears in the financial setting ("I deposited a check at the bank") or in the river setting ("I sat on the river bank after fishing").

---

3 For more on these two approaches, refer to Chapter 6.

4 For more, read the Word2Vec Wikipedia article (*https://oreil.ly/8DHbE*).

Generally, pretrained word embeddings have a few hundred dimensions (typically three hundred). The more dimensions, the more subtle representations you can embed with the word embedding algorithms, but this comes at the cost of computation speed and increased complexity. If you want a better-performing model, it is better to use a word embedding matrix that has more dimensions than fewer for any given word embedding algorithm you choose. If you want a faster/more computationally efficient model, it is better to use a matrix that has fewer dimensions, all else being equal.

GloVe

GloVe, short for Global Vectors, was 'the next major word embedding to come onto the scene; it launched in 2014, a year after Word2Vec. GloVe addressed the first major shortcoming of Word2Vec. Instead of relying on a small window-based model like Word2Vec, GloVe considered the word statistics of the entire corpus when learning the word embedding for each word.

GloVe works similarly to Word2Vec but uses a different approach to learn the vector representations for words. More specifically, GloVe uses unsupervised learning, generating a global co-occurrence matrix to learn the semantic property of the target word given the entire corpus it appears in.[5]

Although GloVe addresses one of the shortcomings of Word2Vec, it still does not consider subword information.

fastText

In 2016, Facebook launched fastText, the third major word embedding approach in recent years. fastText differs from Word2Vec and GloVe; instead of considering each word as the smallest unit, fastText uses n-gram characters as the smallest unit. In other words, fastText uses subword information to generate word embeddings. For example, the word vector "kingdom" could be broken down into n-gram characters such as "ki," "kin," "ing," "ngd," "gdo," and "dom."

Instead of learning vector representations for words by using other words as context, fastText learns vector representations for n-gram characters by using other n-gram characters as context. Because it breaks the units down into a more granular level than either Word2Vec or GloVe, fastText achieves a wider variety and more nuanced set of word embeddings.

---

5 For more on GloVe, read the pdf of the official paper (*https://oreil.ly/RRRSu*).

This use of n-gram characters instead of words as the smallest unit is a material improvement over Word2Vec and GloVe for several reasons. First, fastText requires less training data because it is able to learn a lot more from the various n-gram characters in a set of words than what Word2Vec or GloVe could for the same set of words.

Second, fastText uses subword information and, therefore, generalizes better because new words that fastText hasn't been trained on yet may share n-gram characters with words on which fastText has trained on. For example, if fastText has trained on "fastest" but has not trained on "biggest," it can infer the meaning of "est" in "biggest" from the "est" in "fastest," whereas Word2Vec and GloVe could not. Third, fastText can generate embeddings for OOV words using the average vector representations of n-grams in the OOV words that fastText has embeddings for. This is related to the use of subword information, which neither Word2Vec nor GloVe support.

With fastText, the only major shortcoming is its inability to produce multiple vectors for each word depending on the context.

Context-Aware Pretrained Word Embeddings

As good as they are, word embeddings trained by Word2Vec, GloVe, and fastText are not context-aware. They do not capture the different context-specific semantic properties of words. For example, the word "bank" has the same word vector (and, therefore, the same semantic property) regardless of whether it is used in the sentence, "I deposited a check at the bank," or in the sentence, "I sat on the river bank after fishing."

The large, pretrained language models based on the Transformer architecture, such as ELMo and BERT, that came onto the scene starting in 2018 changed this: they introduce context-aware word representations. With context-aware word representations, the "bank" in a financial setting has a different word vector than the "bank" in a river setting. This should feel intuitive: the same word in different contexts means different things, and, therefore, we should have different word vectors to represent the different meanings of the word depending on the context. More on this soon.

In this section, we just covered the advances in word embeddings over the years. In the next section, we'll explore the advances in modeling approaches in recent years, starting with sequential models.

Sequential Models

Starting in 2016, sequential models began to rise in prominence in the field of NLP, achieving success in tasks such as machine translation, text summarization, conversational bots, and image captioning. Sequential models also captured mainstream attention with the *New York Times* article on Google's new machine–translation-based

Google Translate (*https://oreil.ly/M0VJb*). Dubbed "The Great AI Awakening," the article brought to the world stage for the first time the power of NLP models in solving complex language tasks.

Sequential models are machine learning models that input or output sequences of data, such as text, audio, and time series data. Sequential models are a class of modeling approaches, not just a singular approach, and they include RNNs, LSTMs, and GRUs, all of which we covered in detail earlier in the book. All of these sequential models either take in a sequence of data and output a singular result (for example, classify movie reviews as positive or negative sentiment), take in a singular input and output a sequence of data (for example, take in an image and return a caption that describes the image), or turn one sequence of data (such as text or audio) into another sequence (known as seq2seq modeling). For instance, neural machine translation models take text in one language as the input sequence (e.g., French) and return the text in another language as the output sequence (e.g., English). In other words, the model takes in an input sequence and outputs an output sequence.

 To recap, sequential models handle multiple types of scenarios: (a) sequential input to single output, for scenarios such as sentiment analysis; (b) single input to sequential output, for image captioning; and (c) sequential input to sequential output, for machine translation.

Sequential models are generally composed of an encoder and a decoder. The encoder takes in the input sequence, item by item, and generates a representation; think of this as converting text (such as a sentence) into a vector of numbers that machines can process. In the machine translation task, the encoder "encodes" the representation word by word to form the representation.

Once the encoder processes the entire input sequence, it passes the representation to the decoder, which unravels it into an output sequence, item by item. For example, in the machine translation task, the decoder "decodes" the representation word by word to form the output sentence.

Over the past several years, sequential models have gotten better and better, solving the flaws of their predecessors. Let's explore the nature of sequential data some more, and then we will start with the earliest of the modern-day sequential models, made up of RNNs.

Although we focus on NLP-based sequential modeling applications in this book, it is important to know that sequential modeling has applications well beyond NLP. Within NLP, sequential modeling is relevant for text (e.g., machine translation, text summarization, question answering, and more), audio (e.g., chatbots), and speech (e.g., speech recognition). Outside NLP, sequential modeling is relevant for images (e.g., image captioning), video (e.g., video captioning), anomaly detection on time series data, and time series prediction involving sensor data, stock market data, genomic data, and weather data. Sequential modeling is one of the most relevant and flourishing areas of machine learning in the enterprise, not just for NLP.

Sequential Data and the Importance of Sequential Models

Before we dive into RNNs, let's explore the nature of sequential data and why there is a need for a special class of models (i.e., sequential models) to work with it. Sequential data involves a series of sequentially interdependent/related items; for example, the words in a sentence are related to one another in some sequential fashion and, therefore, are interdependent. The words in a sentence are not sequentially independent of each other.

This is true of other sequential data as well. For example, the phonemes in a spoken sentence (phonemes are the smallest speech utterances, such as the "c" in "cat") are also sequentially dependent on each other. The sounds we make in speech are related to the ones preceding and succeeding each utterance. If we want to model audio, we need a way to capture the sequential connectedness of the data.

A third example of sequential data is stock market prices. Each one-second tick in stock prices is related to the series of ticks before and the series of ticks after. There is a pattern in the data that connects each tick with the rest. To predict stock prices well, a machine learning model that learns from the stock market's price data needs to be able to represent and process the sequential nature of stock prices well. This is true of sensor-type time series data in healthcare and industrial robotics and many other fields.

Traditional feed-forward neural networks treat each input/observation as independent of the one preceding it and the one succeeding it. For example, a computer vision model that classifies images as "cat" or "dog" does not need to consider the preceding or succeeding image in order to successfully classify the current image. The model needs to focus only on the current image.

This singular focus on a single input is, of course, not optimal for sequential data problems. If we had to build a model to translate a sentence from French to English, it would be suboptimal to translate each word in the French sentence to a word in English, word by word. While this would be a literal translation of French to English, the output sentence in English would likely not make much grammatical sense because the rules of French grammar differ from the rules of English grammar.

A more optimal approach would be for the model to generate a representation of the entire input (French) sentence first before attempting to translate it to an output (English) sentence. The model should do this by processing each word, word by word, while taking into consideration the preceding word(s). This is critical because language exhibits a sequential pattern that will help the model generate a better representation of the French sentence than if the model ignored the sequential pattern altogether.

By taking into account the sequential pattern of the French language as it processes the input sentence, the model is better equipped to more accurately translate the sentence into English. This is the crux of sequential modeling; by considering the sequential pattern of data, such as text, audio, and time series data, sequential models generate better performance on tasks than traditional feed-forward neural networks.

With this context, let's dig into the first of the successful sequential models in recent years: RNNs.

RNNs

Sequential models learn about the temporal nature of data, one time step at a time. Let's use an example to demonstrate this. Sequential models that process text "read" each word, one word at a time. Each moment the model reads a word is a time step. As the model processes an entire sentence, it moves from time step 0 to time step x, where x is the length of the sentence. At every time step increment, the model considers the present word while taking into consideration the series of words that preceded it.

 Here's a simple, intuitive way to think of RNNs: they are networks with loops in them, allowing information of the past to persist as "memory," which can be used to process the next input.

The better the memory of the model, the better the model will be able to perform tasks, such as translating a sentence from one language to another or answering questions.

RNNs are a family of machine learning models that can store and use memory of prior sequential data in processing the current data. For example, RNNs have memory of prior words and use this memory to process the current word in a sentence. The major challenge of RNNs is having great memory of sequential data that spans a long time frame. For example, it is easier for an RNN to have memory of the most recent few words it has processed compared to memory of words in a sentence several sentences ago.

Let's start with vanilla RNNs in this section, which have good short-term memory, before we turn to RNNs with gates (e.g., LSTMs and GRUs), which model not only short-term memory but also long-term memory and are better able to capture the long-term dependencies in sequential data that are necessary to solve more complex tasks such as question answering.

 Before RNNs, CNNs were used to solve NLP problems. CNNs have become famous in machine learning for their performance on computer vision tasks, but they also have relevance for natural language tasks. In CNNs, the neural net uses fixed-length windows to represent the data. For example, in text-based problems, the neural network uses a small, bounded context of words to perform tasks such as machine translation. While CNN-based language models are very fast, they have little context of words; they have even less context than the short-term memory of RNNs. This limits the CNNs' performance, which is why researchers switched to RNNs once these became available.

Vanilla RNNs

Unlike conventional feed-forward networks, recurrent neural networks have a temporal dimension; in other words, RNNs take time into account, whereas conventional feed-forward networks do not. Conventional feed-forward networks feed information in one direction (hence, feed forward), but RNNs pass the data forward and then cycle the data back through a loop.

This "recurrent" cycling allows RNNs to have a sense of time, enabling the network to process the current input while retaining some context of the previous inputs. When an RNN processes an event in time step t, it also considers the recent past (e.g., what happened in time steps t-1, t-2, etc.). In other words, RNNs share weights over time. You can think of conventional feed-forward networks as having forgetful memories, whereas RNNs have better memories of recent events. Information in RNNs persists, whereas it does not with conventional feed-forward networks.

In sequential models, both the encoder and decoder could be RNNs. Both the encoder and decoder RNNs take two inputs at each timestamp. In the machine translation case, for example, the two inputs are (a) a word and (b) a hidden state. This hidden state vector is the sequential memory that the recurrent network has preserved from previous time steps.

Each word is represented with a word embedding, which we reviewed earlier in the chapter.

At each timestamp, the encoder RNN processes the input (i.e., the word vector) and the hidden state (also a vector) and generates an output vector and a new output hidden state (also a vector). At the next timestamp, the RNN processes the next input (i.e., the next word vector) and the (output) hidden state from the previous timestamp and generates another output vector and a new output hidden state. This continues until the encoder RNN has finished processing the entire input sequence.

Once the encoder is done, it passes only the last output hidden state it generated to the decoder. This last output hidden state is the "representation" we alluded to earlier. You can think of it as the input sequence represented in a machine-processable format, ready for the decoder to process into an output sequence.

Once the decoder RNN receives the "representation" from the encoder, it unravels it word by word into the output sequence. In other words, the decoder RNN "translates" the hidden state word by word. You can think of this as unraveling what the encoder did but in reverse. This is a very simple explanation of how RNNs work, but check out Chapter 6 for more details.

RNNs can handle all sorts of sequential data, not just text; this includes time series data, for example.

RNNs are an excellent choice for modeling sequential data such as text because they use an internal state to process the sequence. In other words, as the RNN works item by item through a sequence, it relies on its internal state/memory to process each item. This is very important because the items in the sequence (e.g., words in a sentence) are not independent of one another; they are related. Having an internal state/memory of how the inputs are related to one another is crucial for modeling the data effectively.

This should be intuitive. Translating one sentence from one language to another requires representing the input sentence properly first. Each word in the input sentence is dependent on/related to the word(s) prior. By managing the hidden states in the way it does, an RNN uses its internal state/memory (based on the prior words processed) to process each subsequent word.

However, RNNs also have a major flaw: they cannot process very long sequences very well.[6]

LSTM Networks

Vanilla RNNs have memory, but this memory is mostly just short-term; vanilla RNNs really struggle with capturing and storing long-term dependencies in data. Therefore, they have limited performance in solving more complex NLP tasks such as question answering.

LSTM networks also use a recurrent neural network architecture but help solve for the inability of vanilla RNNs to process long sequences very well. LSTMs are able to hold memory of data over longer sequences. They can keep the context of sequential data in mind for much longer using mechanisms known as *gates* as part of their neural network architecture (more on gates soon).

Having longer-term memory is so important because solving an NLP task may require the memory of an item from many time steps before. Think of the following passage, taken from the Wikipedia article on George Washington (*https://oreil.ly/V7Sdh*):

> George Washington was an American political leader, military general, statesman, and Founding Father who served as the first president of the United States from 1789 to 1797. Previously, he led Patriot forces to victory in the nation's War for Independence. He presided at the Constitutional Convention of 1787, which established the U.S. Constitution and a federal government. Washington has been called the "Father of His Country" for his manifold leadership in the formative days of the new nation.

If asked "Who is the first president of the United States?" an NLP model trained using vanilla RNNs may be able to answer the question correctly ("George Washington") because the number of time steps between the mention of "George Washington" and the mention of "the first president of the United States" is reasonably low (fewer than 20 steps).

But, an NLP model trained using vanilla RNNs would have much greater difficulty answering "Who presided at the Constitutional Convention of 1787?" because of the number of time steps between the mention of "George Washington" and the mention of "the Constitutional Convention of 1787" unless the NLP model could hold some form of longer-term memory.

---

6 This is due to the infamous vanishing gradient problem in backpropagation (*https://oreil.ly/9HVht*).

RNNs work perfectly fine when there's a small gap between the relevant information and the point where it is needed, but RNNs begin to struggle as the gap grows and the RNNs' short-term memory is unable to connect the question with information from the distant past. In other words, since RNNs can't preserve information over many time steps, they can only handle tasks that require short-term memory. An NLP model would have greater success answering the question, "Who presided at the Constitutional Convention of 1787," if it could successfully disambiguate the pronoun "he" as "George Washington" as it processes the entire paragraph of text on George Washington. More modern NLP models do this very well using attention mechanisms. We'll discuss this in more detail in "Attention Mechanisms" on page 188.

LSTMs hold long-term memory using a series of three carefully regulated gates, which control how much information flows into and out of the LSTM's memory. These gates enable LSTMs to remember values over arbitrary time intervals. You can think of the three gates as mechanisms that allow the network to add or remove items to its memory depending on how relevant the network deems the items to be.

In other words, an LSTM network updates its memory vector at each time step depending on (a) which information it wants to add from the current input, (b) which information it deems not relevant anymore and wants to forget, and (c) which information it wants to keep. The gates are the mechanisms that learn which items in the sequential data are important to store in the LSTM's memory and which items are not. The gates are neural networks in their own regard, learning how to perform their respective specialized roles best. These three types of gates are as follows:

Input gate
 This determines which information from the current input should be used to modify the memory.

Forget gate
 This type of gate determines which information to forget from memory because the information is no longer relevant.

Output gate
 This determines the information to keep in memory (and pass on to the next time step) given the current input and what the network has chosen to forget.

Using these gates, LSTM allows a neural network to operate on different time scales at once, capturing longer dependencies much better than RNNs would.

The TL;DR is that LSTM is an improved version of RNNs. LSTM has longer-term memory compared to RNNs. LSTM achieves this using mechanisms called gates, which learn which information in the sequential data matters most and which does not.

GRUs

Gated recurrent units (GRUs) are another form of RNNs with gates. They are similar to LSTM but have a simpler structure, using just two gates instead of three. These two kinds of gates are the following:

Update gate
> The update gate determines whether the memory should be updated with new information from the current input.

Reset gate
> This determines how much of the new memory is important (and should be retained and passed on) or not (and therefore reset).

In other words, the update gate controls information that flows into memory, and the reset gate controls information that flows out of memory. The update gate in GRUs is similar to the combination of the input gate and the forget gate in LSTM, while the reset gate in GRUs is similar to the output gate in LSTM.

The performance of GRUs is similar to the performance of LSTMs (but generally not quite as good), but, because of their simpler structure, GRUs are computationally more efficient. They train faster and are also a better choice than LSTM when you have limited training data because GRUs have fewer weights and parameters to update during training.

To recap, RNNs are a family of sequential models that have helped advance the field of NLP, particularly since 2015. Vanilla RNNs have simple, short-term memory, but the gated variants (LSTM and GRUs) have longer short-term memory and capture longer-term dependencies in sequential data better. LSTM and GRUs are the best-performing RNNs in the field of NLP today. Both have similar performance, but GRUs are simpler than LSTM (GRUs use two gates instead of the three in LSTM) and faster to train.

As successful as these RNNs were at the end of 2016, they handled longer-term dependencies poorly, a problem the next breakthrough in NLP—attention mechanisms—sought to address.

Attention Mechanisms

Although LSTM and GRUs have longer-term memories than RNNs, they still have shortcomings that hamper their performance on NLP tasks. This is most apparent on sequence-to-sequence NLP tasks such as machine translation. Both LSTM and GRUs have a hidden state ("memory") that is passed on from one time step to the next. In machine translation, the input sentence is encoded first, and the final hidden state ("representation") is passed on to the decoder to decode/translate the sentence into the output language.

The decoder has only this final hidden state to work off of. It does not have access to the intermediate hidden states of the encoder. This means that there is information left on the table (in the form of the intermediate hidden states of the encoder) that the decoder could use to improve its translation but does not have access to. Because of this limitation, LSTM, for example, cannot preserve information for more than 20 words in machine translation. The bidirectional version of LSTM was invented to solve this (known as Bi-LSTMs), but even Bi-LSTM could not preserve information for more than 40 words.

It should be clear that trying to squeeze the meaning of an entire sentence into one vector (the final hidden state of the encoder) and passing this to the decoder to translate the input sentence is suboptimal. It would be better for the decoder to focus on the relevant locations of the input sentence (via the intermediate hidden states of the encoder) at every time step as the decoder worked on the translation.

In other words, the decoder should focus its attention on the relevant hidden states of the encoder at every time step instead of using just one vector (the final hidden state of the encoder) to perform the translation. Intuitively, this should improve the quality of translation because the decoder would have more relevant information as it worked through the translation of the input sentence.

The mechanisms that enable LSTM to focus their attention are known as *attention mechanisms*.They helped unleash the major breakthroughs in NLP in recent years, starting in 2017. Attention mechanisms in LSTM allow the decoder to access all the hidden states of the encoder, not just the final hidden state. Beyond this, they help the decoder focus its attention on particular hidden states and ignore the others as it translates the input sentence into the output sentence.

By being able to access the entire source input, an LSTM with attention mechanisms can handle longer input sequences better than vanilla LSTM and GRUs (and certainly much better than RNNs). In a nutshell, LSTM with attention mechanisms are less forgetful because they are able to have better and more focused memory.

In an LSTM with attention, the encoder passes all the hidden states to the decoder instead of just the last hidden state, which is the case in an LSTM without attention.

This should feel intuitive. Attention in neural networks mimics cognitive attention in humans. Whether reading a sentence or driving a car, we as humans are not paying equal attention to everything around us all the time. Doing so would not only be mentally exhausting, but it would be impossible for us. We could not hold that cognitive load at once.

Instead, we focus our attention on items that matter most given the task we are performing. If we are reading a sentence, we pay more attention to some of the words—such as the names of the protagonists, where they are, and the activities they are performing—than to filler words such as articles and prepositions and words from many sentences ago. The filler words are less relevant and, therefore, not worth as much of our attention.

This is also true for complex tasks such as driving a car. We focus our attention on the road in front of us, including stop signs, traffic lights, crosswalks, other nearby vehicles, pedestrians, cyclists, and other objects we want to avoid hitting. We are much less focused on what is happening in our peripheral vision or the landscape on the horizon, especially when there is a lot of active traffic in front of us.

In much the same way, attention mechanisms in machine learning help neural networks focus their attention on what matters most for the task at hand while ignoring everything else that is less relevant. This enables neural networks to have better performance on tasks in much the same way that humans who can focus well (free of cognitive impairments such as drugs or alcohol or other distractions) are able to perform tasks better.

After their early success in improving machine translation, attention mechanisms became highly in vogue. A flurry of attention mechanisms came onto the market including self-attention, global/soft attention, and local/hard attention. Moreover, attention mechanisms were used for more than NLP applications; they became popular in computer vision, too. For more on these variants of attention mechanisms and how they work, refer to Chapter 7.

Attention mechanisms also help make models more interpretable and explainable. This allows us to learn what the model is focused on as it translates words or generates a caption for an image, for example.

As these became more popular, researchers began to explore neural network architectures that relied more and more on attention mechanisms and less on the recurrent neural architecture of RNNs. This resulted in the next big breakthrough in NLP: the Transformer architecture.

Transformers

LSTM with attention mechanisms was a major improvement over vanilla LSTM and GRUs, but it had some shortcomings. Most notably, LSTM with attention mechanisms is computationally intensive to train and hard to parallelize.

Soon after LSTM with attention mechanisms became popular in 2017, researchers designed an even better architecture, one that was faster to train and eliminated recurrent networks altogether and relied solely on attention mechanisms. This new architecture is known as the Transformer architecture (or Transformer, for short).

Instead of using a recurrent network-based encoder-decoder, Transformers use a feed-forward encoder-decoder with attention.

Transformers were the catalyst for the ImageNet moment in NLP, heralding the advent of large, pretrained language models such as ULMFiT, ELMo, BERT, GPT-2, and GPT-3. Transformers are very memory-intensive, but parallelize very well. Given the parallelization, it is possible to train Transformers on lots of data super fast across lots of GPUs, which is exactly what has happened at the large tech giants in recent years.

Let's dig into the parallelization some more because it helps explain why the Transformer was such a major breakthrough compared to LSTMs with attention. An LSTM, like all RNNs, needs to process data in order. In other words, the first word of a sentence needs to be processed before the LSTM can process the second word, and the third word, etc. Transformers do not have this requirement; they do not need to process data in order, from beginning to end.

By removing the recurrent processing and relying solely on attention mechanisms, Transformers pass an entire sequence of data to the decoder at once rather than sequentially as the older conventional sequential models do. This innovation around passing blocks of data (such as several sentences) through the network at once was a game changer.

Compared to conventional sequential models, the Transformer learns from more data at any given time and has much more parallelization as a result, reducing training times. Greater parallelization and faster training times have allowed researchers to train on massively large datasets, much larger than the datasets the conventional sequential models could have trained on.

This enabled research teams at Google, Facebook, and other firms to train on very large datasets, much larger than what was possible with LSTM. This breakthrough in parallelization during training led to the advent of very large, pretrained language models.

With this in mind, let's explore the Transformer architecture in more detail. Transformers rely on attention mechanisms alone, without any recurrent sequential processing, to perform tasks. The invention of attention mechanisms made the Transformer possible.

Like LSTM, the Transformer relies on an encoder-decoder architecture. Specifically, the encoding component is a stack of encoders that process the input, and the decoding component is a stack of decoders that process the encodings passed to them by the encoders. The number of encoders equals the number of decoders. Also, all the encoders are identical in structure, and all the decoders are identical in structure.

Let's examine the stack of encoders first. Each encoder has two components (or sublayers): a self-attention mechanism and a feed-forward neural network. The self-attention mechanism takes in the input encodings from the previous encoder and weighs the relevance of the encodings to each other to generate a set of output encodings. The output encodings are fed into the feed-forward neural network, which processes the encodings individually before passing them to the next encoder layers and the decoder layers.

The self-attention mechanism helps the encoder weigh the relevance of the words in the input sentence for the word the encoder is processing. For example, in the sentence, "Washington was the first President of the United States, while Adams was the first Vice President," the self-attention mechanism would assign greater relevance to the words "first" and "President" when processing the word "Washington" than it would assign to the other words, particularly words related to "Adams." This helps the encoder focus on the more relevant information when processing the word at hand, once again highlighting the beauty of attention mechanisms.

The first encoder takes the word embeddings of the input sentence and the positional information of the tokens as its input rather than encodings. Every other encoder uses the encodings generated by the prior encoder in the stack.

The stack of decoders processes the encodings passed by the encoders and generates an output. Each decoder has three components: a self-attention mechanism, an attention mechanism, and a feed-forward neural network. The decoder has a similar structure except for the additional attention mechanism, which helps it weigh the relevant information from the encodings generated by the encoders. This attention mechanism helps the decoder focus on the relevant parts of the input sentence, similar to what the attention mechanism does in LSTMs with attention.

The self-attention layer in the decoder also works a bit differently; the self-attention mechanism is allowed to attend to only earlier positions in the output sentence. All future positions are masked so the transformer is not using the current or future output to generate its output.

After the stack of decoders, the output vector is fed into a final linear transformation and softmax layer to produce the output probabilities over the vocabulary. The word in the vocabulary with the highest probability is generated as the final output of the time step.

After it was introduced in late 2017, the Transformer became the clear standout architecture for solving many NLP problems. Researchers have used it to advance the field dramatically over the past three years, starting with the explosion of activity in 2018, the year of NLP's ImageNet moment.

Transformer-XL

One major limitation of the original 2017 Transformer architecture was the fixed-length requirement for text strings that were fed into the Transformer as input. Because of this limitation, text fed into the Transformer was often fragmented. For example, sentences were split in the middle and fed into the Transformer, meaning that the Transformer had only partial context in processing the split sentence. The text was split without awareness of sentence boundaries or other semantic properties of the text, capping the performance of Transformers.

To address the shortcoming, in 2019, researchers invented the Transformer-XL, which introduced a recurrence mechanism to learn the dependencies between consecutive segments of fixed-length text fed into the Transformer's attention mechanisms. The recurrence mechanism allows the Transformer to access long-term dependencies in the data, retaining information from previous segments the Transformer had already processed.

What is interesting about the Transformer-XL is that it combines two major concepts of deep learning: recurrence and attention. While attention mechanisms (in the form of Transformers) have supplanted recurrent neural networks, the addition of recurrence to Transformers has made recurrence popular again. This highlights how ideas rise in favor, fall in popularity, and are often rediscovered and recycled in innovative ways to advance the field of NLP and machine learning, more generally.

The advances in word embeddings (from Word2Vec and GloVe to subword embeddings such as fastText) and in modeling architectures (from vanilla RNNs, LSTM, and GRUs to attention mechanisms and Transformers) culminated in the watershed year for NLP (the so-called ImageNet moment in 2018), which we will dive into now.

NLP's ImageNet Moment

The invention of the Transformer in 2017 directly led to NLP's ImageNet moment. In 2018, large, pretrained language models came onto the market that had been trained on a lot of data, and these models showed remarkable performance across a variety of NLP tasks. Previously, an NLP model had to be trained for every NLP task to be performant; there was no single model that could perform well on all the tasks at once.

This was a watershed moment for NLP. Now, researchers and applied NLP engineers could leverage the large, pretrained language models released by the likes of Google and OpenAI and apply them to all sorts of domain-specific NLP tasks. In other words, transfer learning from large, pretrained language models became possible, and this led to a flurry of activity in the enterprise in much the same way that computer vision's ImageNet moment led to the explosion of commercial activity around image tagging, object detection, autonomous driving, and more.

A flurry of releases made this moment possible and helped rapidly advance the state-of-the-art performance of NLP models. These releases include ULMFiT, ELMo, BERT, and GPT-1. Since then, the number of Transformer-based models has exploded, including BERT variants such as XLNet and RoBERTa, as well as GPT variants such as GPT-2 and GPT-3.

Let's walk through these releases in more detail to see what each contributed to the field of NLP.

Universal Language Model Fine-Tuning

In May 2018, Jeremy Howard and Sebastian Ruder's paper on Universal Language Model Fine-Tuning (ULMFiT)[7] showed that it was possible for a pretrained language model fine-tuned on a new dataset to have good performance on other NLP tasks as well, not just on the original NLP task the model was trained for. This is possible by first pretraining a language model on a general domain corpus such as Wikipedia articles. This pretraining enables the language model to learn the main properties of language, such as syntax and semantics.

Once the pretraining is complete, the next step is fine-tuning the model to perform a specific task. Because of the pretraining, the model is able to converge a lot faster than if the model were trained to perform the specific task at hand from scratch, which would not only take longer but would require a lot of the domain-specific corpus relevant for the specific task.

---

7 J. Howard and S. Ruder, "Universal Language Model Fine-Tuning for Text Classification," arXiv, May 2018, *https://oreil.ly/DPO8b*.

Language modeling is an NLP task in which the model is trained to predict the next word in a sequence of words. Researchers chose this NLP task to pretrain a model because language modeling does not need labels; it is a form of unsupervised NLP. Because no labels are necessary, researchers can pretrain language models on a massive amount of text data, which allows the model to learn the properties of language very quickly and robustly. If researchers had chosen machine translation on which to pretrain a model, they would have needed to assemble and annotate a massive dataset, which would have been costly and time-consuming.

In other words, pretrained ULMFiT-based models perform very well on small and medium datasets compared to models that have to be trained from scratch. ULMFiT opened up NLP applications for companies and use cases where assembling large amounts of data is difficult (not to mention that the models train much faster).

ELMo

Following the coattails of ULMFiT, AllenNLP released ELMo, which introduced contextualized word representations for the first time. This improved the word embeddings generated by the earlier word embedding algorithms, such as Word2Vec, GloVe, and fastText. With ELMo, it became possible to generate different word representations for the same word, such as "bank," depending on the context it appeared in (financial bank versus river bank).

Moreover, these word representations are character-based, like fastText word embeddings, which allows ELMo-based models to handle OOV tokens that weren't seen during training. Unsurprisingly, adding ELMo's contextualized word representations to existing NLP systems improved the state-of-the-art performance for every task.

BERT

The breakthroughs of ULMFiT (transfer learning) and ELMo (contextualized word representations) led to the bombshell moment for NLP in 2018—Google's open sourcing of BERT, the large, pretrained language model that shattered performance records on many NLP tasks. Bidirectional Encoder Representations from Transformers (BERT) was the culmination of multiple recent advances in NLP (Transformers + transfer learning + contextualized word representations). BERT was a "wow" moment for NLP researchers for the following reasons:

- It was pretrained on billions of annotated training examples, learning the properties of language from a lot of data.

- It could be fine-tuned by anyone in the world to achieve state-of-the-art results on their specific task.

BERT not only leveraged semi-supervised pretraining (similar to ULMFiT) and contextualized word representations (similar to ELMo), but it introduced a bidirectional component to the network by cleverly masking some of the words in a sentence and then havingf the network predict the masked words. BERT was able to do this masked bidirectional pretraining with a deep neural network and also learned how to model relationships between sentences.

BERT leveraged these different advances in NLP to develop an approach that would become the standard process for developing large, pretrained language models. In 2018, Google released two different versions: a base model and a large version. The large version was similar to the base model but had more of everything: larger feedforward networks, more attention heads, and more encoder layers (24 in the large versus just 12 in the base). Since then, several other companies have released versions of large, pretrained language models, each larger than its predecessor.

BERTology

The first BERT-like model to best Google's BERT was XLNet, released in early 2019. XLNet trained on more data than BERT, and for longer, but also improved on the training methodology by predicting tokens in random order (compared to BERT, where only the masked tokens are predicted). XLNet also leveraged the Transformer-XL architecture we referenced earlier (which is essentially the original Transformer architecture with recurrence).

A few months after XLNet and several months after Google released BERT, Facebook optimized the architecture further and released its own BERT-based version called RoBERTa. In particular, Facebook modified key hyperparameters in BERT; it removed BERT's next-sentence pretraining and trained the model with much larger mini-batches and learning rates. Facebook also trained on more data and for a longer amount of time. With the design changes, RoBERTa achieved state-of-the-art performance on many of the tasks BERT had set records in.

GPT-1, GPT-2, GPT-3

OpenAI also entered the NLP race by designing its own Transformer-based models. These models are known as GPT models, short for Generative Pretrained Transformer. The first of the GPT models, GPT-1, was released in 2018 and used an unsupervised pretraining and supervised fine-tuning process similar to ULMFiT. GPT-2 was released in 2019; compared to its predecessor, it trained on more data and with more parameters, helping it achieve state-of-the-art performance on many tasks in zero-shot settings.

In zero-shot learning, a model is given no examples to train on but must understand the task to perform given the instruction provided. For example, a zero-shot learning task may require a model to translate an English sentence into German, but the model would not be given English-to-German sentences to learn from. In few-shot learning, a model is given a few examples to learn from, but usually not many.

OpenAI released GPT-3 in 2020. Compared to GPT-2, GPT-3 trained on an even larger dataset and had an even larger number of parameters. GPT-3 bested its predecessor and set a new standard for zero-shot and few-shot learning. It is considered to be the most performance-generative NLP model to date.

 As you may have noticed, models have gotten bigger and bigger and have trained on more and more data over the years. This, along with design changes, larger models, and more data, has helped push the state-of-the-art performance in NLP.

Conclusion

In this chapter, we tied all the major concepts in the book together, including word embeddings, RNNs, attention mechanisms, the Transformer architecture, and contextualized word representations. Collectively these advances helped bring about NLP's ImageNet moment in 2018, the year when large, pretrained language models became available to the public and set new performance records on NLP benchmarks.

With the rise of the pretrained language models, it has become possible for applied NLP engineers to fine-tune large models on their domain-specific NLP tasks and achieve remarkable performance. Now that we've covered the major NLP concepts you need to know to develop NLP models, let's discuss how to productionize NLP models once you've developed them.

## PART III

Outside the Wall

Congratulations! You now know enough about NLP to actually read and understand the latest research and implement every part of the pipeline to solve the most common NLP tasks from scratch.

But when deploying models in production, there are many more things to consider. Where do you run your model—on the client or a server? How do you handle multiple simultaneous requests? How do you integrate your PyTorch model, which is only accessible from Python, in a JavaScript web app? How do you train on new, real user data that comes in? How do you detect and handle errors in your model while it's in production? How do you scale training across very large datasets and multiple nodes?

Many of these questions actually do not have a perfect answer, but in this section, we'll try to shine some light on the tools and technologies that are important to real-world productionization of models.

A lot of the topics discussed in these next few chapters are not, strictly speaking, directly related to NLP. They're what we called "outside the box" concepts in Chapter 1. Nonetheless, they are important to consider when taking your NLP models from a fun side project to large-scale research and a real-world deployment that has an impact on real humans.

## CHAPTER 9

Tools of the Trade

In the preceding section, we covered all the foundational elements of NLP and how to develop NLP models. Starting with this chapter, we'll cover what you should begin to think about as you come out of the wonderful world of training magnificent models on carefully curated datasets and into the mess that is the real world.

In this chapter specifically, we will discuss mainstream machine learning software and the choices you will face as you decide what to include in your stack. Then, in Chapter 10, we build custom web apps for machine learning and data science using an easy-to-use open source Python library called Streamlit (*https://streamlit.io*), and we will conclude this section (in Chapter 11) with model deployment at scale using software from the industry leader, Databricks (*https://databricks.com*). By the end of these three chapters, you will have a good understanding of how to productionize machine learning models as web apps, APIs, and machine learning pipelines.

Let's start with a topic many developers love spending inordinate amounts of time arguing over: tools.

People who should probably be spending their time coding, love hashing out the standard TensorFlow versus PyTorch or best programming language debates on endlessly long Twitter threads, but we want to take a step back and talk about some of the more practical decisions you'll have to wrestle with in the real world. After all, "applied" is in the title of this book.

Here are a few obligatory disclaimers:

- It is almost certain that what we recommend today will become outdated over time. Instead of being overly prescriptive with our advice, we want to help you develop intuition for what matters when you make decisions about what to include in your tech stack.

- We recognize that you probably have your own set of restrictions—for example, your company may already have a set of tools you are obligated to use. Or, you might be part of a large team where the choice of programming language, cloud provider, etc., has already been made for you. But hopefully, this chapter will still provide you with a sense of what else is out there.

- Making choices for your tech stack can be overwhelming. There are so many different providers offering similar competing services, and the prices and features they offer change frequently. This makes picking the absolute best a nearly impossible exercise. The sheer variety of competing providers can lead to decision fatigue. We will try to do our best to keep the choices you have to make to a minimum. In fact, we will go a step further. We, the authors of this book, will pick our own favorite tools to work with when building NLP applications!

- The list here is neither comprehensive nor definitive (nor is it in any particular order or ranking). The tools we list here are simply the ones that we, the authors, have found useful, popular, or interesting. The decision on what to use is, as always, up to you.

- What may work for one person in the field may not work for you. Take our suggestions with a grain of salt, and think critically about what makes the most sense for you.

- In the end, what's most important is not what tools you use but how you use them. In fact, you'll find that a lot of the deep learning frameworks, programming languages, etc., are often very similar, and it's not too hard to learn one once you've learned another.

We've split the tools into a few categories and have listed a few under each. At the end of each section, you'll find two specific recommendations, labeled "Ankur's Pick" and "Ajay's Pick" in the classic style of The Motley Fool (*https://www.fool.com*). These are our *individual personal* favorites:

Ankur's picks
These will tend to be more production-oriented, with a focus on tools that are stable and popular in industry, and that scale well.

Ajay's picks
These will be more experimental and research-oriented. These tools are designed for rapid experimentation and prototyping and will help you stay on the bleeding edge of modern research.

By the end of this chapter, you should be well acquainted with the landscape of tools available to you as you build NLP applications, both to prototype and to deploy in production.

Deep Learning Frameworks

Let's start with the deep learning frameworks. These frameworks are the core building blocks for nearly all of NLP (that's relevant to us), and we will use them extensively throughout this book. Most deep learning frameworks do the same exact thing—they perform tensor computations on GPUs.

What differentiates them is the way they implement the various high-level features and abstractions as well as how they manage the less obvious backend implementation that governs the actual performance of your code.

Over the last decade, multiple frameworks have phased in and out of existence. Older and increasingly less popular ones that you might have heard of in passing are Theano, Chainer, Lua, Torch, and Caffe. As of 2020, we think these smaller frameworks are, for the most part, obsolete and not worth exploring in great detail.

The big ones that you're familiar with and perhaps have used already are PyTorch and TensorFlow. These two frameworks were launched by two of the most successful technology companies today—Facebook and Google, respectively. Partly because of their dominance in the tech space, these two companies have been able to spur large developer communities to adopt and support their deep learning frameworks. Both frameworks have several things in common: they are both open source and interface with Python as the primary programming language. But there are a few differences between the two, which we will highlight in detail.

 PyTorch is based on the Torch framework, and TensorFlow is based on the Theano framework. Even though Torch and Theano have declined in popularity, their derivatives are now the most dominant in the deep learning space.

However, there are also a few new kids on the block, which you're probably less familiar with. Jax, Julia, and Swift for TensorFlow all promise killer new features, far better performance/speed, and are fairly drastic departures from what we've seen so far. They are still not as fleshed out as PyTorch and TensorFlow in terms of stability, community, and hardware support, but they show a lot of potential and have good development momentum, so be prepared to dip your toes in those as well.

PyTorch

Let's start with PyTorch, the fastest growing deep learning framework over the past several years. It was developed by Facebook's AI Research lab (FAIR) and released publicly in October 2016. The consensus is that PyTorch is now more popular among researchers.

At the core of PyTorch lies the torch.tensor object. It's a type of multidimensional array, almost identical to a numpy.ndarray, that can live in GPU memory and be used for fast parallel computation. Almost all of PyTorch is built for manipulating these tensors with operations such as matrix multiplication, convolution, etc.

The other big component of PyTorch is autograd. This feature automatically calculates a quantity called the *gradient* whenever you use PyTorch tensor operations, which is extremely useful for training neural networks.

Beyond this, the easiest way to describe PyTorch would be to call it "NumPy on the GPU" with added convenience functions for deep learning. Typically, deep learning involves repeatedly performing similar computations on large tensors, which is where GPUs excel. NumPy performs computation on the CPU, which, in most cases, is much slower than running lower-precision computations in parallel on the GPU.

For most Python programmers, PyTorch will feel natural and "Pythonic" since its interface is very similar to NumPy. This is one of the main reasons that PyTorch has continued rising in popularity over the last few years, despite the fact that it was released after TensorFlow.

Both PyTorch and TensorFlow offer distributed computation features, but PyTorch has better optimization for training because it has native support for asynchronous execution.

The job of deep learning frameworks can be described as executing a "graph" of computations on tensor data structures. In PyTorch you define the graph at runtime, which allows you to easily go back and forth between planning and execution. The ability to evaluate operations immediately, without compiling graphs explicitly, is known as *eager execution*.

Eager execution allows you to prototype faster and create new types of architectures, but at the cost of speed. Think of this as the difference between compiled and interpreted languages.

This used to be a big deal a few years ago since TensorFlow used static graphs back then, requiring you to define the entire graph first before pushing data through. However, both frameworks now support eager execution by default, and this has since been adopted as the go-to industry standard.

Following are itemized lists of things to consider before you start using PyTorch. First the pros:

- Easier to learn and more intuitive; Python-like coding
- Dynamic graph
- Excellent for fast experimentation and prototyping
- Requires less reading through documentation

- Better integration with other Python packages
- Rapidly gaining popularity among researchers

Here are some of the cons of using PyTorch:

- Relies on third party for visualization (e.g., Visdom)
- Has a less-robust native system for edge device deployments (requires API server)

Now, let's compare PyTorch with TensorFlow, the framework that remains the most popular in the industry today despite PyTorch's rapid ascent.

TensorFlow

Developed by the Google Brain team for internal Google use, TensorFlow 1.x was released in late 2015. It has a larger user base in industry, though this is likely due to the fact that it was released earlier and many companies have existing TensorFlow experience and legacy code. For the same reasons, TensorFlow has a larger community base overall.

In general, we would not recommend the 1.x version of TensorFlow, since it has a very bloated API and is generally more verbose and less user friendly than PyTorch (and actually slower in some cases due to problems with the backend).

However, with TensorFlow 2.0, the differences between TensorFlow and PyTorch have narrowed. TensorFlow now offers the ability to build dynamic graphs, instead of static graphs. TensorFlow 2.0 also fully integrates Keras, a very popular high-level API for TensorFlow. While TensorFlow 2.0 has resolved a lot of its issues with a complete redesign of the framework, it has also faced criticism for the drastic changes it introduced, which breaks nearly all 1.x code.

Compared to PyTorch, TensorFlow has excellent built-in visualization capabilities (e.g., TensorBoard) and has better support for mobile platforms with TensorFlow Lite (though this is changing with PyTorch Mobile). Because of this, TensorFlow can be easier to deploy in a production setting thanks to tools like TensorFlow Serving, which uses REST client APIs.

TensorFlow, in general, consists of a lot more than the Python framework, though. There are now more variants than we can count, including TensorFlow Lite, TensorFlow Extended, TensorFlow Serving, TensorFlow.js, TensorFlow.jl, TensorFlow Probability, and many more. This could be a helpful ecosystem or a confusing nuisance to deal with, depending on your perspective.

We recommend TensorFlow to developers that are ready to build production-ready applications and who may have existing code/infrastructure built on the TensorFlow ecosystem.

Following are itemized lists of things to consider before you start using TensorFlow. First, the pros:

- With Keras in TensorFlow 2.0, has a simple built-in high-level API
- Now supports eager mode
- Excellent visualization (TensorBoard)
- Production-ready (TensorFlow Serving)
- Great mobile support
- Large developer community and comprehensive documentation
- Has better performance at very large scale
- The dominant framework in industry

Following are some cons in using TensorFlow:

- Many people complain that TensorFlow still carries the baggage from its 1.x version, which was completely different from the TensorFlow we have today and was generally much harder to use.
- It has a steeper learning curve, and can feel at tims like a new language.

While PyTorch and TensorFlow are the two most popular deep learning frameworks available today, let's explore some of the fast-rising newcomers that may eventually challenge the incumbents.

Jax

Jax is a new numerical computing library introduced by Google very recently. It takes the idea of "NumPy on GPUs" popularized by PyTorch to a whole new level. At its core, Jax provides autograd functionality (the ability to calculate gradients of chained functions without explicitly specifying a derivative, which is extremely important for deep learning frameworks) directly on top of the standard NumPy and Python functions. This means Jax's autograd can handle loops, conditionals, closures, and other native Python constructs without any modification to your code!

But why is Google making a new library that has very similar functionality to Tensor-Flow? Who knows? The Jax project uses components and tools like XLA that stemmed from TensorFlow, but it seems to be a much cleaner rewrite of it. Will it eventually replace TensorFlow? Maybe. Only time will tell. But what we have now seems to indicate a promising new direction for deep learning frameworks focused on high performance on accelerators and reducing boilerplate code and syntax.

Julia

Julia, unlike others on this list, is not just another framework or library, it is an entirely new programming language. Its creators expressed concerns that many suboptimal decisions were made from a performance perspective when Python was created. It was, after all, designed to be easy-to-use first and everything else second.

But today, we're using Python tools to manage large datasets, run complex scientific simulations, and train deep neural networks with billions of parameters. This doesn't seem like something that should be done in a language that sacrifices performance for simplicity.

Julia was designed from the ground up for numerical and scientific computation. While Python has many use cases, including server backends, databases, and scripting, Julia focuses on the traditional "data science stack" that Python programmers use (i.e., NumPy, pandas, matplotlib, SciPy, etc.).

We won't be covering Julia extensively in this book, but we highly recommend checking it out yourself.

Honorable Mention: Swift for TensorFlow

Swift for TensorFlow (sometimes abbreviated to S4TF) attempted to solve an issue similar to the one Julia does—the fundamental limitations of Python.

The project made valuable contributions to the space of differentiable programming, compilers, and numerical computing in general, but unfortunately stopped development in 2021. We thank the S4TF team for their efforts, which have now introduced a number of upstream changes to the Swift programming language itself; its example has inspired other projects that attempt to build mainstream differentiable programming languages.

Without further ado, here are our personal picks:

Ankur's pick

> This is a very difficult choice for me. On one hand, I love to prototype in PyTorch, given how "Pythonic" it is. On the other hand, TensorFlow is so well entrenched in industry that it's hard not to invest heavily in learning and developing in TensorFlow. My recommendation is to learn TensorFlow because you will likely come across it if you work in the enterprise. But, for everything else, I prefer the ease and simplicity of PyTorch, which is my top pick personally.

Ajay's pick

> My deep learning framework of choice is PyTorch. While I'm super excited about some of the new ones and can't wait for deep learning frameworks to expand into other programming languages, PyTorch still seems to be the most reliable solution at the moment. It's a great tool for research, and a lot of the latest academic literature is implemented in PyTorch, which makes tweaking and testing new architectures, optimizers, etc., extremely easy.

Next, we will discuss visualization and experiment tracking software for your deep learning training needs.

Visualization and Experiment Tracking

Often, you'll start training one model, then another, then the next, and "Oh wait, maybe if I try this…"

Once you've set up your training pipeline, it becomes extremely easy to quickly run multiple experiments, perhaps even simultaneously. At this stage, most of your effort as a deep learning practitioner will not go into writing code but into making tweaks to a few key components of your model, data, or training loop.

As you start this rapid experimentation phase, you might need to run hundreds of experiments to find the best solution. Without software to visualize and track your experiments, it would be challenging to keep track of which experiments were most promising and which directions are worth pursuing further. Debugging these models is also difficult and time-consuming without good visualization software. Also, because most of machine learning today is highly collaborative, you'll need software to track your work within a team and share progress with others to avoid issues like redundant experiments.

That's what this section is all about—tools that help you track experiments, monitor performance, version control your experiments, and share your results with the rest of your team.

TensorBoard

TensorBoard is TensorFlow's built-in visualization software. It's open source and free and has a very large community of users. It allows us to visualize the graph, track and visualize metrics such as loss and accuracy, view histograms of weights and biases over time, project embeddings into a lower-dimensional space, and display images, text, and audio data.

With TensorBoard, we can run multiple experiments and track which experiments are leading to better/worse performance. This helps us optimize model performance by tuning hyperparameters more easily, for example. It is also easier to troubleshoot machine learning models with TensorBoard.

The latest version of TensorBoard, TensorBoard.dev, even allows us to host, track, and share our experiments with others; this is especially useful for collaboration within and among teams. Prior to TensorBoard.dev, we had to submit screenshots of TensorBoard to others to collaborate on work.

While TensorBoard is a good built-in solution for TensorFlow, it lacks a lot of the collaborative features that other players in the space offer. The main advantage of TensorBoard lies in the fact that it's an official, first-party, built-in tool, something that PyTorch currently does not offer.

Weights & Biases

Some machine learning practitioners rely on tracking ML experiments with a spreadsheet. Unless you're from the 20th century, this approach is both brittle and nonscalable in industry. Given the need for great deep learning visualization and experiment tracking software, companies such as Weights & Biases have sprung up.

Founded in 2017, Weights & Biases allows teams to track their ML experiments, visualize, and optimize model performance, and maintain versioning of datasets and models with just a few lines of code. TensorBoard was designed for individuals to experiment independently, but Weights & Biases was designed with collaborative teams in mind.

Weights & Biases automatically tracks hyperparameters, metrics, etc., and logs them to the cloud. You can then visualize results through an interactive dashboard that updates in real time. You can log practically anything you might care about, including plots, sample predictions, audio, video, 3D models, and even raw HTML. This tool also offers tags, filtering, grouping, and the ability to export to a wide variety of formats to keep your experiments well-organized.

Neptune

Much like Weights & Biases, Neptune allows us to track experiments and organize work for our team. The best part about Neptune is it easily hooks into multiple frameworks and is a very lightweight tool. It works very easily in notebook environments (e.g., Jupyter, JupyterLab, and Google Colab).

Neptune is best for users who want a lightweight experiment management tool for all model training (classic machine learning, deep learning, reinforcement learning, etc.). It also offers great notebook tracing (for Jupyter and JupyterLab). If you do most of your machine learning work in notebooks, Neptune is a top contender for experiments tracking.

Comet

Comet is great for any model training, not just deep learning. It also offers meta machine learning capabilities (e.g., AutoML) that the other experiment tracking software platforms lack. Like Weights & Biases, Comet is a robust piece of software, one we recommend to industry practitioners.

MLflow

Developed in 2018 by the creators of Databricks, one of the leading data science platforms today (more on Databricks soon), MLflow is a free open source technology to track machine learning experiments, register models, and deploy models. In other words, MLflow helps manage the entire machine learning life cycle from prototyping to deployment. While MLflow is helpful to individuals who need to track many experiments, it really shines with teams. Teams can collaborate better by reproducing results of their peers and leveraging prior experimentation and the modeling others have already done. Since models are registered at a central repository, MLflow also makes it clear to team members which models are in production and how to access them.

MLflow is unlike TensorBoard and Weights & Biases because it manages the entire machine learning life cycle; in other words, it is more than just experiments-tracking software. But, it does have light experiments-tracking features.

The major downside of MLflow is the lack of visualization capabilities that the likes of TensorBoard, Weights & Biases, Comet, and Neptune offer. In fact, MLflow has a very limited user interface altogether. Moreover, MLflow works best when used with Databricks. As a standalone technology, it lacks many of the features enterprises will need, such as user management.

In Chapter 11, we will revisit MLflow and show where it shines best: model registry and model deployment.

Here are our picks:

Ankur's pick
> The single best pick here is Weights & Biases. The team there truly understands how to develop software to help with machine learning work. The founders of Weights & Biases previously founded a very popular and successful data annotation firm called Figure Eight (formerly known as CrowdFlower), which I have used in the past and has since been acquired by Appen. If you want to make your experimentation process more organized with better process, Weights & Biases is your solution. Weights & Biases also integrates well with nearly all the major data science frameworks and platforms, including Databricks, which we use in Chapter 11.

Ajay's pick

I'm biased here, since I've been using Weights & Biases much more than anything else. But that's because it's the first tool I tried, and I found it perfect for what I do. The way I look at it, Weights & Biases really helps you move from working in code space to idea space. Having all my models and results in one place has really improved my productivity as a deep learning practitioner.

Now, let's move on to automated machine learning, which may help you with your training process.

AutoML

Machine learning has become more mature and increasingly in demand. As a result, startups that specialize in automated machine learning (AutoML) have become a hot topic of conversation in the data science community in recent years. Let's explore the current major players in AutoML and how they could be helpful in building NLP applications.

The standard machine learning pipeline includes the following steps:

1. Import data.
2. Preprocess data (e.g., handle missing values and outliers, check and convert data types, etc.).
3. Perform feature scaling, engineering, and selection.
4. Structure data (e.g., create training, cross-validation, and test sets, etc.).
5. Define evaluation metric and choose which algorithms to test.
6. Set up algorithms, and choose and test models with various hyperparameters.
7. Select model(s) to deploy in production.
8. Refactor code, write tests, and push into production.
9. Monitor and maintain model in production.
10. Collect actual results, and retrain model, as necessary.

AutoML is machine learning that has been automated to some extent, reducing the effort required from human coders. AutoML may include the following:

- Automated data preparation (e.g., imputation of missing values, feature scaling, feature selection, etc.)
- Automated grid search and hyperparameter optimization
- Automated evaluation of multiple algorithms

- Automated ensembling of models (e.g., ensemble selection and stacking)

By automating some portions of the standard machine learning pipeline, AutoML frees up time for us to work on data preprocessing, feature engineering, and model deployment and maintenance.

H2O.ai

Founded in 2012, H2O.ai is an open source machine learning platform that helps programmers build ML applications very quickly. It is very well-funded, having raised $151 million as of early 2021. It supports both classic machine learning (e.g., random forests, gradient boosting, generalized linear models, etc.) and deep learning. At the core of the platform is the ability to run multiple algorithms with multiple hyperparameters to produce a leaderboard of the best models. In other words, it helps find the best model for your problem, performing tasks such as algorithm selection and hyperparameter optimization.

Supporting both Python and R, H2O is robust. It also offers a no-code graphical notebook–based interactive UI for users to run experiments with a few clicks of a button; the UI is known as H2O Flow. H2O's AutoML automatically ensembles individual models to improve overall performance. H2O is built for big data problems, supporting distributed, in-memory machine learning.

It has some support for NLP; H2O is able to convert text strings into features using techniques such as TFIDF, CNNs, and GRUs. These features are then fed into either classic machine learning or deep learning algorithms.

H2O is a useful platform for data scientists to speed up model training and evaluation, but experienced data scientists and ML engineers will prefer to have more control over their models by leveraging deep learning frameworks such as PyTorch or TensorFlow coupled with their choice of experiment-tracking software.

Dataiku

Dataiku is another major data science platform; it was founded in 2013 and has raised $247 million as of early 2021. Dataiku is a collaborative data science software platform, bringing together multiple data players (e.g., data scientists, data analysts, data engineers, etc.) within an organization.

Whereas H2O is strictly a machine learning platform (to quickly train and evaluate multiple ML models), Dataiku is built for more generalized data science work, including data exploration, feature engineering, model building, data analysis, and deployment of insights and models. Like H2O, Dataiku supports both coders and noncoders with a no-code, click-friendly UI.

Dataiku is a great way to quickly move from development to test to preproduction to production very quickly. It manages a lot of the overhead, such as creating data workflows, automating data pipelines, monitoring performance, versioning models, and rolling back to prior versions, as necessary. It also manages other thorny elements you will encounter as you push data pipelines and models into production; this includes items such as governance, security, and monitoring.

DataRobot

Another well-funded player in this space is DataRobot, having raised $751 million as of early 2021, just nine years since its founding in 2012. Like Dataiku, DataRobot is an end-to-end data science platform supporting model building, deployment, and management. It is a great blend of the AutoML features H2O offers and the full end-to-end data science and engineering capabilities of Dataiku.

DataRobot has made some amazing acquisitions to build out what we consider is the single best data science software platform on the market today. Not only does it have AutoML, it also includes MLOps (via its acquisition of ParallelM in 2019). This allows us to deploy, monitor, manage, and govern machine learning models in production. It supports all the modern production infrastructures such as Kubernetes and Spark, either on-premise or on a cloud provider, e.g., Amazon Web Services (AWS), Google Cloud Platform (GCP), and Azure. It supports real-time monitoring and alerts and auditing of actions for models, which you will want to have once you take your ML applications into production.

In other words, DataRobot considerably speeds up the process to prepare our data, train and evaluate our models, and deploy into production. It also offers us ways to visualize the data and the model.

Here are our picks:

Ankur's pick
> My top pick is DataRobot, given its string of acquisitions. It has the most robust capabilities to support the end-to-end data science and machine learning pipeline.

Ajay's pick
> I personally have never used any AutoML, since I primarily train my own models from scratch. No pick from me here!

In the next section, let's explore the options to access compute resources to train our machine learning models.

ML Infrastructure and Compute

The most annoying and expensive part of deep learning is getting access to compute.

If you want to do any serious deep learning today, you're going to need an Nvidia GPU. Nvidia is pretty much the only brand you'll be able to use reliably, since all deep learning frameworks primarily target CUDA, which is proprietary Nvidia technology. Hopefully, in the future, there will be plenty of other competitive options for compute, but that's not the case today.

You can either invest in your own graphics card for a workstation, or connect to a cloud instance that has a GPU set up for you. If you're a beginner, it's probably better to get started with a cheap cloud service, rather than pay for your own GPU upfront. Setting up your workstation also involves a lot more effort than just connecting to a one-click Jupyter Notebook from your browser. However, when you eventually find yourself running many experiments daily and are paying out of your pocket for compute hours, you can save some money by using your own GPUs.

The big three cloud providers—AWS, GCP, and Microsoft Azure—all offer state-of-the-art GPU hardware for training. For the most part, the decision on which service to use comes down to one factor: cost. This varies a lot over time, so for a more up-to-date resource, GitHub user zszazi put together an excellent table (*https://oreil.ly/q8wLz*) that compares most of the cloud service providers that you'll see for the next few years.

In this section, we'll present some of the newer players in the training infrastructure space, describe the unique features they offer for deep learning engineers, and as usual, tell you our picks.

Paperspace

Founded in 2014, Paperspace is a niche machine learning–focused cloud computing company; it provides an ML development platform to individuals and teams that want to develop and deploy machine learning models using GPUs. Paperspace is a good choice for teams focused solely on building GPU-based machine learning applications. Instead of building custom GPU workstations, which are very expensive upfront and require a good bit of hardware setup, data scientists can utilize cloud-based GPUs on demand and pay as they go (typically by the hour).

Compared to the likes of AWS, Azure, and GCP, Paperspace has a more intuitive set of offerings with more transparent pricing. It allows teams to spin up a virtual machine with the right set of GPUs, train machine learning models using any framework (including TensorFlow and PyTorch), version models, share code within teams, scale out the training and inference operations, and make the models available via APIs.

Instead of spending an hour or more setting up the infrastructure on AWS, we can set up the infrastructure to train machine learning models within minutes using Paperspace.

Paperspace's core product is Paperspace Gradient; it offers all the infrastructure we need to develop and deploy machine learning models. With a few clicks, we can set up our cloud environment, load and explore data, develop a model via Jupyter Notebook (we also have the option to leverage a single instance or scale up with distributed training), monitor model performance, and deploy our model as an API endpoint using either GPUs or CPUs with the ability to scale based on request volume. To boot, Gradient also offers continuous integration service with GitHub.

FloydHub

FloydHub is similar to Paperspace, providing data scientists a managed cloud platform to train, test, and deploy machine learning models. Like Paperspace, FloydHub provides cloud infrastructure in a nicely packaged product, letting data scientists code without worrying about managing the infrastructure they need to do their work. This includes DevOps as well (e.g., provisioning the infrastructure, orchestrating the jobs, managing logging, security, etc.). Both FloydHub and Paperspace offer experiment-tracking software, too, allowing us to track, organize, and share our work.

FloydHub's core product is FloydHub Workspace, which is powered by JupyterLab and similar to Paperspace Gradient in terms of capabilities.

Compared to more established players such as AWS, Azure, and GCP, Paperspace and FloydHub are newer and support much smaller communities. As a result, there is less community-sponsored documentation and support compared to the cloud computing giants.

Google Colab

By far the simplest and cheapest (free!) cloud service for training machine learning models is Google Colab ("Colaboratory"), a free cloud service hosted by Google. Google Colab requires zero configuration, offers free access to GPUs, and makes sharing very easy. At its core, Colab notebooks are online cloud-based Jupyter Notebooks that use Google's cloud instances to perform the compute necessary for model training.

The Colab notebooks are all stored in a Google Drive account, and the notebook environment allows users to access data and code from Google Drive, GitHub, and many other sources. Colab comes preinstalled with many major Python libraries used in data science and machine learning, including NumPy, pandas, TensorFlow,

PyTorch, and Scikit-learn. Installing new libraries is also very easy; Colab allows shell commands directly in the notebook environment.

There are some downsides. Colab can run code for up to 24 hours on CPU and for up to 12 hours on GPU. After this duration, the notebook is disconnected from the VM, interrupting any ongoing training. We do have the option to connect to our local runtime and train for an unlimited duration, though.

Kaggle Kernels

Kaggle, the online machine learning competition platform owned by Google, offers its own Jupyter Notebook environment for users to find and publish datasets, build models, and share their work; it is known as Kaggle Kernels. Kaggle Kernels allow users to write and share code to make their work reproducible and to invite collaborators to collaborate on ongoing projects. Kaggle Kernels store code, comments, environment variables, required input files, and outputs; all of this runs on Docker containers.

Docker containers are self-contained packages of code and all necessary dependencies to run applications in an isolated environment, ensuring that the software works uniformly regardless of the machine it is run on.

The Docker container is preloaded with the most common data science libraries and with the project-specific dataset. The Kernel connects to this Docker container over the web, allowing users to quickly perform their data science and machine learning work via a web browser, without requiring any setup on their local machine. There are two Kernel types. You are able to create either a script that runs the entire code from start to finish or a notebook that supports data exploration and insights.

Compared to Google Colab, Kaggle Kernels is slower and offers even shorter duration execution times (9 hours of total executions versus 12 for Google Colab using GPUs). For students, academics, researchers, data science enthusiasts, and data science competitors, Kaggle Kernels is a great way to learn more about machine learning, develop and share models, and engage with the broader data science community, but it is not a viable option to train models in enterprise.

Lambda GPU Cloud

Another newcomer to the GPU cloud space is Lambda Labs. Lambda Labs is best known for its deep learning workstations and hardware (which might be worth considering if you aren't interested in building your own from scratch), but it recently also started offering the Lambda GPU Cloud. This is a player to keep an eye on, but it doesn't yet offer anything as robust and complete of a solution as the other compute providers here.

Here are our picks:

For students and price-sensitive developers, Google Colab is the best place to start because it's free and easy to use; it is available to all Gmail users with a single click of the button.

For moderate, noncompany developers, Paperspace or FloydHub are the best options. They are easy and intuitive to use and do not require any IT overhead to maintain.

For moderate or heavy developers (e.g., professionals), especially in the enterprise, AWS, Azure, and GCP are the best options. These companies offer a wide variety of cloud services that your IT organization will need to support your machine learning work. If your company is early stage, you might qualify for startup discount programs. If your company is well established, you should be able to negotiate discounts for longer-term contracts.

And here are our individual picks:

Ankur's pick
> Unless you work in a large organization that is already deeply wedded to AWS, GCP, or Azure, I recommend leveraging GPUs in the cloud through a UI/UX-friendly platform. That's why Paperspace is my favorite pick today. It is easy to spin up GPUs, train multiple ML models in parallel, and then spin down the GPUs after you're done. You can also use Paperspace to make the models available as APIs; it's more pain-free to use versus the services offered by AWS, GCP, and Azure.

Ajay's pick
> I've tried plenty of cloud services and set up multiple workstations for deep learning, but today, I mostly find myself using Colab and a university-provided compute cluster. Of course, not everyone has access to compute clusters, so in general, Colab is what I recommend. Apart from the obvious advantage of being free, what I love about Colab is how easy it is to get into a Jupyter Notebook. In fact, for me, launching a Colab instance is faster than spinning up a local Jupyter Notebook server!

Edge/On-Device Inference

When it's time to deploy your model in production, there are two ways you can run inference: in the cloud or on-device. For the most part, the advantages/disadvantages are what you'd expect.

Running inference in the cloud will, in most cases, provide a faster experience for the end user, since you can leverage cloud GPUs and run inference any way you want. You also don't have to worry about supporting multiple platforms, devices, and hardware configurations because you can use one unified backend that's accessible via an API.

But what makes offline or on-device inference appealing is that your users won't need an internet connection to use your model, which can be a huge consideration, depending on your application. Also, by offloading the compute onto the users' devices, you can save a lot in cloud service bills, especially since GPU instances are significantly more expensive than traditional web servers.

We will compare on-device inference first, and then we will explore the major cloud service providers.

ONNX

Open Neural Network Exchange (ONNX) is the most significant project to address inference on multiple devices and platforms. Instead of a library, framework, etc., that's limited in scope, ONNX presents a new format for storing machine learning models that can be run on all sorts of inference engines, programming languages, devices, etc. It's an approach that splits inference into a "frontend" and "backend," with ONNX models being the backend. ONNX supports all major deep learning frameworks, and there are many popular client implementations that allow you to run your ONNX models in a browser, mobile device, and more.

Fair warning, though: this is not as straightforward as it seems. The process of exporting your models to the ONNX format and loading them into your application can get quite complicated and may not always work. However, the sad truth is that this is the state of on-device machine learning today. ONNX seems to be the main tool that has widespread support from deep learning frameworks.

Core ML

Core ML is a framework by Apple designed to work with most Apple devices using the Swift programming language. It takes advantage of the CPU, GPU, and the "neural compute engine" that newer iPhones have. Although Core ML is specific to Apple devices, it seems to have a fair amount of support. Hugging Face, one of the top NLP software development companies today, also released a few demos to run state-of-the-art models like GPT-2 and BERT with Core ML and Swift on an iPhone.

Edge Accelerators

In the last few years, a few companies have started creating custom hardware for inference on edge devices. Among these are Intel's Movidius compute stick, Google's Edge TPU, and the Nvidia Jetson family of developer boards.

These devices aren't designed for web or mobile usage. Rather, they're meant to be used with custom IoT devices, smart appliances, and robotics applications. If you're building a product like this, you probably already know what to use. Also, these are generally more relevant for computer vision than NLP, so we won't discuss these in detail.

Given how new these tools are, we do not have a favorite yet.

Next, let's cover the major cloud providers on the market today; this will be one of the most important decisions you will have to make for your software stack.

Cloud Inference and Machine Learning as a Service

Today, the three most dominant cloud instance providers are AWS, GCP, and Microsoft Azure. Choosing the right cloud provider will require you to consult with your entire IT organization, which makes it hard to provide a recommendation here. That being said, let's review the pros and cons of the cloud providers with respect to machine learning.

All of the big three offer machine learning as a service (MLaaS), handling tasks such as data preprocessing, model training, model evaluation, and model deployment, so we'll factor this in as well.

AWS

AWS is by far the largest and most dominant of the cloud providers. It has a third of the entire market share, whereas second-ranked Microsoft has an 18% market share. Google, however, is particularly strong in AI and is growing rapidly as AI applications continue to flourish.

AWS has the largest set of available services and the most comprehensive network of worldwide data centers. It has the most mature, enterprise-ready offering of any of the cloud providers. That being said, AWS has poor transparency around its cost structure and is not the easiest for newcomers to understand. It is also entirely in the public cloud game and does not support hybrid cloud deployments like Microsoft does.

Amazon's MLaaS offering is called Amazon SageMaker. It is a fully managed service and handles end-to-end machine learning work, allowing us to train, fine-tune, deploy, and manage models. SageMaker also now offers many of the same capabilities of the experiment-tracking software we discussed earlier.

Amazon has several speech and text processing APIs for out-of-the-box NLP, too. These include Amazon Lex (chatbot), Amazon Transcribe (speech-to-text), Amazon Polly (text-to-speech), Amazon Comprehend (text analysis, e.g., named entity recognition, language recognition, sentiment analysis, and topic modeling), and Amazon Translate (machine translation).

Microsoft Azure

Microsoft has a major advantage when it comes to enterprise clients; many of its enterprise clients are well-accustomed to using Microsoft products such as Windows and Office 365. Azure is tightly integrated with these other Microsoft products, making it easier for enterprise clients to adopt Azure. Tight product coupling also allows Microsoft to offer discounts to its enterprise customers.

Microsoft's MLaaS offering is called Azure Machine Learning. Compared to Sage-Maker, Microsoft has more beginner-friendly options, offering a graphical drag-and-drop interface.

Microsoft also offers high-level NLP APIs for speech and text analysis.

Google Cloud Platform

Google is the newcomer on the block but has among the best offerings for data and machine learning work. It doesn't feature nearly the same scale and variety of offerings as Amazon or Microsoft, however, so the rest of your IT organization may prefer to use AWS or Azure over GCP.

Google has two MLaaS options: Cloud AutoML and Google Cloud Machine Learning Engine. Google Cloud AutoML is for beginners, allowing users to upload datasets, train models, and deploy them as APIs pretty quickly. Google Cloud ML Engine is for more experienced users, offering more flexibility in exchange for ease of use. It is pretty similar to Amazon SageMaker.

Google, like Amazon and Microsoft, offers high-level NLP APIs, but its main advantage over competitors is the ability for users to train custom models using Google's AutoML platform.

Here are our picks:

Ankur's pick
> My pick is AWS. It is the most widely adopted cloud provider in enterprise, with the largest and most robust set of offerings. That being said, which cloud provider you pick should be based on what the rest of your organization uses.

Ajay's pick
> In my experience, running inference on a server is the simplest way to deploy your model because this allows you to run PyTorch code without having to worry about exporting your model to a special format. With that in mind, my recommendation would be to use whatever cloud provider your application already uses. Other than perhaps pricing, there are no significant differences among the deep learning offerings of AWS, Azure, and GCP. The deciding factor here should be what benefits the other components of your application best.

Next, let's discuss tools to help us automate the process of testing before deploying any changes to our models in production.

Continuous Integration and Delivery

In this chapter, we have discussed all of the ML infrastructure and software we will need to train, deploy, and manage machine learning models in production except for one last item: continuous integration and delivery (CI/CD). CI/CD is a set of practices to help developers like us deliver code changes in production frequently and reliably. You can think of CI/CD as the process that allows us to maintain ML models in production (e.g., replacing current models with newly retrained models) without a prolonged interruption in the service our model provides.

Let's unpack CI/CD. CI is the set of practices that recommends developers implement small changes to the codebase frequently (as opposed to large changes all at once) and version their code by frequently pushing it to version code repositories. However, to support all the small changes developers are pushing to the code base, there needs to be an automated process that integrates and validates all the changes being made, accepting changes that comply with certain standards set by the developers and rejecting changes that fail to pass such tests. This is what CI governs.

It is easier to identify problems with the code changes when the commits are small and frequent (ideally daily) versus very large and infrequent.

CD is the set of practices responsible for automating the delivery of our applications to downstream infrastructure environments. CD, for example, may restart services on the various environments to deploy newer versions of the applications.

Here are our picks:

Ankur's pick
My pick is GitHub Actions. GitHub is the dominant player among code repositories and code versioning, and GitHub Actions integrates well with the existing features GitHub offers. That being said, keep an eye out for GitLab; it is taking some market share away from GitHub.

Ajay's pick
GitHub Actions! Since Actions are already built into GitHub, they are extremely easy to intergrate with your repos. The GitHub marketplace provides ready-to-use actions for publishing to pip, testing, style-checking, and more. GitHub seems to be doing a great job adding new features and functionality to Actions as well, so expect to see more development in this product. Fun fact: there's also a GitHub Action for wandb (*https://oreil.ly/aDeeO*).

Conclusion

In this chapter, we explored many of the major machine learning tools you will encounter during your work in NLP, including deep learning frameworks, visualization and experiment tracking, AutoML, ML infrastructure and compute, edge/on-device inference, cloud inference and machine learning as a service, and CI/CD. We also provided our personal picks, which should help inform your own choices. That being said, be mindful of what others in your organization are adopting/have adopted, too.

Before we dive into model deployment at scale using Databricks in Chapter 11, let's explore simple web app deployment for machine learning using Streamlit. Web apps are one way for nontechnical audiences to access and interact with machine learning applications that you build.

## CHAPTER 10

Visualization

In the previous chapter, we covered some of the most popular machine learning tools on the market today and shed light on the choices you'll have to make for your ML software stack. Hopefully we didn't leave you with a case of analysis paralysis.

But to ensure that you don't get stuck in the "finding the right tool for the job" phase, let's go a step further towards productionization and build a machine learning web app together. A web app is software that can be run from a web browser. This means your users don't have to go through the extra step of installing your app before using it. More often than not, web apps also interact with web servers, which are remote computers that do more complicated things that you cannot expect a client to do, such as managing a database or, in our case, running inference on an NLP model.

Building a web app is useful because most humans do not derive satisfaction from scouring GitHub repos and dealing with CUDA out of memory errors. Creating a graphical user interface may seem like something that is not "real" NLP or deep learning. But having a simple graphical interface that's accessible online is the most common way to have nontechnical users interact with your model. It's also a great way to share your projects online, since most people (including deep learning researchers) would rather just click a link and see a demo than figure out what version of matplotlib to pip install because you forgot to include a *requirements.txt*.

Fully built, production-ready web apps require dedicated engineering resources to develop and deploy (using languages such as JavaScript, Java, and Python and front-end frameworks such as React and Angular). As machine learning practitioners, we would collaborate closely with these engineering teams to stand up a true machine learning web application.

In this chapter, we will use the popular tool Streamlit (*https://www.streamlit.io*) to build a simple web app for data and machine learning. Streamlit allows data scientists and ML engineers to turn their work into web apps without requiring any frontend experience.

It may not be the next Airbnb, but it *will* allow you to take your spaCy named entity recognition model, which was, until now, a bunch of numbers and progress bars, and then deploy it as a web app that people can actually use.

 Streamlit is an easy-to-use open source Python library for us to demonstrate what a machine learning web app looks like and how to develop and deploy it. Keep in mind that this is more of a proto-type web app than anything that we would consider production-ready. Nevertheless, the web app we build together will be illustrative of machine learning web apps and their potential.

Our First Streamlit App

We will build and deploy the app using Google Colab. As always, to follow along, refer to the corresponding notebook in our book's GitHub repo (*https://github.com/nlpbook/nlpbook*).

First, let's connect to our Google Drive, make an *apps* directory in our *Applied-NLP-in-the-Enterprise* directory, and switch to the *apps* directory.

To read the data successfully in the next snippet, you will need to copy the *train_pre-pared.csv* we created in Chapter 3 (also available on our AWS S3 bucket as */data/ag_dataset/prepared/train_prepared.csv*) into the *Applied-NLP-in-the-Enterprise/data/ag_dataset/prepared/* directory on Google Drive:

```
# Connect to Google Drive
from google.colab import drive
drive.mount('/content/drive', force_remount=True)

# Make and switch to Apps directory
%mkdir '/content/drive/My Drive/Applied-NLP-in-the-Enterprise/apps'
%cd '/content/drive/My Drive/Applied-NLP-in-the-Enterprise/apps'
```

Build the Streamlit App

Next, we will create a new Python script in this *apps* directory called *ner_app_agnews.py*. This app will read in the AG News Dataset (the same one we used in Chapter 3) and display widgets to allow the user to explore the data. The app will also perform named entity recognition using both the base spaCy model and the custom spaCy model we trained in Chapter 3 and display the results.

To write the file, we can add a simple command at the start of the script:

```
%%writefile ner_app_agnews.py
```

Next, let's import the libraries we need, set the title of the web app using Streamlit, and read and cache the AG News Dataset:[1]

```
# Load libraries
import spacy
import streamlit as st
import spacy_streamlit
import numpy as np
import pandas as pd
import random

# Set title
st.title(':star: AG News Dataset')

# Define function to read data
@st.cache
def read_data(file):
    read_path = '/content/drive/My Drive/Applied-NLP-in-the-Enterprise'
    data = pd.read_csv(read_path+file)
    return data

# Read data
data = read_data('/data/ag_dataset/prepared/train_prepared.csv')
```

Next, we will define a function to select the category of interest (Business, Sci_Tech, Sports, or World), and we will surface sidebar widgets to allow the user to select whether they'd like to view the full data or a single article, which category they'd like to explore, and which article they'd like to display within that category:

```
# Define function to select category
@st.cache
def select_category(data, category_option):
    return data.loc[data.class_name==category_option]

# Set up sidebar widgets
st.sidebar.header("Parameters")
display_selections = st.sidebar.multiselect(
  "Which data would you like to display?",
  ["Full Data","Single Article"], None)

category_option = st.sidebar.radio(
  'Which category would you like to explore?',
  data.class_name.unique())

article_option = st.sidebar.number_input(
  'Which article would you like to explore?',
  data.loc[data.class_name==category_option].index.min(),
  data.loc[data.class_name==category_option].index.max(),
```

---

1 If you would like more detail, refer to the official Streamlit API Documentation (*https://oreil.ly/blbmj*).

```
                        data.loc[data.class_name
                            ==category_option].index.min())
```

Notice how we set the widgets using very simple Streamlit functions, such as multise
lect, radio, and number_input. Streamlit makes it easy to modify these widgets and
customize them for your own web app.

Let's set up the display behavior for the data based on what the user selects:

```
# Set display behavior for data
if "Full Data" in display_selections:
    st.header("Full Data")
    st.write(select_category(data,category_option
                        .loc[:,["title","description"]],
                        width=1980, height=200)

if "Single Article" in display_selections:
    st.header("Single Article")
    st.subheader("Title")
    st.write(data.loc[article_option,"title"])
    st.subheader("Description")
    st.write(data.loc[article_option,"description"])
```

Finally, let's perform NER now using our two spaCy NER models (the base and the
custom model):

```
# Set text
default_text = data.loc[article_option,"description"]

# Show NER Results
st.header("NER Results")
base, custom = st.beta_columns(2)

# Base spaCy model
with base:
    base_model = spacy_streamlit.load_model("en_core_web_lg")
    doc_base = base_model(default_text)
    ner_labels = ["ORG","PERSON","GPE"]
    show_table = True
    title = "Base SpaCy Model"
    sidebar_title = "Base SpaCy Model"
    spacy_streamlit.visualize_ner(doc_base,
                            labels=ner_labels,
                            show_table=show_table,
                            title=title,
                            sidebar_title=sidebar_title)

# Custom spaCy model
with custom:
    custom_ner_model = spacy_streamlit.load_model(
        '/content/drive/My Drive/Applied-NLP-in-the-Enterprise/
        models/ag_dataset/ner-base-V3/model-best')
    doc_custom = custom_ner_model(default_text)
    ner_labels = ["ORG","PERSON","GPE","TICKER"]
```

```
    show_table = True
    title = "Custom SpaCy Model"
    sidebar_title = "Custom SpaCy Model"
    spacy_streamlit.visualize_ner(doc_custom,
                                  labels=ner_labels,
                                  show_table=show_table,
                                  title=title,
                                  sidebar_title=sidebar_title)
```

Notice how we take the user-selected text and apply each of the NER models to it. We then pass in custom titles to Streamlit and display the results using the Streamlit function visualize_ner.

This will make much more sense when we deploy the web app in the next section.

Deploy the Streamlit App

Now that we've built the Streamlit app for performing NER on the AG News Dataset, let's deploy it. To follow along, refer to the notebook in our book's GitHub repo (*https://github.com/nlpbook/nlpbook*).

To deploy the app, let's import our basic libraries and install spacy and spacy-Streamlit:

```
# Import libraries
'''Main Libraries'''
import numpy as np
import pandas as pd

# Install spacy
!pip install -U spacy[cuda100]
!pip install -U spacy-lookups-data
!pip install cupy-cuda100==7.3.0

# Download pretrained language model (core model)
!python -m spacy download en_core_web_lg

# Install spacy-streamlit
!pip install spacy-streamlit
```

 You will need to restart your runtime after installing spacy-Streamlit.

We also need to install Streamlit (of course!) and ngrok to create a tunnel to our web app from Google Colab:

```
# Install Streamlit
!pip install streamlit

# Install ngrok
!pip install pyngrok
```

Let's also connect to Google Drive:

```
# Connect to Google Drive
from google.colab import drive
drive.mount('/content/drive', force_remount=True)
```

Next, we will modify the Streamlit config file to remove automatic displays to the web app. By default, Streamlit displays data that is written on a standalone line, but we want to control what data gets displayed instead of showing data unnecessarily.

Let's define a function to deploy our Streamlit app. This function kills any existing ngrok tunnels and connects a new ngrok tunnel for our web app. Once the function is defined, let's deploy the app by calling the function and passing to it the path to the Streamlit app we created in the previous section:

```
# Define deploy function
def deploy(path):
  # Kill app
    try:
        ngrok.kill()
        print("All ngrok jobs aborted.")
    except:
        print("No ngrok jobs to kill.")

    # Set app location
    app_location = path

    # Import ngrok
    from pyngrok import ngrok

    # Set up a tunnel to the streamlit port 80
    public_url = ngrok.connect(port='80')
    print(public_url)

!streamlit run $app_location --server.port 80 >/dev/null

# Deploy app
deploy('/content/drive/"My Drive"/Applied-NLP-in-the-Enterprise/\
 apps/ner_app_agnews.py')
```

Once you deploy the app, you should see an output in Google Colab similar to the following ngrok tunnel:

```
No ngrok jobs to kill.
NgrokTunnel: "http://b45166a8492f.ngrok.io" -> "http://localhost:80"
```

Click the first URL (*http://b45166a8492f.ngrok.io*), and you should see the Streamlit web app open up in a separate web browser tab. The app should look similar to Figure 10-1.

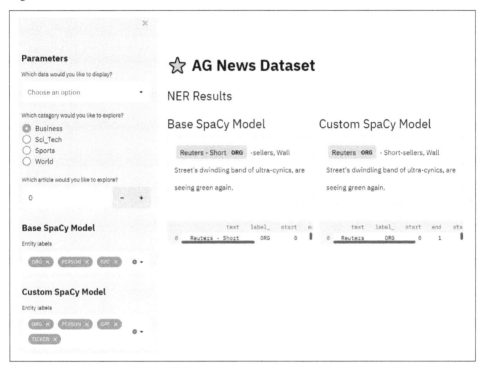

Figure 10-1. AG News Dataset NER app

Perfect. We have built and deployed a Streamlit web app for our NER models on the AG News Dataset.

Explore the Streamlit Web App

Let's explore this app in more detail. It may be helpful for you to review this web app alongside the Python script we created in "Build the Streamlit App" on page 222.

As you see on the righthand side of the web app (the main panel), there is a title that we generated (*star* AG News Dataset) along with the NER results of our two spaCy models (the base and the custom).

On the lefthand side of the web app, there is a sidebar panel with the various widgets we created. The first widget allows you to select whether you wish to view the "Full Data" or a "Single Article." You could select one or both. If you select both, you should see the righthand side of the app load both the full data and a single article (see Figure 10-2).

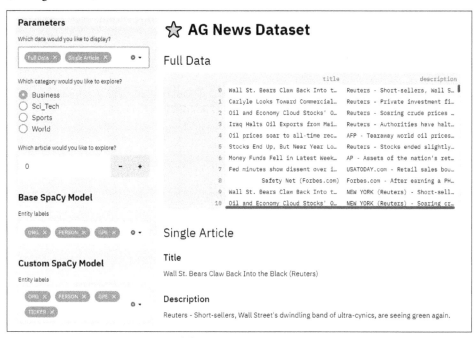

Figure 10-2. AG News Dataset sidebar

You could also select the category to explore and the article number on which to perform NER. For instance, if we select "Sports" and "article 457," the spaCy models will generate the NER outputs of the following sentence:

```
KOHLER, Wisconsin (Reuters)—Tiger Woods failed to make the
most of a red-hot start in the U.S. PGA Championship third round on
Saturday, having to settle for a three-under-par 69.
```

Figure 10-3 shows the results from the web app.

You could also select or deselect the entity labels you'd like to display using the sidebar in the web app.

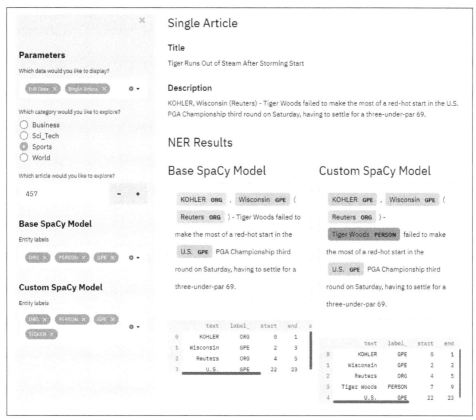

Figure 10-3. Single article

This concludes the exploration of our first Streamlit web app. Next, we will build a Streamlit web app to perform NER on custom, user-input text rather than on the AG News Dataset.

Build and Deploy a Streamlit App for Custom NER

Now, instead of performing NER on the AG News Dataset, let's perform NER on custom text that the user enters. We want to show how easy it is to modify the Streamlit app we built earlier and deploy it using Streamlit. To follow along, refer to the *ch10_build_streamlit_app.ipynb* in our book's GitHub repo (*https://github.com/nlpbook/nlpbook*).

We will use the same process we used before to build a Streamlit app with slightly different code. The most significant difference is the following line:

```
default_text = st.text_area("Enter text to analyze.", heights=500)
```

We also removed the lines that load the AG News Dataset and allow the user to explore it:

```
%%writefile ner_app_custom.py
# Load libraries
import spacy
import streamlit as st
import spacy_streamlit
import numpy as np
import pandas as pd
import random

# Set title
st.title(':star: Custom NER')
st.header("Custom Text")
default_text = st.text_area("Enter text to analyze.",
                            height=250)

# Show NER results
st.header("NER Results")
base, custom = st.beta_columns(2)

# Base spaCy model
with base:
    base_model = spacy_streamlit.load_model("en_core_web_lg")
    doc_base = base_model(default_text)
    ner_labels = ["ORG","PERSON","GPE"]
    show_table = True
    title = "Base SpaCy Model"
    sidebar_title = "Base SpaCy Model"
    spacy_streamlit.visualize_ner(doc_base,
                                  labels=ner_labels,
                                  show_table=show_table,
                                  title=title,
                                  sidebar_title=sidebar_title)

# Custom spaCy model
with custom:
    custom_ner_model = spacy_streamlit.load_model(
    '/content/drive/My Drive/Applied-NLP-in-the-Enterprise/
    models/ag_dataset/ner-base-V3/model-best')
    doc_custom = custom_ner_model(default_text)
    ner_labels = ["ORG","PERSON","GPE","TICKER"]
    show_table = True
    title = "Custom SpaCy Model"
    sidebar_title = "Custom SpaCy Model"
    spacy_streamlit.visualize_ner(doc_custom,
                                  labels=ner_labels,
                                  show_table=show_table,
                                  title=title,
                                  sidebar_title=sidebar_title)
```

Now, let's deploy it using the deploy function in our other Google Colab notebook called *ch10_deploy_streamlit_app.ipynb*. Remember to kill the web app that is already running by clicking the stop button in the Google Colab notebook:

```
# Deploy NER App for Custom Text
deploy('/content/drive/"My Drive"/Applied-NLP-in-the-Enterprise/\
    apps/ner_app_agnews.py')
```

Once you click the ngrok URL, you should see a Streamlit web app screen similar to the one in Figure 10-4.

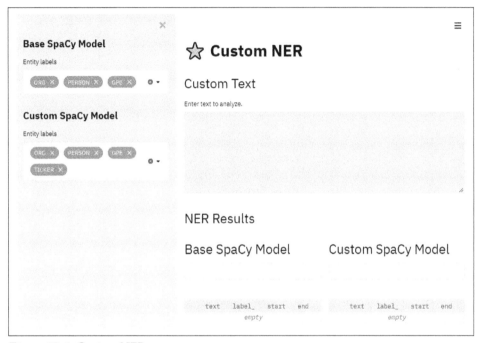

Figure 10-4. Custom NER app

Notice that the app provides a blank text box for the user to enter in the text of their choice. Let's enter in the following text and see the NER results from our two spaCy models:

```
The book you are reading is published by O'Reilly Media and is written by
    Ankur Patel and Ajay Arasanipalai.
```

Go ahead and press Ctrl-Enter, and you should see output similar to that in Figure 10-5.

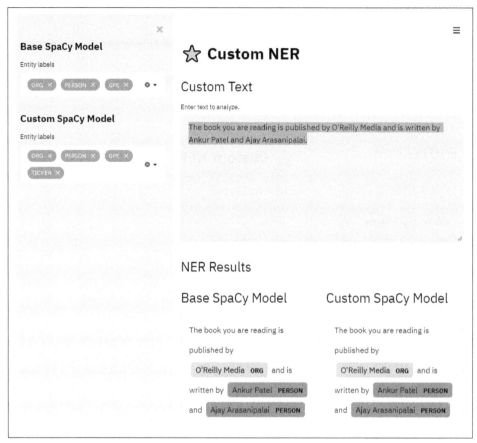

Figure 10-5. Custom NER app output

Now, let's build two more Streamlit apps: one for text classification on the AG News Dataset and one for text classification on custom, user-defined text.

Build and Deploy a Streamlit App for Text Classification on AG News Dataset

Let's go back to our notebook and write the code to build a Streamlit app for text classification on the AG News Dataset.

Here is the code:

```
%%writefile textcat_app_agnews.py
# Load libraries
import spacy
import streamlit as st
import spacy_streamlit
import numpy as np
import pandas as pd
import random

# Set title
st.title(':star: AG News Dataset')

# Define function to read data
@st.cache
def read_data(file):
    read_path = '/content/drive/My Drive/Applied-NLP-in-the-Enterprise'
    data = pd.read_csv(read_path+file)
    return data

# Read data
data = read_data('/data/ag_dataset/prepared/train_prepared.csv')

# Define function to select category
@st.cache
def select_category(data, category_option):
    return data.loc[data.class_name==category_option]

# Set up sidebar widgets
st.sidebar.header("Parameters")
display_selections = st.sidebar.multiselect(
 "Which data would you like to display?",
 ["Full Data","Single Article"], None)

category_option = st.sidebar.radio(
 'Which category would you like to explore?',
 data.class_name.unique())

article_option = st.sidebar.number_input(
 'Which article would you like to explore?',
 data.loc[data.class_name==category_option].index.min(),
 data.loc[data.class_name==category_option].index.max(),
 data.loc[data.class_name==category_option].index.min())

# Set display behavior for data
if "Full Data" in display_selections:
    st.header("Full Data")
    st.write(select_category(data,category_option)
            .loc[:,["title","description"]],
            width=1980, height=200)

if "Single Article" in display_selections:
    st.header("Single Article")
    st.subheader("Title")
```

```
st.write(data.loc[article_option,"title"])
st.subheader("Description")
st.write(data.loc[article_option,"description"])

# Set text
default_text = data.loc[article_option,"description"]

# Custom spaCy model
custom_model = spacy_streamlit.load_model(\
'/content/drive/My Drive/Applied-NLP-in-the-Enterprise/\
models/ag_dataset/textcat-prodigy-V3-base-full/model-best')
doc= custom_model(default_text)
title = "Text Classification"
spacy_streamlit.visualize_textcat(doc, title=title)
prediction = max(doc.cats, key=lambda key: doc.cats[key])
confidence = str(np.round(doc.cats[prediction],2))
st.header("Prediction: " + prediction)
st.subheader("Confidence: " + confidence)
```

Notice that the overall structure is similar to the structure for the first two Streamlit web apps we built. Walk through the code and, if you have questions, do not hesitate to reach out to us over Slack, or via email at *authors@appliednlpbook.com*.

Now, let's deploy the web app using the *ch10_deploy_streamlit_apps.ipynb* notebook:

```
# Deploy text classification app for AG News
deploy('/content/drive/"My Drive"/Applied-NLP-in-the-Enterprise/\
  apps/textcat_app_agnews.py')
```

Once the app is up and running, you should see a screen similar to that in Figure 10-6.

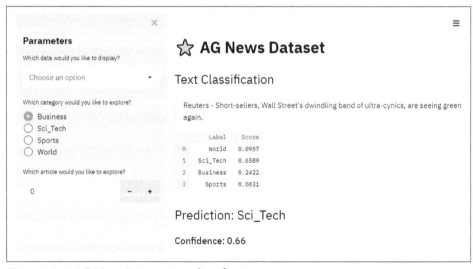

Figure 10-6. AG News Dataset text classification app

Notice that the web app loads our custom spaCy text classification model and applies it to the AG News Dataset article of our choice. For the first article description, the model outputs a prediction of "Sci_Tech" with a confidence score of 0.66, which is wrong. Fortunately, for the second article, the model outputs a prediction of "Business" with a confidence score of 0.78, which is right. You can explore the widgets on the sidebar panel on your own time; by now, you should have a good feel for how easy it is to use Streamlit.

Build and Deploy a Streamlit App for Text Classification on Custom Text

Finally, let's build and deploy a text classification app on custom text. In the *ch10_build_streamlit_app.ipynb* notebook, let's run the following code:

```
%%writefile textcat_app_custom.py
# Load libraries
import spacy
import streamlit as st
import spacy_streamlit
import numpy as np
import pandas as pd
import random

# Set title
st.header(":star: Text Classification")
default_text = st.text_area("Enter text to analyze.")

# Custom SpaCy Model
custom_model = spacy_streamlit.load_model(\
'/content/drive/My Drive/Applied-NLP-in-the-Enterprise/\
models/ag_dataset/textcat-prodigy-V3-base-full/model-best')
doc= custom_model(default_text)
title = "Text"
spacy_streamlit.visualize_textcat(doc, title=title)
prediction = max(doc.cats, key=lambda key: doc.cats[key])
confidence = str(np.round(doc.cats[prediction],2))
st.header("Prediction: " + prediction)
st.subheader("Confidence: " + confidence)
```

This code is considerably simpler since we do not have to load the AG News Dataset.

Let's now deploy this using the deploy function and app file path in the *ch10_deploy_streamlit_app.ipynb* notebook. The web app has a blank text box to start, but let's enter the opening paragraph of Elon Musk's Wikipedia bio (*https://oreil.ly/YAdyw*) and see what prediction our model generates. The results are shown in Figure 10-7.

 **Text Classification**

Enter text to analyze.

> Elon Reeve Musk FRS (/ˈiːlɒn/ EE-lon; born June 28, 1971) is a business magnate, industrial
> designer and engineer.[3] He is the founder, CEO, CTO and chief designer of SpaceX; early
> investor,[b] CEO and product architect of Tesla, Inc.; founder of The Boring Company; co-

Text

Elon Reeve Musk FRS (/ˈiːlɒn/ EE-lon; born June 28, 1971) is a business magnate, industrial
designer and engineer.[3] He is the founder, CEO, CTO and chief designer of SpaceX; early
investor,[b] CEO and product architect of Tesla, Inc.; founder of The Boring Company; cofounder of Neuralink; and co-founder and initial co-chairman of OpenAI. He was elected a
Fellow of the Royal Society (FRS) in 2018.[6] Also that year, he was ranked 25th on the Forbes
list of The World's Most Powerful People,[8] and was ranked joint-first on the Forbes list of the
Most Innovative Leaders of 2019.[9] A centi-billionaire,[10] Musk became the richest person in
the world in January 2021.[11]

	Label	Score
0	World	0.0000
1	Sci_Tech	0.0003
2	Business	0.9997
3	Sports	0.0000

Prediction: Business

Confidence: 1.0

Figure 10-7. Custom text classification app

The model successfully predicts "Business" with nearly 100% confidence.

Congratulations! This concludes our work in Streamlit. You have successfully built
and deployed several Streamlit web apps for our spaCy models.

Conclusion

Visualizations are a powerful, useful, and simple way to present your results to other
humans without bogging them down in technical details and numbers. In this chapter, we introduced a new tool—Streamlit—that allows you to quickly prototype web
apps to show off your model.

What makes Streamlit so useful to machine learning practitioners is that it allows you to build cool dashboards and visualizations using only Python. No HTML, CSS, or design skill required. We demonstrated this by building web apps for:

- NER on the AG News Dataset
- NER on custom text
- Text classification on the AG News Dataset
- Text classification on custom text

All in just one Jupyter Notebook!

In the next chapter, we will explore one of the single best platforms for data science and machine learning work today: Databricks, the so-called unified data analytics platform. Databricks is a platform to develop and deploy machine learning models using any deep learning framework you choose. It leverages cloud infrastructure from either AWS or Azure (your choice) and offers MLflow to manage the entire machine learning life cycle. We will use it to deploy machine learning APIs and machine learning pipelines, adding two more options for us to productionize machine learning in addition to the web deployment that we covered in this chapter.

## CHAPTER 11

Productionization

The difficulty of the move from prototyping to production is where many companies fail and is one of the main reasons many companies derive such a low return on investment on machine learning initiatives they launch. In the previous chapter, we discussed how to productionize machine learning as a web app. However, the primary way for companies to productionize machine learning and truly unlock the value of these models in a production setting is not via a simple web app; it is via APIs and automated pipelines, both of which we will cover in this chapter. We will also discuss the various roles that are involved in deploying, maintaining, and monitoring machine learning models in production, and explore Databricks, one of the current market-leading platforms to perform data science and machine learning work in the enterprise.

Data Scientists, Engineers, and Analysts

Before we dive into how to productionize machine learning models, let's review the different individuals who will be involved during the entire machine learning development and deployment cycle. Understanding the roles of these individuals and their preferences for programming language and programming environment is important because we want to reduce the friction in moving from prototyping models to deploying them in production; in other words, we need to consider ease of collaboration to ensure success in running machine learning in production.

Prototyping, Deployment, and Maintenance

There are three distinct technical stages in the machine learning cycle: prototyping, deployment, and ongoing monitoring and maintenance. In the prototyping stage, data scientists take into consideration the objectives of the business (usually informed by a product manager) and prepare data, perform feature engineering, choose algorithms to test, define cost functions, train and evaluate multiple models, and select the best-performing model as the winner—all of which you are very familiar with.

During this prototyping stage, data engineers may help with some of the extraction, transform, and load (ETL) work required to consolidate the data from multiple sources into one centralized location and make it available to data scientists for machine learning development. Data analysts may perform data exploration and preparation to assist the data scientists and may help evaluate the results of the machine learning models. But, data scientists are largely the primary players during this model development phase, while engineers and analysts perform support roles.

During the model deployment stage, data and machine learning engineers become the primary players, supported by the data scientists who developed the machine learning models during the prototyping stage. The engineers typically refactor the code developed by the data scientists so that the model is performant (i.e., can scale to large datasets) and robust (i.e., can handle errors and edge cases gracefully). The engineers also need to position the model in the company's software architecture so the model does what it needs to in the larger workflow. These data and ML engineers are the crucial players in getting models from prototype to production.

Data scientists support the engineers by pair programming, working alongside each other as the engineers write a more performant, robust version of the data scientist's original code. The data scientist explains how the model works and answers any other questions the engineers may have.

During model deployment, data analysts have a very limited role to play. However, once the model has been deployed, data analysts take on the primary role of interpreting the model's outputs and interfacing with the nontechnical consumers of the model, both internally in the organization and potentially externally with clients.

The data and ML engineers and analysts are also the first line of defense in case the model behaves poorly. Data and ML engineers will monitor the model to ensure it has near-100% uptime, is scaling well to large volumes of data, and is generating successful responses instead of errors. Data analysts also help identify when there are errors in the model's outputs and flag when the model's performance deteriorates, which will happen over time as new data flows through the model that perhaps is not well-represented by the training data used to develop the model.

If the issues with the model are engineering-related, the engineers will resolve the situation themselves. But, if the issues are model-related, the engineers and analysts will engage the data scientists to dig deeper into why the model is performing poorly. One common resolution is model retraining: the data scientists will have to periodically retrain the model on new data that is representative of the data the model is performing inference on in production.

Once the data scientists finish retraining the model, the data and ML engineers will deploy it in production, and the data analysts will interpret the results and confirm that the model is indeed performing better. And, the cycle goes on.

Notebooks and Scripts

A common point of contention is using Jupyter Notebooks for production work. As a consequence of history, notebooks have gotten a bad rep for encouraging poor software engineering practices and nonreproducible code. For the most part, a lot of these concerns have now been mitigated, but it's still important to think about where it might be useful to use notebooks versus scripts.

During the prototyping stage, most data scientists develop models in a notebook-based environment, such as Jupyter Notebook, JupyterLab, IPython, Google Colab, and even a VS Code extension. Notebook-based environments are great for prototyping because you can write short blocks of code and run them immediately using the Shift-Enter keystroke and see an output right below the block of code you edited.

This has a very surprising and profound impact on developer productivity. It allows programmers to iterate quickly and run many experiments very fast, which is the key to success in machine learning. Notebooks, in general, are excellent for fast prototyping and experimentation. They really do bring us close to the "code at the speed of thought" adage.[1]

However, your "thoughts" may not necessarily have unit tests or PEP compliance, and they generally don't need to work with a distributed version control system with frequent force pushes to main...

---

[1] Recently, many people have been comparing Jupyter Notebooks to the idea of literate programming, a paradigm proposed by Donald Knuth, where model code is something to be interpreted first and foremost by humans, not computers. In literate programming, code is interspersed with its own natural language documentation, and parts of it are generated through macros. Don't you think notebooks embody this idea? Knuth was way ahead of his time.

So after the data scientists are finished developing the model in these notebook-based environments, engineers typically refactor the code into scripts, writing functions and organizing them into classes to make it easier to reproduce results, experiment at scale, and debug in production.

Data scientists prefer notebooks because it allows them to experiment and iterate quickly. Engineers prefer scripts because they work with the broader set of tools required for deployment. Once the models are in production, the data and ML engineers still need to monitor the models for performance and robustness, and the data scientists still need to maintain the quality of the model by occasionally retraining it, so the desire to go back and forth between notebooks and scripts still exists.

Data analysts, who typically interface more with business functions and are less involved in developing and deploying machine learning models, will need to engage with the model's outputs and interpret the results. The needs of these data analysts will also need to be accommodated.

Companies that want to do machine learning in production need to be aware of these various roles—data scientists, data and ML engineers, and data analysts—and how to establish a unified platform for work across all three functions. Note that different organizations may refer to these roles by different names. There is no standardized convention, and many times a single person may wear many hats. But at the end of the day, the crucial tasks can be split into building new models, integrating them into a production pipeline, and analyzing/interpreting results to produce valuable insights to the organization.

Databricks: Your Unified Data Analytics Platform

Fortunately there is a platform today that accommodates these varying needs and makes it easier to push machine learning models into production: Databricks. Databricks is the industry leader for collaborative data science and machine learning work for large-scale production use cases today. It accommodates data scientists, data and ML engineers, and data analysts and supports the entire ML life cycle from model development to testing and deployment to monitoring and maintenance.

Let's explore Databricks and use it to deploy one of the machine learning models we developed earlier in the book.

While there are alternatives to Databricks, such as Amazon Sage-Maker and Saturn Cloud (discussed later in the chapter), Databricks is by far the market leader today for several reasons:

- It has been around the longest, which means that many practitioners are already familiar with the technology.

- It currently has the most mature offering for organizations, including the security and compliance features most companies will need.

- It is built for big data and continues to innovate on this front; in fact, the creators of Databricks were the original creators of the most popular big data processing framework today (Spark, which we'll cover in the next section).

We expect the landscape to become more competitive in the coming years, so spend time exploring alternatives to Databricks, too, as you advance in your career.

Support for Big Data

When developing machine learning models, many data scientists do not fully consider how to make them performant on very large datasets or how to handle streaming use cases (e.g., where data is flowing through the model for real-time inference). Data scientists typically work on small to medium-sized datasets that are prepared for model training. But, once in production, these models may need to perform inference quickly on orders of magnitude larger datasets.

To perform machine learning at scale, it is impractical to use a single machine to perform inference. Rather, many machines are required; these machines, when linked together for a task, are often referred to as a cluster of machines.

This is also where big data technologies such as Hadoop and Spark come into play. Hadoop is the original big data technology, starting out as a Yahoo project in 2006. Hadoop allows users to perform data operations in parallel across many machines in a cluster and string them back together as an output; this mechanism to farm out data operations and generate results is known as MapReduce. For example, if a user wanted to add a scalar to every element in a 10-billion row dataset, the user could use a 10-machine cluster to perform the task nearly 10 times faster than if the task had been performed on a single machine.

Spark, the newer big data technology, was developed in 2012 at the AMPLab at UC Berkeley. It is similar to Hadoop in many ways; Spark processes data in parallel across a cluster, just like Hadoop. However, Spark performs these data operations in memory (also known as RAM), whereas Hadoop reads and writes files to its filesystem format (Hadoop Distributed File System, or HDFS), which is on disk.

While Hadoop is still popular, Spark is the clear winner and rising star in big data. Spark can run 100 times faster in-memory and 10 times faster on disk compared to Hadoop. Spark is also much faster on machine learning applications and supports abstractions that are preferred by data scientists (Spark DataFrames, which are similar to Python's pandas and R packages) and by data analysts (Spark SQL, which is similar to SQL tables in relational data stores).[2]

Databricks is built on Spark, and one of Databricks' cofounders, Matei Zaharia, is also the founder of Spark. Although Spark is an open source framework and supported by the Apache Software Foundation, the Databricks version of Spark is a commercially focused and further optimized instance of Spark and yet another reason Databricks is the preferred platform for data and machine learning work.

Support for Multiple Programming Languages

One of the major challenges for data scientists, engineers, and analysts is the disconnect in programming languages. Data scientists typically code in Python (and R, although decreasingly so), data and machine learning engineers prefer Scala or PySpark (both of which leverage Spark), and data analysts prefer SQL.

Databricks makes it easy to transition from one programming language to another (from Python to Scala to SQL) and supports a notebook-based environment (which data scientists typically prefer) as well as scripts, programmatic access, and APIs (which engineers will need to deploy, monitor, and maintain systems in production efficiently).

The beauty of this multilanguage approach is that data scientists, engineers, and analysts can all work on a single platform. Once the models are developed, Databricks makes it easy to deploy these models fast; no need to switch from one platform to another to take a model from prototype to production. Databricks dissolves the organizational and technological silos that data scientists, engineers, and analysts traditionally encounter.

Support for ML Frameworks

Figure 11-1 shows how Databricks describes the challenges and their solutions. The challenges include the need to support multiple programming languages, multiple machine learning frameworks, and multiple DevOps tools as well as the need to reduce friction among teams that are preparing data, building models, and moving the models into production. And, security and compliance are crucial considerations for any mature organization.

---

2 For more on Hadoop versus Spark, check out this excellent piece on Logz.io (*https://oreil.ly/mf1Uy*).

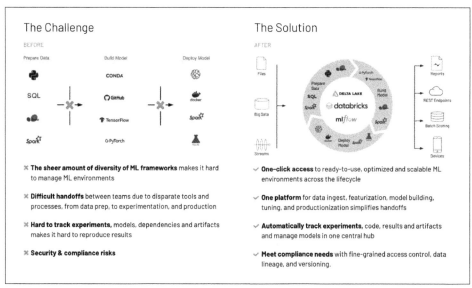

The Challenge — The Solution

Figure 11-1. Databricks platform (courtesy of Databricks (https://oreil.ly/iX7SW))

Databricks' solution to these challenges is a ready-to-use, optimized, and scalable machine learning environment with built-in support for the most common data science programming languages and many of the most popular machine learning frameworks, such as PyTorch, TensorFlow, and Scikit-learn. This environment is available for use with just a few clicks (after some initial setup), allowing data scientists to quickly spin up clusters of machines to perform data science and develop machine learning models and then spin the clusters down once the work is done. These environments are also customizable, allowing data science and ML teams to import libraries and run init scripts, as necessary.

Spark also comes with its own Spark-optimized machine learning library, MLlib, which is available for use on Databricks. MLlib supports the more common machine learning algorithms such as classification, regression, clustering, and collaborative filtering, and allows data scientists to develop more performant machine learning pipelines.

Support for Model Repository, Access Control, Data Lineage, and Versioning

Finally, Databricks provides the ability to track experiments, register and version machine learning models, grant access and permissions based on roles, and track how data flows through the data pipeline. Databricks comes with many of the compliance features larger enterprises will need as they scale their machine learning operations.

To sum up, see Figure 11-2, whiich shows the ML life cycle on Databricks. This figure shows how data from multiple data sources (e.g., flat files, big data, and streaming data) flows into Databricks, which has multiple layers to support the work required (everything from collaborative workspaces, AutoML features, feature engineering stores, experiment tracking, model registry, model deployment options, and security and compliance support). The work done on Databricks powers both analytical use cases such as reports and dashboards as well as operational AI via APIs, batch scoring, and edge device deployment.

Figure 11-2. Machine learning life cycle (courtesy of Databricks (https://oreil.ly/iMuq7).)

Databricks provides a unified platform for data scientists, engineers, and analysts to develop and deploy machine learning models at scale, work in multiple programming languages, access a variety of ML frameworks and libraries with a few clicks, and collaborate on every stage from model prototype to production.

Databricks Setup

With that overview, let us get started with Databricks.

First, let's register for Databricks (*https://oreil.ly/NQmX6*). Once you submit your details to register, you should see a screen similar to the one in Figure 11-3.

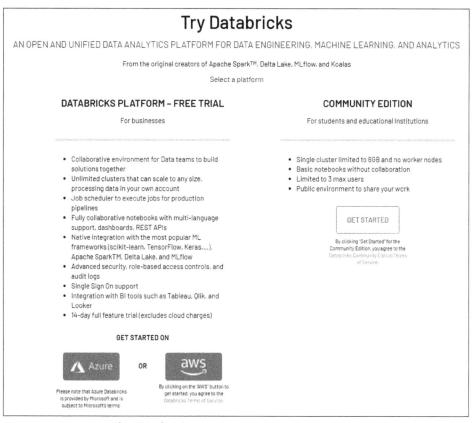

Figure 11-3. Register for Databricks

Databricks offers two versions of its product: the full-fledged Databricks Platform, and the free, lightweight Community Edition. This latter version is a fine one to use to get started with Databricks; it offers a single cluster with 6 GB of RAM.

However, to support machine learning in production, you will need access to the full-fledged Databricks Platform. This is what we will use. Databricks leverages cloud compute from cloud computing giants Azure and AWS; Databricks does not operate its own cloud computing infrastructure but instead runs its software on top of these cloud providers.

To proceed with the Databricks Platform, you will need to choose one of the cloud providers. Both offer comparable prices, so the selection is dependent on your company's choice (or your personal choice, if you are learning how to productionize machine learning on your own). We will proceed with AWS.

You will have to pay for the cloud compute instances you use at Azure or AWS as well as the Databricks Platform. Both Azure/AWS and Databricks charge by the hour, and the cost per hour depends on the size of the cluster you use.

Next, you will receive an email, requiring you to validate your email address and create a new password. Once you are done, you'll see a page similar to the one shown in Figure 11-4.

	STANDARD	PREMIUM	ENTERPRISE
	One platform for your data analytics and ML workloads	Data analytics and ML at scale across your business	Data analytics and ML for your mission critical workloads
JOBS COMPUTE Run data engineering pipelines to build data lakes and manage data at scale. See details.	From **$0.07/** DBU	From **$0.10/** DBU	From **$0.13/** DBU
SQL COMPUTE (PREVIEW) Run SQL queries for BI reporting, analytics, and visualization to get timely insights from data lakes.	–	**$0.15/** DBU	**$0.15/** DBU
ALL-PURPOSE COMPUTE Run interactive data science and machine learning workloads. Also good for data engineering, BI and data analytics.	**$0.40/** DBU	**$0.55/** DBU	**$0.65/** DBU
Compare compute options	Calculate price	Calculate price	Calculate price

Figure 11-4. Databricks plan

Here you will have to select a Databricks plan type. For more details, visit the Databricks on AWS pricing page (*https://oreil.ly/dZML2*). To get started, we will select the Standard Plan. Note the rates you will be charged: $0.40/DBU for all-purpose compute and $0.07/DBU for jobs compute.

The pricing here can become quite complex, but here's a high-level overview. One DBU (Databricks unit) is approximately one hour on a standard cloud compute instance (e.g., a cloud compute EC2 instance on AWS). In other words, if you use Databricks for one hour on a standard cloud compute instance, you will consume one DBU.

All-purpose compute is compute associated with code running on an interactive environment such as a notebook, while jobs compute is compute consumed by an automated data or machine learning pipeline. Typically, most of the coding data scientists will do (e.g., in a notebook-based environment) will be classified as all-purpose compute, while pipelines deployed by data and ML engineers will be classified as jobs compute. All else being equal, it is considerably cheaper to consume cloud compute on Databricks using automated pipelines rather than working in notebooks.

Once you choose Standard Plan and click Select Plan, you will be prompted to enter your billing details. Next, we will set up AWS access for Databricks. You should see a page similar to the one shown in Figure 11-5.

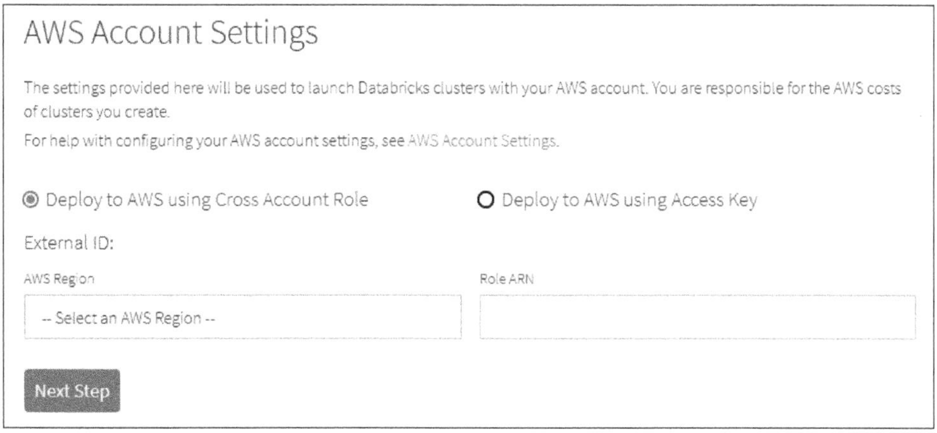

Figure 11-5. AWS account settings

To configure AWS access for Databricks, you will need to have access to an AWS account (or create a new AWS account, if you don't have one).

For those without an AWS account, you can create one using the AWS account creation page (*https://oreil.ly/asqPY*). As a new user, you will have 12 months of free-tier access to basic services such as compute and storage.

Once you have created an AWS account, log in to the account. Now, let's go back to the Databricks page and begin linking Databricks to AWS. For detailed step-by-step instructions on how to perform the configuration, visit the official AWS configuration page on Databricks (*https://oreil.ly/O0lZB*).

After you complete the AWS Account Setup, Databricks will have access to your AWS account. With this access, Databricks will spin up cloud compute clusters (called EC2 instances) on AWS and use the clusters to run code you develop and deploy on Databricks.

Next, you will be prompted to set up the AWS storage for your account-wide Databricks assets such as libraries, logs, registered models, etc. Just like before, follow the official step-by-step instructions (*https://oreil.ly/OW4mD*) to get the storage set up properly.

After you complete the AWS Storage Setup, Databricks will be able to read and write to cloud storage on AWS (called S3 buckets). The storage access you have just set up allows Databricks to read and write account-wide Databricks assets to a single S3 bucket (which you created), but does not grant read and write privileges to all of your S3 buckets on AWS. In other words, if you want Databricks to have access to training data on S3, for example, you will have to configure read and write access to the S3 bucket with training data later on (which we will cover soon).

Great! Now, your deployment should be active, and you should see a link to your active Databricks deployment. This should be similar to the link shown in Figure 11-6. We can now get started with the Databricks Platform.

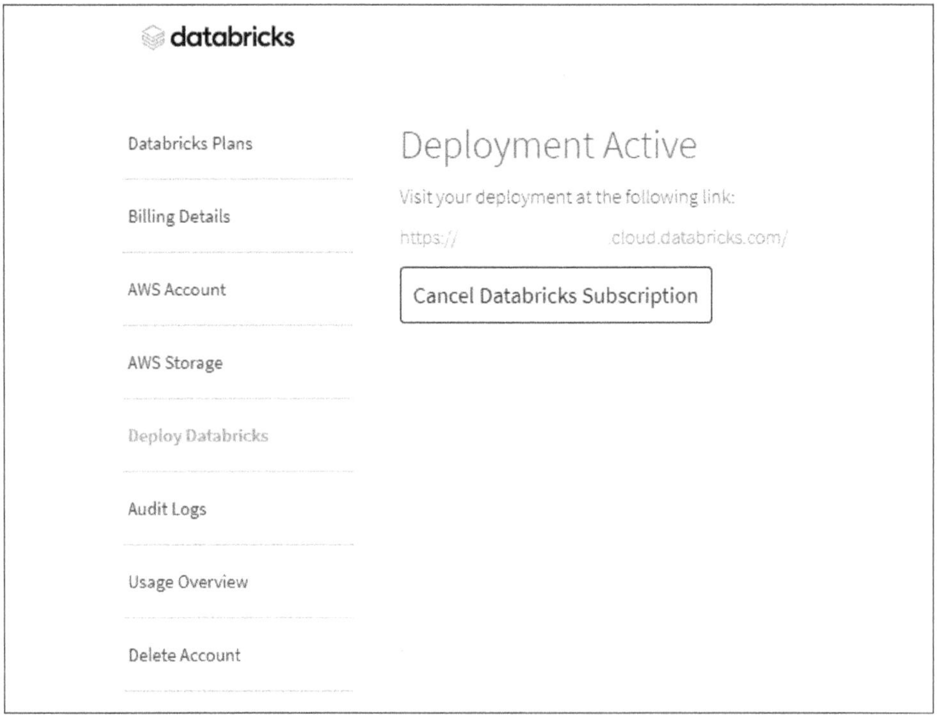

Figure 11-6. Active deployment

Set Up Access to S3 Bucket

Once you log in to your Databricks deployment, you should see a "Welcome to Databricks" home page similar to the one shown in Figure 11-7.

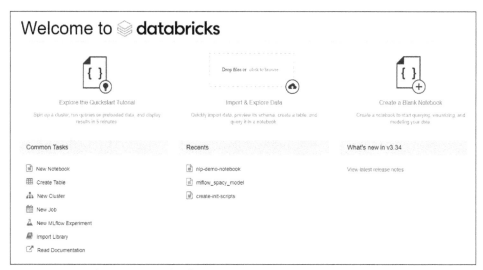

Figure 11-7. Welcome to Databricks

To get started quickly, click Explore the Quickstart Tutorial and try importing and exporting data using the Import & Export Data widgets on the Databricks home page. You can do this on your own, following the step-by-step instructions provided by Databricks. Once you've finished these tutorials, let's proceed.

As we mentioned in the previous section, we granted Databricks access to your AWS account and provided it read and write access to a single S3 bucket. However, Databricks does not have access to any other S3 buckets. Let's grant Databricks access to an S3 bucket that has the training data for the AG News Dataset we introduced in Chapter 3.

Before we proceed, let's set up an S3 bucket on AWS with the training data for the AG News Dataset. First, log into your AWS account (*https://oreil.ly/vsIpx*). Search for S3 in the search bar at the top of the page. Once you navigate to the S3 Management Console, click the orange button that says "Create bucket." Enter in a bucket name (we named ours *nlp-demo*, which you will see us refer to later), select your region, and click the orange "Create bucket" at the bottom of the page. Within the newly created bucket, create a folder called *ag_dataset*, and upload the *train_prepared.csv* under data → ag_dataset → prepared folder on our book's GitHub page to this newly created S3 bucket.

While we are here, let's also create a folder called *models* in our bucket and upload the three models under models → spaCy → packages on this book's GitHub repository (*https://github.com/nlpbook/nlpbook*). We will use these packages (*tar.gz* files) to install our models on a Databricks cluster soon.

Let's return to the instance profiles. AWS identities are known as Identity and Access Management (IAM) roles, and these roles have permission policies that determine what the identities can and cannot do in AWS. To give Databricks access to additional S3 buckets, we have to create a new IAM role with the proper S3 privileges.

To make this easier for us, we will use instance profiles. Instance profiles are containers for IAM roles that we can pass to EC2 instances we spin up. In other words, when we spin up a cluster, the instance profile attached to the cluster will dictate the S3 access permissions the EC2 instance will have based on the IAM role the instance policy contains. To set up an instance profile, use Databricks' step-by-step guide (*https://oreil.ly/nI4Vo*).

Excellent! Now, you will be able to use instance profiles to access data on S3 directly from your Databricks notebooks.

Set Up Libraries

Before we spin up an EC2 cluster to begin coding, let's add libraries to our Databricks workspace. From the Databricks home page, click Workspace on the lefthand bar (see Figure 11-8).

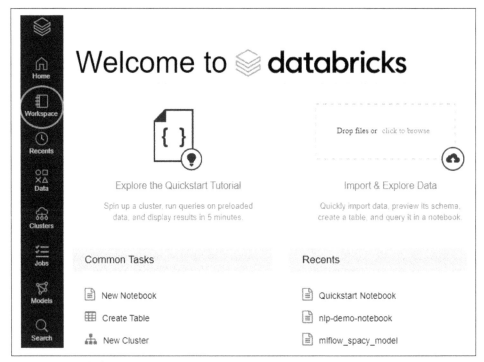

Figure 11-8. Workspace

Next, navigate from Workspace to Users to your email address. Create a new folder called *Workspace Libraries*.

In the *Workspace Libraries* folder, right-click to create a library. You should see a prompt similar to the one in Figure 11-9.

Figure 11-9. Create library

We need to install spaCy for use in our EC2 cluster. To make spaCy available as a library to install, click PyPI on the Create Library widget, enter **spacy** in the Package search bar, and click Create. If this is successful, you should see "spacy" under Workspace Libraries in the Workspace tab.

You can add more libraries using the same widget.

Create Cluster

We have now established S3 access using an instance profile and created libraries for our Workspace. This is where the fun really begins. Let's now spin up a cluster.

From the Databricks home page, click Clusters on the lefthand bar (see Figure 11-10).

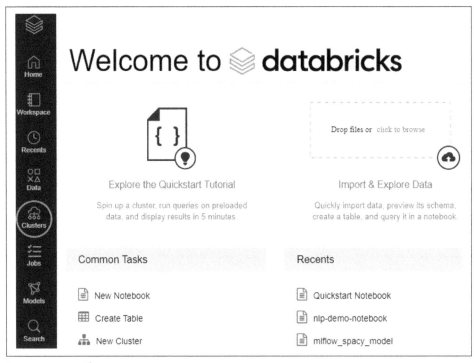

Figure 11-10. Clusters

In the Clusters view, you will see three tabs: All-Purpose Clusters, Job Clusters, and Pools. We want to create a cluster for use in a notebook, so the All-Purpose Clusters (which should be the default choice) is the correct selection.

Click the blue Create Cluster button. There are a lot of potential selections available, but let's cover the basics. First, enter the Cluster Name. Next, select the Cluster Mode. The "Standard" Cluster mode is the default choice if you want to leverage multiple machines in an EC2 cluster (e.g., if you need many machines working simultaneously to process your data operations). For our small AG News training dataset, we can select Single Node but, for larger datasets in production, you will want to select Standard. Let's select Standard to demonstrate how to work with large datasets.

Next, select the Databricks Runtime Version. These are constantly updated, but let's select the latest ML runtime as of January 2021 (7.5 ML). In the Autopilot Options section, enable autoscaling, autoscaling local storage, and set a termination period (if the cluster is inactive for this period of time, it will automatically shut off, saving you from experiencing unnecessary costs for inactive, idle machines).

Next, let's select the Worker and Driver Types. The driver is the primary node, and it sends instructions to the worker nodes to execute commands. We can scale the number of workers if we want to speed up the time for data operations, which is the magic of distributed computing and why Spark is really well-suited for machine learning in large-scale production.

The default number of minimum workers is 2, and the maximum number is 8. Let's select an EC2 instance. Since our needs for the AG News Dataset are modest, let's select the m4.large Worker Type. The Driver Type is set to the same as the worker. Note, that this machine has 8 gigabytes of memory and 2 cores and costs 0.4 DBUs per hour. We will pay 0.4 DBUs × $0.40 per DBU per hour ($0.16 per hour) per EC2 instance.[3] In other words, if we want to have 1 driver and 8 workers, we will need to spin up 9 EC2 instances (with 2 cores per instance), which would cost 9 instances × 0.4 DBUs × $0.40 per DBU per hour ($1.44 per hour), which is pretty reasonable.

Your configuration for the new cluster should look similar to the one shown in Figure 11-11 now.

---

3 Note that these rates change all the time.

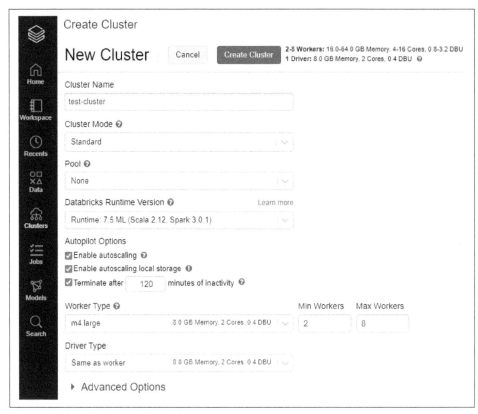

Figure 11-11. Cluster configuration

Next, let's set the instance policy for the cluster under Advanced Options. The default value is None. From the drop-down, select the instance profile you've created. In our case, it is called *databricks-nlp-demo* (see Figure 11-12).

Figure 11-12. Instance profile

Perfect. Now we are ready to start the cluster. Go ahead and click the blue Create Cluster button at the top.

Your cluster will take a few minutes to spin up. While it is starting up, let's go ahead and install the `spacy` library. From the Clusters view, navigate to the Libraries tab, click Install New, select Workspace, navigate to the `spacy` library you saved, and click Install. Your navigation pane should look similar to the one shown in Figure 11-13.

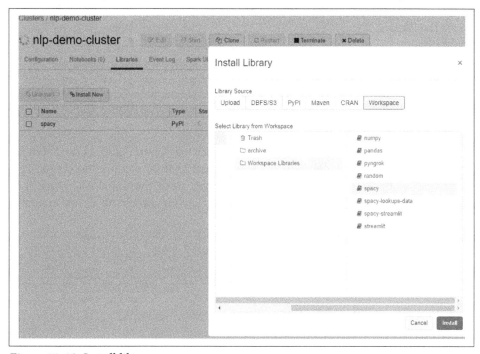

Figure 11-13. Install library

If you did this successfully, you should soon see `spacy` installing on the cluster (see Figure 11-14).

Figure 11-14. Successful installation

Create Notebook

Now, let's create our first Databricks notebook. Our first Databricks notebook will create an init script to pip install the `spacy` libraries we will use, and then we load the script into the Databricks File System (DBFS). We will add this init script to our cluster configuration so that the init script will run every time we spin up a cluster. In other words, the cluster will run the init script (pip installing the `spacy` libraries we need), and we will then be able to load the `spacy` libraries for the NLP work we will do on Databricks.

DBFS is mounted into a Databricks workspace and available on Databricks clusters. Think of it as storage mounted onto the cluster you create. It is storage that persists files even after you terminate a cluster.

On the navigation pane to the left, click Workspace (shown in Figure 11-8). From the Workspace, navigate to your *user* folder and right-click to create a notebook. Let's name the notebook "create-init-scripts." When you open the notebook, attach it to the cluster you just created. If successful, the top of your notebook should resemble Figure 11-15.

Figure 11-15. New notebook

Perfect. Let's write some code now.

First, let's make a directory for our models on DBFS:

```
# Make directory in DBFS
dbutils.fs.mkdirs("dbfs:/databricks/models/spacy")
```

Next, let's copy the model packages we uploaded to S3 to the directory you just created on DBFS:

```
# Copy files from S3 to DBFS
dbutils.fs.cp("s3a://nlp-demo/models/spacy/",
              "dbfs:/databricks/models/spacy/", True)
```

You can confirm that the files successfully copied over to DBFS using the following command:

```
# Confirm files in DBFS
display(dbutils.fs.ls("dbfs:/databricks/models/spacy/"))
```

If successful, you'll see output similar to the one in Figure 11-16.

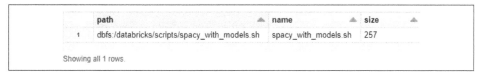

	path	name	size
1	dbfs:/databricks/models/spacy/en_core_web_lg-2.3.1.tar.gz	en_core_web_lg-2.3.1.tar.gz	782740864
2	dbfs:/databricks/models/spacy/en_ner_base_V3-0.0.0.tar.gz	en_ner_base_V3-0.0.0.tar.gz	782715804
3	dbfs:/databricks/models/spacy/en_textcat_prodigy_V3_base_full-0.0.0.tar.gz	en_textcat_prodigy_V3_base_full-0.0.0.tar.gz	783834261

Showing all 3 rows.

Figure 11-16. spaCy models on DBFS

Let's create a directory for our init script on DBFS, too:

```
# Make directory in DBFS
dbutils.fs.mkdirs("dbfs:/databricks/scripts/")
```

Finally, let's create an init script that pip installs the spaCy packages we just uploaded:

```
# Put script in DBFS
dbutils.fs.put("dbfs:/databricks/scripts/spacy_with_models.sh", \
"""pip install /dbfs/databricks/models/spacy/en_core_web_lg-2.3.1.tar.gz \
pip install /dbfs/databricks/models/spacy/en_ner_base_V3-0.0.0.tar.gz \
pip install /dbfs/databricks/models/spacy/\
en_textcat_prodigy_V3_base_full-0.0.0.tar.gz""", True)
```

Let's confirm that this init script is now on DBFS:

```
# Confirm file in DBFS
display(dbutils.fs.ls("dbfs:/databricks/scripts/spacy_with_models.sh"))
```

If successful, you'll see output similar to the one in Figure 11-17.

	path	name	size
1	dbfs:/databricks/scripts/spacy_with_models.sh	spacy_with_models.sh	257

Showing all 1 rows.

Figure 11-17. Init script

Excellent! We have now uploaded the spaCy model packages and an init script to install these packages to DBFS.

Enable Init Script and Restart Cluster

Now that the spaCy models and init script are ready, let's go back to the Clusters tab. Navigate to the cluster you created. Under Advanced Options, navigate to Init Scripts and copy the path to the init script you uploaded in the previous section. Your init script path should be similar to the one in Figure 11-18. Click Add to add the init script to the cluster configuration.

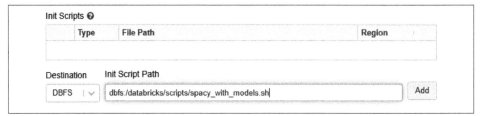

Figure 11-18. Adding init script

Let's now restart the cluster. When the cluster restarts, it will run the init script we just configured. This init script will pip install the three spaCy model packages we uploaded in the previous section (recall that we copied these packages from S3 to DBFS, which will persist the files even after you terminate your cluster). The cluster will also install the spacy library we configured earlier.

Run Speed Test: Inference on NER Using spaCy

Once the cluster is up and running, we are ready to perform an inference speed test using our spaCy NER model on the AG News Dataset. We will compare how fast the spaCy NER model runs on Databricks versus the same model on Google Colab. We should find the time to perform inference to be considerably shorter on Databricks compared to Google Colab, highlighting the power of distributed computing and showcasing how to develop machine learning pipelines in production.

Once the cluster is ready to go, let's create a new notebook using the Workspace → Create Notebook flow we went through earlier. We will name this notebook "nlp-demo-notebook."

Let's load the libraries that we will need for our work:

```
# Load libraries
# Python
import spacy
import numpy as np
import pandas as pd

# PySpark
from pyspark.sql.functions import udf
from pyspark.sql.types import *
```

Load data into a PySpark DataFrame. You will need to modify the S3 path depending on your directory structure and directory names on S3:

```
# Load data
inputPath = "s3a://nlp-demo/ag_dataset/prepared/train_prepared.csv" \
 # path to your S3 bucket
df = spark.read.format('csv').options(header='true', inferSchema='true', \
 quote="\"", escape= "\"").load(inputPath)
```

Although not necessary, we can cache this data in memory using the following command:

```
# Cache
df.cache()
```

To confirm that the data loaded properly, we can print the shape of the data:

```
# View shape of data
print((df.count(), len(df.columns)))
```

Now, we are ready to perform inference using our spaCy model. We will perform inference using the en_core_web_lg spaCy model, which we already pip installed using the init script in the previous section.

Before we define the function to apply the spaCy model to our PySpark DataFrame, let's define the output schema for the model. For each of the 120,000 article descriptions in the AG News Dataset, we want to tag each entity in the text with the appropriate entity label. We also want to extract the relevant text and the starting and ending characters for each entity. In other words, for each of the 120,000 descriptions, we will generate an array of text, starting character, ending characters, and an entity label.

Here's the code to define the schema:

```
# Define schema
schema = ArrayType(StructType([
    StructField("text", StringType(), False),
    StructField("start_char", IntegerType(), False),
    StructField("end_char", IntegerType(), False),
    StructField("label", StringType(), False)
]))
```

Let's now define the function to generate the entities per this schema using the spaCy model:

```
# Define function to get entities
def get_entities(text):
    global nlp
    try:
        doc = nlp(str(text))
    except:
        nlp = spacy.load('en_core_web_lg')
        doc = nlp(str(text))
    return [[e.text, e.start_char, e.end_char, e.label_] for e in doc.ents]

get_entities_udf = udf(get_entities, schema)
```

The get_entities function should be fairly straightforward and similar to what we did in Chapter 3. The only difference is that we have to create a user-defined version of this function (UDF) to apply it to the PySpark DataFrame. We also need to pass our desired output schema to the UDF.

Let's create a new PySpark DataFrame called documents_df that takes the original data and applies the spaCy model to generate a new column called "entities":

```
# Get entities
documents_df = df.withColumn('entities', get_entities_udf('description'))
```

Spark has lazy execution, so this function won't execute until we run an action that requires performing this inference.

To force this inference, let's write the documents_df PySpark DataFrame as a Parquet file. This will determine how long it takes Spark to perform inference on our 120,000-row dataset:

```
# Write parquet
documents_df.write.parquet(\
  "s3a://nlp-demo/ag_dataset/prepared/write_test.parquet", \
  mode="overwrite")
```

Depending on how large your multi-node cluster is and what node type you selected, this should take between 5 and 15 minutes to run. It took us less than 7 minutes to run on a modest cluster of 8 workers and 1 driver using an m4.large instance/node type.

Let's now run the same inference in Google Colab and test how long it takes.

First, let's load the necessary libraries, connect to Google Drive, and install spacy:

```
# Import libraries
'''Main Libraries'''
import numpy as np
import pandas as pd

# Connect to Google Drive
from google.colab import drive
drive.mount('/content/drive', force_remount=True)
write_path = '/content/drive/My Drive/Applied-NLP-in-the-Enterprise'

# Install spaCy
!pip install -U spacy
!python -m spacy download en_core_web_lg
```

Now, let's run a simple code snippet to time how long it takes to run inference using the same spaCy model on the same 120,000-row AG News training dataset:

```
# Load libraries
import spacy
import numpy as np
import pandas as pd
import time

# Start timer
start_time = time.time()
```

```
# Define function to read data
def read_data(file):
    read_path = '/content/drive/My Drive/Applied-NLP-in-the-Enterprise'
    data = pd.read_csv(read_path+file)
    return data

# Read data
data = read_data('/data/ag_dataset/prepared/train_prepared.csv')

# Load model
nlp = spacy.load("en_core_web_lg")

# Load time
load_time = time.time()
print("Time to load data and model: ", np.round(load_time-start_time,2))

# Apply NLP model
data["entities"] = data["description"].apply(lambda x: \
 [(e.text, e.start_char, e.end_char, e.label_) for e in nlp(x).ents])

# End timer
end_time = time.time()
print("Time to perform NER: ", np.round(end_time-load_time,2))
print("Total time: ", np.round(time.time()-start_time,2))
```

Great. This will take a while, but the code should finish in 20 to 30 minutes.

As you can see for yourself, the same model took considerably less time on Databricks than it did on Google Colab. Speed, however, is only one of the considerations for deploying machine learning models in production. We also need to have the means to trigger machine learning models automatically based on events or a schedule; we cannot rely on running our code snippets in a notebook like we would do during the model prototyping phase.

Machine Learning Jobs

Now that we've finished showcasing the speed of Databricks in running machine learning models, let's build a machine learning pipeline on Databricks. We will show how to trigger the machine learning pipeline based on two mechanisms: (1) a schedule we set and (2) events.

One of the beautiful things about Databricks is that we can select a notebook to run as part of a machine learning pipeline. Although it is best practice to create a script to run your machine learning model in production (with CI/CD, etc.), we can get started with a simple machine learning pipeline for production with just notebooks.

Production Pipeline Notebook

Let's first create a notebook to run as part of our machine learning pipeline. This will be very similar to the notebook we created earlier. Click "Workspace," on the lefthand tab in Databricks, navigate to the notebooks directory under your name, and create a new notebook called "nlp-demo-pipeline."

In this notebook, let's enter some basic building blocks for the application of our spaCy model to the AG News Dataset. Let's load libraries first:

```
# Load libraries
# Python
import spacy
import numpy as np
import pandas as pd

# PySpark
from pyspark.sql.functions import udf
from pyspark.sql.types import StringType, ArrayType
from pyspark.sql.types import *
```

Next, let's load the data. Note that the `inputPath` is a parameter that we will define later when we configure our machine learning pipeline job:

```
# Load data
inputPath = getArgument("inputPath", "default")
df = spark.read.format('csv').options(header='true', inferSchema='true', \
  quote="\"", escape= "\"").load(inputPath)
```

Here's our schema as before:

```
# Define schema
schema = ArrayType(StructType([
    StructField("text", StringType(), False),
    StructField("start_char", IntegerType(), False),
    StructField("end_char", IntegerType(), False),
    StructField("label", StringType(), False)
]))
```

Here's our function to perform inference and retrieve named entities:

```
# Define function to get entities
def get_entities(text):
    global nlp
    try:
        doc = nlp(text)
    except:
        nlp = spacy.load('en_ner_base_V3')
        doc = nlp(text)
    return [[e.text, e.start_char, e.end_char, e.label_] for e in doc.ents]

get_entities_udf = udf(lambda x: get_entities(x), schema)
```

Next, we apply the function on the "description" column of the AG News Dataset:

```
# Get Entities
documents_df = df.withColumn('entities', get_entities_udf('description'))
```

Finally, we will write the PySpark DataFrame as a Parquet file. Note that the output path is also a parameter (similar to the input path), which we will define in the next section:

```
# Write Parquet
outPath = getArgument("outputPath", "default")
documents_df.write.format("parquet").mode("overwrite").save(outPath)
```

We are now ready to create a scheduled job.

Scheduled Machine Learning Jobs

From the Databricks home page, click Jobs (see Figure 11-19). From here, click the Create Job button. Let's now set up the job details. Enter "NLP Demo" for the job name. Select the notebook we created before (*nlp-demo-pipeline*) to apply the spaCy model to the AG News Dataset and perform inference.

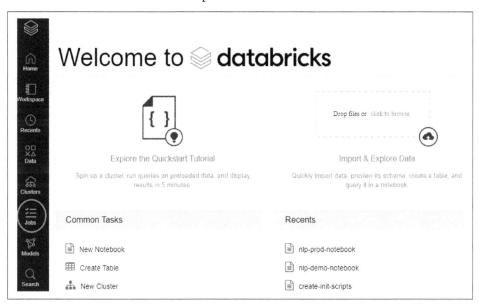

Figure 11-19. Jobs

Under Parameters, click Edit. Let's now enter the inputPath and outputPath. The paths should be locations on your S3 bucket where the input data resides (*train_prepared.csv*) and where you would like the output file (the Parquet file) to be written, similar to what is shown in Figure 11-20.

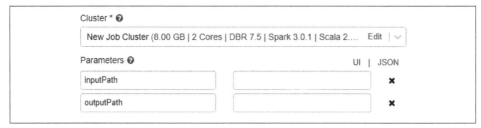

Figure 11-20. Set parameters

Under Dependent Libraries, click Add, navigate to the spacy library we added to your Workspace, and click OK.

For Cluster, click Edit. Here you can define a new cluster configuration for jobs. You could opt for an existing all-purpose cluster (such as the one we configured earlier), but it is better to create a new job cluster because, as we discussed earlier, job compute is considerably cheaper than all-purpose compute on Databricks, $0.07 per DBU for job compute versus $0.40 for all-purpose compute.

Under Cluster Mode, select either Standard or Single Node; Standard is more expensive but will be faster. Select 7.5 ML or a more up-to-date ML runtime. Enable autoscaling and autoscaling local storage. Let's select the same worker and driver types as before (m4.large).

Under Advanced Options, we need to select our instance profile under Instance Profile. We also need to add the init script path under the Init Scripts tab. We did all of this before for our first cluster configuration, but we have to repeat these steps for our new cluster configuration.

Once you are ready, click the blue Confirm button at the top.

Finally, click Edit next to schedule the frequency at which you would like the notebook to run.

Great job! You've now scheduled an automated machine learning pipeline.

If you would rather run the job now, you can click Run Now under Active Runs. Go ahead and test this out for yourself.

Your runs will automatically generate logs, which you can view at the bottom of the page (see Figure 11-21).

Completed in past 60 days						

Latest successful run (refreshes automatically)

‹ Previous 20   Next 20 ›

Run	Run ID	Start Time	Launched	Duration	Spark	Status	
Run 14	14	2020-12-29 18:55:52 EST	Manually	8m 22s	Spark UI / Logs / Metrics	Succeeded	✗
Run 13	13	2020-12-29 14:01:51 EST	Manually	6m 49s	Spark UI / Logs / Metrics	Succeeded	✗
Run 12	12	2020-12-29 13:50:25 EST	Manually	10s	Spark UI / Logs / Metrics	Cancelled ⓘ	✗
Run 11	11	2020-12-29 11:31:58 EST	Manually	10s	Spark UI / Logs / Metrics	Cancelled ⓘ	✗
Run 10	10	2020-12-29 11:28:14 EST	Manually	10s	Spark UI / Logs / Metrics	Cancelled ⓘ	✗
Run 9	9	2020-12-29 11:09:46 EST	Manually	19s	Spark UI / Logs / Metrics	Cancelled ⓘ	✗
Run 8	8	2020-12-29 10:00:07 EST	Manually	9m 35s	Spark UI / Logs / Metrics	Succeeded	✗
Run 7	7	2020-12-29 08:42:29 EST	Manually	2m 37s	Spark UI / Logs / Metrics	Succeeded	✗
Run 6	6	2020-12-28 23:00:15 EST	Manually	9m 23s	Spark UI / Logs / Metrics	Succeeded	✗
Run 5	5	2020-12-28 21:43:31 EST	Manually	2m 3s	Spark UI / Logs / Metrics	Failed	✗
Run 4	4	2020-12-28 21:36:30 EST	Manually	2m 11s	Spark UI / Logs / Metrics	Failed	✗
Run 3	3	2020-12-28 21:26:30 EST	Manually	8m 53s	Spark UI / Logs / Metrics	Failed	✗
Run 2	2	2020-12-28 20:51:14 EST	Manually	16m 6s	Spark UI / Logs / Metrics	Failed	✗
Run 1	1	2020-12-28 20:50:46 EST	Manually	25s	Spark UI / Logs / Metrics	Cancelled ⓘ	✗

Figure 11-21. Completed runs

Event-Driven Machine Learning Pipeline

While scheduled machine learning jobs are very helpful for recurring machine learning tasks in production, often you will want to have the machine learning jobs trigger only on events such as new writes to an S3 bucket. Event-driven pipelines are better to use when you want your machine learning model to run and refresh the outputs as soon as new data is available for use; otherwise, if you choose a scheduled job, the machine learning model will not run on new data immediately and will rely on a schedule instead. There are many instances where you would much rather have an event-based pipeline than a scheduled process; for example, if you had a news recommendation app, you would want the app to refresh news recommendations as soon as news updates were available rather than wait for the scheduled job to run.

Instead of a scheduled job, let's set up an event-driven machine learning pipeline that is triggered based on new data hitting an S3 bucket on AWS. To set this up, we will use an AWS Lambda Function (*https://aws.amazon.com/lambda*), which will trigger our machine learning job on Databricks whenever new writes occur to the S3 bucket of our choice.

AWS Lambdas are great because they trigger compute resources only when we need it, and once the work is done, the compute resources are released.

Let's set up the Lambda function. Navigate to the Lambda Service on your AWS account (*https://oreil.ly/V2iN8*) and click the orange Create function button. We will author a function from scratch so make sure the Author from scratch tab is selected.

Enter a name for your function. We will use Node.js to write the function. Hit the orange Create function button.

In the body of the Function code section, enter in the following snippet. You will need to modify the script in three places. First, enter in the Job ID from the Jobs tab in Databricks. This should be the Job ID for the job we created together in the previous section (see Figure 11-22). Then enter your Databricks URL under Host.

Figure 11-22. Job ID

Third, you will need to secure a personal access token in Databricks (*https://oreil.ly/ drg2u*) and pass this token to AWS in order to grant AWS access to run the Databricks job. Enter your personal access token next to Bearer in the following script:

```
const https = require("https");

exports.handler = (event, context, callback) => {
  var data = JSON.stringify({
    "job_id": XXX
  });

  var options = {
    host: "XXX-XXXXXXX-XXX.cloud.databricks.com",
    port: 443,
    path: "/api/2.0/jobs/run-now",
    method: "POST",
    // authentication headers
    headers: {
      "Authorization": "Bearer XXXXXXXXXXXXXXXXXXXXXXXXXXXXXXXX",
      "Content-Type": "application/json",
      "Content-Length": Buffer.byteLength(data)
    }
  };

  var request = https.request(options, function(res){
    var body = "";

    res.on("data", function(data) {
      body += data;
    });

    res.on("end", function() {
      console.log(body);
    });

    res.on("error", function(e) {
```

```
      console.log("Got error: " + e.message);
    });

  });

  request.write(data);
  request.end();
};
```

Once you are done modifying the script, let's add a trigger. Under Designer, in the Lambda Function page, click Add trigger, and then under Trigger configuration, select S3. Under Bucket, enter the name of the bucket that you would like the Lambda function to monitor.

We will trigger the Lambda function on all object create events, so you can leave the Event type as is.

Under Prefix, enter the prefix of the path in the bucket where you would like to drop the *train_prepared.csv* file to kick off the Lambda function. We used ag_dataset/ input/ as a prefix. Enter **.csv** under Suffix, since the file will end in *.csv*. You don't have to enter a suffix, but doing so will prevent your Lambda function from triggering erroneously. Finally, click Add at the bottom of the page.

Great, we are almost ready to test the Lambda function.

First, let's go back to Databricks and modify the inputPath parameter under Parameters for our Job. You can navigate to this by clicking Jobs on the lefthand pane on Databricks, selecting the job we created earlier, and clicking Edit next to Parameters. Make sure the outputPath parameter is set to where you would like the output Parquet to be written.

Now, we are ready to go. To test the Lambda function, upload *train_prepared.csv* to the S3 bucket and path you chose for the Lambda function trigger. In our case, this is *<bucket-name>/ag_dataset/input/*.

If everything worked successfully, you should see a newly created run under Active Runs under the Job we created in Databricks (see Figure 11-23). This will take several minutes to run, but, once the run completes, you should see the output parquet file in the output path you set under Parameters for the Job.

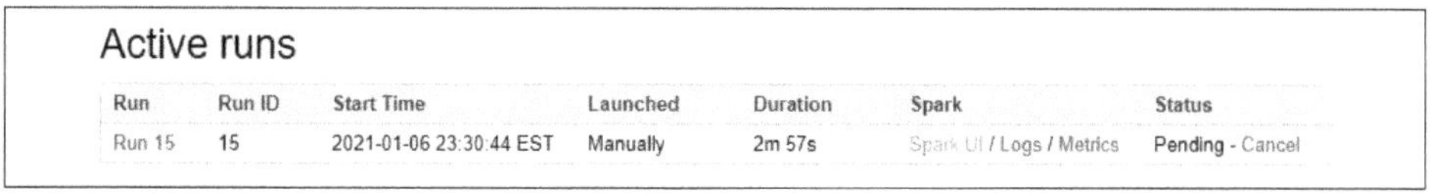

Active runs						
Run	Run ID	Start Time	Launched	Duration	Spark	Status
Run 15	15	2021-01-06 23:30:44 EST	Manually	2m 57s	Spark UI / Logs / Metrics	Pending - Cancel

Figure 11-23. Active runs

Also note that the cluster that gets spun up for this job is a Job Cluster. You can check this by navigating to Clusters → Job Clusters on Databricks (see Figure 11-24).

	Name ▽	State ▽	Nodes ▽	Runtime ▽	Driver ▽
☆ ○	job-3-run-15	Pending ❷	0	7.5 (includes Apache Spark 3.0.1, Scala 2.12)	m5a.large

Figure 11-24. Job clusters

Congratulations! You've built both a schedule-based and an event-based machine learning pipeline, and this pipeline can scale to very large datasets in production using the appropriate cluster configurations on Databricks and AWS.

MLflow

Now that we have showcased Spark's speed in handling ML operations and deployed scheduled and batch-based ML pipelines, let's serve our model as a REST API using the open source machine learning platform known as MLflow. The creators of Databricks also created MLflow (in 2018), which is available for use both as a free open source technology and packaged into the commercial offering at Databricks.[4]

MLflow helps manage the entire machine learning life cycle, including experiment tracking, model registry, and deployment. While MLflow is good for individuals, too, teams are the primary beneficiaries of the capabilities MLflow brings to machine learning. Teams can collaborate better by reproducing results of their peers and leveraging prior experimentation and modeling others have already done. Since models are registered at a central repository, MLflow also makes it clear to the members of the team which models are in production and how to access them.

Before we deploy our model and serve it as a REST API, let's log and register our model with MLflow.

Log and Register Model

Instead of our spaCy named entity recognition model, we will log and register the spaCy text classification model we trained on the AG News Dataset in Chapter 3. Recall that this model takes in article descriptions and generates a classification prediction for four classes: Business, Sci_Tech, Sports, and Business. If you need a refresher, review the relevant sections in Chapter 3.

---

4 For more, read the introductory blog post on MLflow (*https://oreil.ly/JQ5d7*).

Let's get started. From the Databricks home page, create a new notebook under Workspace called `mlflow_spacy_model`. Next, go ahead and open the `mlflow_spacy_model` notebook.

 Make sure you have a cluster up and running; if not, go ahead and start the cluster we created earlier under the list of available Clusters and connect your notebook to the cluster. Make sure the cluster runs with the init script we created earlier.

Let's load the necessary libraries for MLflow and our spaCy model:

```
# Load libraries
# spaCY
import spacy

# MLflow
import mlflow
import mlflow.spacy

# Load model
nlp = spacy.load("en_textcat_prodigy_V3_base_full")
```

We can review the metadata for the model to confirm the text classification details:

```
# Print metadata
nlp.meta
```

The description of this model reads: "Text classification model using AG News Dataset training labels." The model has a `textcat_score` of 91.774875419.

Let's now use MLflow to log the model.[5] To start the MLflow run, we use the prompt `mlflow.start_run` and pass a run_name. Now, we can log parameters for the run, such as tags for the run (these are key-value pairs such as `model_flavor: spacy`):

```
# MLflow tracking
with mlflow.start_run(run_name='SpaCy-TextCat-Prodigy-V3-Base-Full'):
    mlflow.set_tag('model_flavor', 'spacy')
    mlflow.spacy.log_model(spacy_model=nlp, artifact_path='model')
    mlflow.log_metric('textcat_score', 91.774875419)
    my_run_id = mlflow.active_run().info.run_id
```

To log our model, we can use the MLflow command for logging spaCy models; this command is called `mlflow.spacy.log_model`.[6] We pass to this command our spaCy model ("nlp") and the artifact path ("model"). We can also log the accuracy metric

---

5 Visit the official MLflow documentation (*https://oreil.ly/4fHIT*) if you'd like more detail than what is provided here.

6 For more on this command, visit the MLflow documentation for spaCy models (*https://oreil.ly/LJ8uw*).

(textcat_score of 91.774875419). Finally, let's capture the `run_id` of our active MLflow run.

Once the code finishes running, click the Experiment tab in the upper righthand corner of the page. You should see the Experiment tab open up, and it should display your run and details similar to what is shown in Figure 11-25.

Figure 11-25. Experiment

Next, click the expand window icon next to the latest run (the icon highlighted by the red circle in Figure 11-25). This will open a separate window with all of your run details, including your notes, parameters, metrics, and tags. You should see the metric you recorded earlier (textcat_score: 91.77 under Metrics) as well as your tag (model_flavor: spacy under Tags).

Navigate to the bottom of the page and find the Artifacts section. Select "model." You should see the details of the MLflow model appear in the righthand section of the widget, similar to Figure 11-26.

Figure 11-26. Artifacts

Now, click the blue Register Model button in this widget. Yes, it's that simple. We have finished loading our model, logging it using MLflow, and registering it to the Models Repository. Before we proceed, note that you can load the model as a Spark UDF or as a PyFuncModel using the instructions shown in the widget (see Figure 11-26). In other words, this model is available for use in your Databricks notebooks, if you desire.

MLflow Model Serving

Instead of using the model as a Spark UDF, let's deploy the model and serve it via REST API. To start, click Models in the lefthand panel on Databricks (see Figure 11-27).

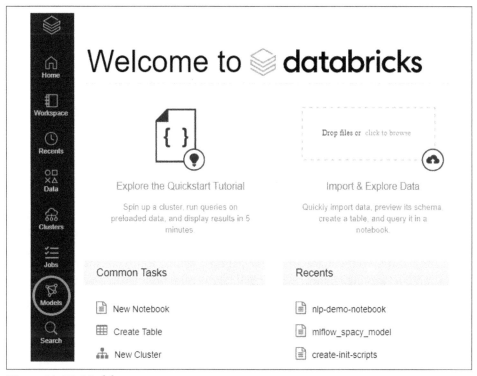

Figure 11-27. Models

Here, you should see the spaCy text classification model we just registered. It should have the name "nlp-demo-textcat-prodigy-V3-base-full." Click the model name, then click Version 1. Here you can see all the details for this version of the model. These details are great for collaboration within and across teams at your organization. We won't dig into too much of this here, but note the types of details that can be logged and tracked. For instance, we can change the stage of the model from "None" to "Staging" to "Production" to help track where in the model testing and model deployment cycle we are. Let's move the model to Staging.

Now, let's return to the previous screen. Click the Serving tab, highlighted in red in Figure 11-28.

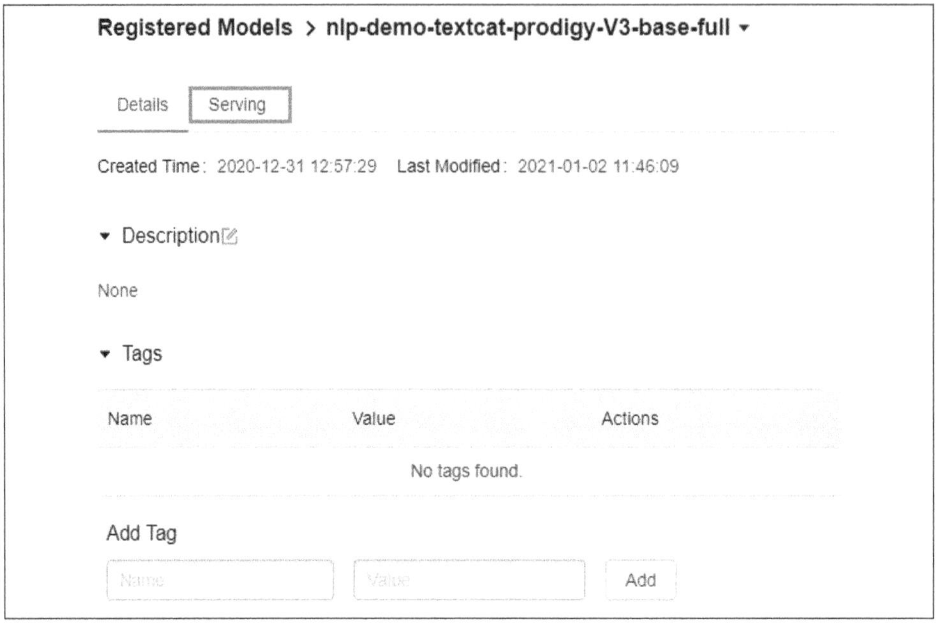

Figure 11-28. Serving

In the Serving tab, we have the option to enable serving by clicking on the blue Enable Serving button. Note that this will launch a single-node cluster.[7]

Click the button. You will see an amber Pending status, which means the cluster to perform model serving is starting. This will take several minutes to boot up.

Once the cluster is up, we are ready to test the REST API surfaced by MLflow. There are three options to call the model: via the browser, cURL, or Python.

Let's try the browser method first. In the Request box, we need to enter text in a properly formatted list such as this (which are also the first 10 article descriptions from the AG News Dataset):

```
[
    "Reuters - Short-sellers, Wall Street's dwindling band of ultra-cynics, are
    seeing green again.",
    "Reuters - Private investment firm Carlyle Group, which has a reputation for
    making well-timed and occasionally controversial plays in the defense
    industry, has quietly placed its bets on another part of the market.",
    "Reuters - Soaring crude prices plus worries about the economy and the outlook
    for earnings are expected to hang over the stock market next week during the
    depth of the summer doldrums.",
    "Reuters - Authorities have halted oil export flows from the main pipeline in
```

---

7 For more on MLflow model serving on Databricks, visit the official guide (*https://oreil.ly/fkn4l*).

```
    southern Iraq after intelligence showed a rebel militia could strike
    infrastructure, an oil official said on Saturday.",
    "AFP - Tearaway world oil prices, toppling records and straining wallets,
    present a new economic menace barely three months before the US
    presidential elections.",
    "Reuters - Stocks ended slightly higher on Friday but stayed near lows for
    the year as oil prices surged past \\$46 a barrel, offsetting a positive
    outlook from computer maker Dell Inc. (DELL.O)",
    "AP - Assets of the nation's retail money market mutual funds fell by $1.17
    billion in the latest week to $849.98 trillion, the Investment Company
    Institute said Thursday.",
    "USATODAY.com - Retail sales bounced back a bit in July, and new claims for
    jobless benefits fell last week, the government said Thursday, indicating the
    economy is improving from a midsummer slump.",
    "Forbes.com - After earning a PH.D. in Sociology, Danny Bazil Riley started to
    work as the general manager at a commercial real estate firm at an annual base
    salary of $70,000. Soon after, a financial planner stopped by his desk to
    drop off brochures about insurance benefits available through his employer.
    But, at 32, \"buying insurance was the furthest thing from my mind,\"
    says Riley.",
    "NEW YORK (Reuters) - Short-sellers, Wall Street's dwindling band of
    ultra-cynics, are seeing green again.",
    "NEW YORK (Reuters) - Soaring crude prices plus worries about the economy
    and the outlook for earnings are expected to hang over the stock market next
    week during the depth of the summer doldrums."
]
```

Once you copy this into the Request box and click the blue Send Request button, you should see the predictions in the "Response" box on the righthand side (see Figure 11-29).

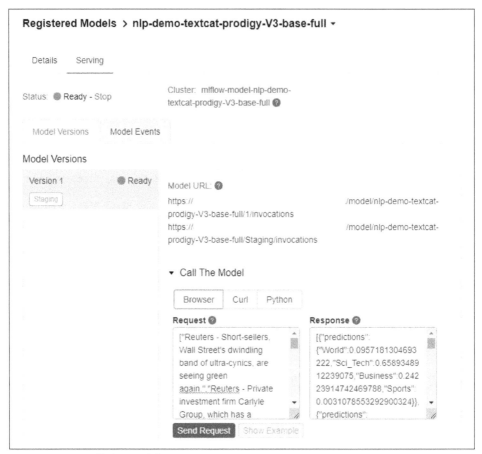

Figure 11-29. Call the model

Here are the responses. Note that for each of the 10 article descriptions we sent, the model returned predictions for each of the four classes (World, Sci_Tech, Business, and Sports) as expected:

```
[
  {
    "predictions": {
      "World": 0.0957181304693222,
      "Sci_Tech": 0.6589348912239075,
      "Business": 0.24223914742469788,
      "Sports": 0.0031078553292900324
    }
  },
  {
    "predictions": {
      "World": 0.002171833999454975,
      "Sci_Tech": 0.21052186191082,
```

```
      "Business": 0.7844370007514954,
      "Sports": 0.002869191113859415
    }
  },
  {
    "predictions": {
      "World": 0.003616414498537779,
      "Sci_Tech": 0.0010920974891632795,
      "Business": 0.9949613809585571,
      "Sports": 0.00033012236235663295
    }
  },
  {
    "predictions": {
      "World": 0.8058245182037354,
      "Sci_Tech": 0.0005569260101765394,
      "Business": 0.19326980412006378,
      "Sports": 0.00034875082201324403
    }
  },
  {
    "predictions": {
      "World": 0.2849672734737396,
      "Sci_Tech": 0.007292506285011768,
      "Business": 0.7071781158447266,
      "Sports": 0.0005621095770038664
    }
  },
  {
    "predictions": {
      "World": 0.0023397665936499834,
      "Sci_Tech": 0.00239493977278471,
      "Business": 0.9952585101127625,
      "Sports": 0.000006784629476896953
    }
  },
  {
    "predictions": {
      "World": 0.003856266150251031,
      "Sci_Tech": 0.02379118837416172,
      "Business": 0.9723222255706787,
      "Sports": 0.000030239543775678612
    }
  },
  {
    "predictions": {
      "World": 0.00020332192070782185,
      "Sci_Tech": 0.00014183521852828562,
      "Business": 0.9996367692947388,
      "Sports": 0.00001810084722819738
    }
  },
```

```
{
    "predictions": {
        "World": 0.00003446835762588307,
        "Sci_Tech": 0.0063316719606518745,
        "Business": 0.9936137795448303,
        "Sports": 0.000020146884708083235
    }
},
{
    "predictions": {
        "World": 0.196404829621315,
        "Sci_Tech": 0.375182181596756,
        "Business": 0.4262356758117676,
        "Sports": 0.002177357906475663
    }
},
{
    "predictions": {
        "World": 0.004218680318444967,
        "Sci_Tech": 0.00035350999678485096,
        "Business": 0.99529629945755,
        "Sports": 0.00013148739526513964
    }
}
]
```

This is great news. The model served via the REST API works as expected. Now, let's send a request via cURL using Google Colab. To follow along, refer to the corresponding notebook in our book's GitHub repo (*https://github.com/nlpbook/nlpbook*).

First, connect to your Google Drive:

```
# Connect to Google Drive
from google.colab import drive
drive.mount('/content/drive', force_remount=True)
```

To send a request via cURL, let's prepare a JSON file of the article descriptions. To do so, load the AG News Dataset:

```
# Load libraries
import numpy as np
import pandas as pd

# Define function to read data
def read_data(file):
    read_path = '/content/drive/My Drive/Applied-NLP-in-the-Enterprise'
    data = pd.read_csv(read_path+file)
    return data

# Read data
data = read_data('/data/ag_dataset/prepared/train_prepared.csv')
```

Let's convert the first 10 descriptions to JSON and save the file:

```
# Convert to JSON
data.loc[:10,"description"].to_json(path_or_buf= \
       '/content/drive/My Drive/Applied-NLP-in-the-Enterprise/data/\
       ag_dataset/prepared/sample.json', orient="records")
```

Now, we are ready to send the cURL request. On the Databricks page, select the "Curl" tab under "Call The Model." You should see a sample cURL request that looks like this:

```
curl \
 -u token:$DATABRICKS_TOKEN \
 -H "Content-Type: application/json; format=pandas-records" \
 -d@data.json $MODEL_PATH
```

To make our cURL request in Colab, we will use a similar format. Note the different parameters we need to pass in. First, we need to pass in our Databricks token. Second, we need to reference a JSON file. Finally, we need to pass the path to the model, which is a URL that begins with the URL to your specific Databricks instance.

Let's go back to Google Colab and submit the cURL request using this format:

```
# Call the Model - CURL
MODEL_VERSION_URI = XXXXXX #the model path
DATABRICKS_TOKEN = XXXXXX #secret access token
JSON_PATH = XXXXXX #path to the JSON we created earlier in Colab

!curl -u token:$DATABRICKS_TOKEN -H \
 "Content-Type: application/json; format=pandas-records" \
 -d@$JSON_PATH $MODEL_VERSION_URI
```

To send this request successfully, fill in the values for your parameters (MODEL_VER SION_URI, DATABRICKS_TOKEN, and JSON_PATH). Once you submit the request, you should see the following response in Google Colab. This is the same response we received earlier when we sent the request via our browser:

```
[
  {
    "predictions": {
      "World": 0.0957181304693222,
      "Sci_Tech": 0.6589348912239075,
      "Business": 0.24223914742469788,
      "Sports": 0.0031078553292900324
    }
  },
  {
    "predictions": {
      "World": 0.002171833999454975,
      "Sci_Tech": 0.21052186191082,
      "Business": 0.7844370007514954,
      "Sports": 0.002869191113859415
    }
  },
```

```
{
  "predictions": {
    "World": 0.003616414498537779,
    "Sci_Tech": 0.0010920974891632795,
    "Business": 0.9949613809585571,
    "Sports": 0.00033012236235663295
  }
},
{
  "predictions": {
    "World": 0.8058245182037354,
    "Sci_Tech": 0.0005569260101765394,
    "Business": 0.19326980412006378,
    "Sports": 0.00034875082201324403
  }
},
{
  "predictions": {
    "World": 0.2849672734737396,
    "Sci_Tech": 0.007292506285011768,
    "Business": 0.7071781158447266,
    "Sports": 0.0005621095770038664
  }
},
{
  "predictions": {
    "World": 0.0023397665936499834,
    "Sci_Tech": 0.00239493977278471,
    "Business": 0.9952585101127625,
    "Sports": 0.000006784629476896953
  }
},
{
  "predictions": {
    "World": 0.003856266150251031,
    "Sci_Tech": 0.02379118837416172,
    "Business": 0.9723222255706787,
    "Sports": 0.0000303239543775678612
  }
},
{
  "predictions": {
    "World": 0.00020332192070782185,
    "Sci_Tech": 0.00014183521852828562,
    "Business": 0.9996367692947388,
    "Sports": 0.00001810084722819738
  }
},
{
  "predictions": {
    "World": 0.00003446835762588307,
    "Sci_Tech": 0.0063316719606518745,
```

```
      "Business": 0.9936137795448303,
      "Sports": 0.000020146884708083235
    }
  },
  {
    "predictions": {
      "World": 0.196404829621315,
      "Sci_Tech": 0.375182181596756,
      "Business": 0.4262356758117676,
      "Sports": 0.002177357906475663
    }
  },
  {
    "predictions": {
      "World": 0.004218680318444967,
      "Sci_Tech": 0.00035350999678485096,
      "Business": 0.99529629945755,
      "Sports": 0.00013148739526513964
    }
  }
]
```

Finally, you can also send a request to the REST API using Python. This is the function to call the model:

```python
# Define Function to Call the Model in Python
import requests

def score_model(model_uri, databricks_token, data):
    headers = {
        "Authorization": 'Bearer '+ databricks_token,
        "Content-Type": "application/json; format=pandas-records",
    }
    data_json = data if isinstance(data, list) else data.to_list()
    response = requests.request(method='POST', headers=headers,
        url=model_uri, json=data_json)
    if response.status_code != 200:
        raise Exception(f"Request failed with status {response.status_code},
            {response.text}")
    return response.json()
```

Let's use the function to return a response:

```python
# Score the Model
MODEL_VERSION_URI = XXXXXX # the model path
DATABRICKS_TOKEN = XXXXXX # secret access token

score_model(MODEL_VERSION_URI, DATABRICKS_TOKEN, data.loc[:10,"description"])
```

Once you enter values for the two parameters (MODEL_VERSION_URI and DATA BRICKS_TOKEN), you should receive a JSON response that is similar to the responses we received via the browser and cURL.

Congratulations! You just deployed the model and served it via REST API and accessed it across all three methods (browser, cURL, and Python).

> Remember to stop serving the model once you are done; otherwise the cluster to serve the model will remain up and running, and you may incur unnecessary Databricks expenses as a result.

This concludes our tour of Databricks. You have seen firsthand the ability of Spark to help perform machine learning at scale (with larger and larger clusters, as necessary). You also set up pipelines to perform both scheduled and event-based batch inference. Finally, you deployed a model using MLflow, served it via REST API, and used the REST API to perform inference. You now know the basics of productionizing machine learning models!

Alternatives to Databricks

Although we have spent all of this chapter discussing how to productionize machine learning models using Databricks, Databricks is not the only major player in town; there are several other good alternatives. Although we cannot review all of them in detail, here are the two top alternatives for you to consider.

> Instead of using a third-party vendor, you could choose to deploy Spark on your own, either on prem or in the cloud; it is, after all, an open source technology. Note that it is a considerable engineering feat to deploy on premise for an organization, but high data privacy industries such as finance and healthcare regularly deploy Spark on prem, so it is certainly an option.

Amazon SageMaker

Amazon's cloud machine learning platform, SageMaker (*https://oreil.ly/D3h1J*), integrates nicely with AWS services. SageMaker allows developers to create, train, and deploy machine learning models in the cloud, much like Databricks does. SageMaker even supports deployment on edge devices and has pretrained ML models that can be deployed as is. Although not as user friendly (especially to nonengineers) as Databricks, it is one of the strongest competitors of Databricks today for machine learning model training and deployment, especially given the dominant market share of AWS in cloud services.

Saturn Cloud

Saturn Cloud (*https://www.saturncloud.io*) is similar in many ways to Databricks; it is a platform for data science and machine learning that runs on AWS and is built to help you run machine learning up to 100x faster. But, instead of running on Spark, it runs on Dask (*https://dask.org*), the open source distributed Python framework. Dask is very new; it was initially released in October 2018. Dask is a Python-based alternative to Spark and is gaining a strong following, especially among developers who want to stay with Python instead of having to use PySpark or Scala as required for Spark. It is not as mature of an offering and does not have as much of an adoption as Databricks, but it is worth closely following and investing some time in.

Other alternatives include Microsoft Azure Machine Learning Studio (*https://oreil.ly/Qg1Wm*), the Google Cloud AI Platform (*https://oreil.ly/7DLGR*), and up-and-coming MLOps players such as Algorithmia (*https://algorithmia.com*).

Conclusion

In this chapter, we explored how to productionize machine learning models. First, we established the different roles that are involved in deploying, maintaining, and monitoring machine learning models in production. Data scientists, data and machine learning engineers, and data analysts are all involved in machine learning work, and their specific needs (such as programming environment and programming language of choice) need to be considered when choosing the appropriate platform for your organization to do machine learning.

The platform that we recommend is Databricks, especially since it is built on top of Spark, which is the best distributed machine learning technology available today; it is the optimal choice when doing machine learning at scale. We used Databricks to create both scheduled and event-based machine learning pipelines, and we then used these pipelines to perform batch inference with our spaCy NER model. We also used MLflow on Databricks to deploy and serve our spaCy text classification model via a REST API, and we then tested the REST API using the browser, cURL, and Python. And, in the previous chapter, we used Streamlit to build and deploy multiple web apps using our spaCy models.

This concludes our section of productionizing machine learning models; at this point we've covered web apps, APIs, and scheduled and event-based batch pipelines. What we have not covered is how to perform machine learning on streaming data, which is beyond the scope of this book.[8]

---

8 But, if you're interested to learn more, drop us a note via Slack or our email.

Prior to this section, we had developed machine learning models, but we had not pushed any into production. The push into production is essential to seeing a return on investment from all the machine learning research and development you do. We cannot emphasize this enough: the difficulty of the move from prototyping to production is where many companies fail and is one of the main reasons many companies derive such a low return on investment on the machine learning initiatives they launch. The more you learn how to productionize your machine learning work, the more value you will be able to deliver to your organization. While we were able to give you a quick introduction to machine learning production, we sincerely hope you devote many more hours to learn more. If you would like additional resources or help, reach out to us.

In the next chapter, we will conclude with 10 final lessons to help you take what you've learned in this book and build NLP applications of your own.

## CHAPTER 12

Conclusion

This brings us to the end of our journey together. Over the course of 11 chapters, we introduced the origins of natural language processing and retraced how the field has advanced over the past decade. We delved into the nitty-gritty details of the space, including preprocessing and tokenization and several types of word embeddings, such Word2Vec, GloVe, and fastText.

We covered everything from vanilla recurrent nets to gated variants such as LSTM and GRUs. And, we explained how attention mechanisms, contextualized word embeddings, and Transformers helped shatter previous performance records. Most importantly, we used large, pretrained language models to perform transfer learning and fine-tune models and discussed how to productionize the models using various tools of the trade.

Instead of getting bogged down in theory, we focused mostly on applying state-of-the-art NLP techniques to solve real-world problems. We hope this helped you build greater intuition about NLP, how it works, and how to apply it well.

By now it should be clear that getting up and running with NLP is relatively easy, partly thanks to the open sourcing of large, pretrained language models by research teams at Google, Facebook, OpenAI, and others. Companies such as spaCy, Hugging Face, AllenNLP, Amazon, Microsoft, and Google have introduced great tooling for NLP, too, making it less painful to develop NLP models of your own from scratch or fine-tune existing models.

Ten Final Lessons

But, as we said in the Preface, many organizations today still struggle with developing and productionizing NLP applications and fail to get a good return on the investment in time, effort, and money that they make. With this in mind, we want to share with you some parting advice from hard-learned lessons we've experienced along the way.

Lesson 1: Start with Simple Approaches First

While it is tempting to turn to the latest state-of-the-art models to build NLP applications and to strive to beat industry benchmarks in performance, it is generally better to start with simple approaches first. Based on our experience, the newer and the more complex the modeling approach, the longer it will take to build the application and push it to production.

This is bad for several reasons:

1. First, it delays the time to tangible impact from any modeling you do. Your organization could benefit faster from a simpler model that takes less time to develop and push to production.

2. Next, a long model development cycle may be demoralizing not only to the machine learning team but to the leadership team and to the investors that have backed the machine learning initiatives at your organization. It is best to ship early and often in the early stages of any machine learning initiative to deliver quick wins to all interested parties and to show that machine learning can help the organization, even if the gains are more modest at first.

3. Finally, you learn a lot more about the problem at hand by working on the machine learning solution end to end. You may also get more real-world intel on the problem once your simple model is in production and you begin to see how it performs on live data. You may begin to ask and answer questions such as: what edge cases did we fail to account for during the development process? Where does the simple model fail most dramatically? How could we better design the model given what we know now?

Simple models are not only simpler to develop and deploy, but they are also easier to interpret than more complex models. For example, a simple NLP model using Light Gradient Boost Machine (LightGBM) (*https://oreil.ly/9xiBY*) with some NLP-specific feature engineering is a lot easier to interpret than a more complex neural network-based model. Simple models also require far less compute resources and time to train, whereas the latest state-of-the-art models are generally much larger and more compute-intensive.

Of course, the definition of what is simple changes over time. For example, BERT was state of the art in 2018 and considerably more difficult to use back then than it is today. Contextualized word representations and Transformer-based pipelines are now the norm in NLP model development, too. If you started your model development with these techniques today, it would be fairly straightforward and simple (but not necessarily in 2018 when the techniques were first publicly released).

While neural networks are now the norm, there is also room for classical, non-neural, network-based NLP applications in enterprise, too. To develop classical NLP models, you will need to perform your own feature engineering using steps such as preprocessing, tokenization, and vectorization. Sometimes these classical NLP approaches quickly lead to pretty good results for the problem at hand, whereas the latest neural networks would take considerably longer.

Even rule-based methods might have a place and should not be shunned in enterprise; not everything has to be model-based. The goal should be to deliver value to the organization fast and reliably, eventually replacing the stopgap measures with better performing ones. As Voltaire said, perfect is the enemy of good.

Lesson 2: Leverage the Community

This brings us to another reason for starting with simple approaches first. The more simple approaches today are the ones that have been tried and tested over at least some reasonable amount of time. They are not purely theoretical and experimental; rather, they are battle-tested. Tried and tested is better than new and flashy for applied work.

These approaches have better documentation and fewer bugs, and they support a larger community of practitioners on sites such as Stack Overflow (*https://stackover flow.com*), which you will be able to tap into when you run into issues with your model development and deployment. These communities are full of helpful tips and suggestions.

There is comfort knowing that others have tried and tested the more simple approaches you are starting your NLP build with today, so you are unlikely to have to pave the way for others from scratch. You are going down a well-paved road with open community support along the way.

Once you have achieved some modest success with the simpler approaches and deployed your model to production, you will have bought yourself more time, and you can invest more energy in the more complex and more experimental state-of-the-art approaches. Even if you run into issues building the more complex model, at least your organization has a modest-performing model delivering tangible value in production as a stopgap measure.

This should be your mantra: ship models early and often in the early days to buy yourself more time to invest in longer R&D cycles. You will get more believers and champions for your initiatives as you show tangible impact along the way.

Lesson 3: Do Not Create from Scratch, When Possible

Before you invest a substantial amount of time and resources into building a solution to solve your problem, spend a modest chunk of time and resources exploring open source or third-party alternatives. Perhaps there is a decent pre-built model available as an API for your particular problem; why build a model from scratch when you could cheaply access an existing model?

Even if the open source or third-party solution is not a perfect long-term fit for your problem, it is generally better to use the solution in the interim since it will deliver immediate value to your organization while you build the in-house solution for your organization's long-term strategic needs.

Do not build what already exists. At the very least, do not start building until you've done the research to evaluate and rule out third-party options. It is very tempting as a programmer to want to build models and applications from scratch, wholly owning the process from start to finish. Building from scratch feeds the ego, but the better option may be to buy what you can from existing players and build only what you cannot find in the market.

The more generic and universal your problem is (such as receipt extraction), the more likely that a decent solution already exists for you to buy. The more custom and specific your problem is, the more likely that you will have to build in-house. Choose wisely what to spend your time working on.

Lesson 4: Intuition and Experience Trounces Theory

Our stance here remains consistent throughout the book: get your hands dirty fast with code and data if you want to advance in the field quickly. While it is certainly important to learn the theory, it is not where you should spend the majority of your time as an applied NLP practitioner.

Theory is most vital for researchers that want to build on top of the work of prior researchers and develop newer state-of-the-art approaches. But, if your goal is to deliver tangible value to your organization fast, it's best to start working with code and data as early as you can.

Our recommendation is for you to start with applied books such as this one (kudos to an excellent start already!) and software that have wrappers that allow you to easily work with large, pretrained language models. Our favorite places to start include spaCy, Hugging Face, and fast.ai, all of which we have explored in this book.

These companies have toy datasets and starter code to help you advance in your NLP journey fast. All three players, like us, favor intuition over theory and are biased toward action. Of the three, fast.ai has the best course materials and will help you build more of your foundational knowledge of NLP. spaCy and Hugging Face are better to explore once you have worked your way through several toy datasets and are ready to transition to performing NLP on larger datasets.

Even if you are a seasoned vet, you will likely need a resource to absorb the latest advances in NLP since the field is constantly changing; fast.ai is the place to go to make this continuing education as painless as possible. Afterward, you can turn to the official blog posts, research papers on arXiv, third-party blog posts, Medium, You-Tube, and other resources.

One last caveat: while we recommend that you start on toy datasets if you are new to NLP, it is critical that you transition to a real-world project before long. Working on a real-world problem (and all the other issues that come from working with data in the wild) will really push you to develop as an applied practitioner in a way that working on toy datasets simply won't.

Lesson 5: Fight Decision Fatigue

As a newcomer to NLP, it is easy to succumb to decision indecision, especially when choosing among all the various tools of the trade that we explored in Chapter 9. Do not succumb; fight the urge. We recommend starting simply and being biased toward action, as always.

Start with fast.ai as a resource. Choose one of the two main frameworks; we recommend PyTorch if you are new to machine learning. Begin coding on Google Colab or on your local environment. Do not worry about all the different cloud compute providers or experiment tracking or productionizing models just yet. All of this can come later with experience and practice. The main goal is getting started as fast and painlessly as possible.

Lesson 6: Data Is King

While we have spent the majority of the book discussing how to develop and productionize NLP models, what makes or breaks performance on many applied use cases is not the modeling approach, but rather the quality and quantity of data you have available to train the model. The more data, the better.

It is best to leverage publicly available datasets for your problem, where possible. You may also find datasets available for purchase online. But, to develop a truly performant model, you will likely need to build first-party data capture into your application so that you control the data off of which you build models. At the very least, you will likely need to have a partnership with a player that has great data capture.

Once you have data, annotations are vital. You could perform the annotation yourself, which we recommend you do initially to get started fast and to learn more about how to annotate the data well. Or you could hire an annotation firm, such as Appen or Scale AI. You could also hire low-cost labor through firms such as Invisible

Technologies or Odetta to perform the annotation. Amazon Mechanical Turk is also a good option, but requires more hands-on oversight than the other annotation companies.

There is good off-the-shelf and open source annotation software to perform the annotations, including Prodigy, which we explored in Chapter 3. However, to have the highest-quality annotations, you may need your organization to build a custom annotation UI. But again, start with off-the-shelf third-party tools, where possible. Don't build from scratch unless you absolutely need to.

Lesson 7: Lean on Humans

When developing an ML-based product, you will need to leverage humans in the loop to handle edge cases that the model fails on and to perform active learning, which is the process of having humans annotate data points where the model performs poorly. Without the human in the loop, even if your NLP application is 90% good, it may not be ready for production because your users demand more than 99% accuracy. To deliver this accuracy to your users, you can leverage the humans in the loop to deal with the 10% of cases in which your model performs poorly. AI is not magic. For AI to be production ready, you will likely need to pair it with humans, at least initially.

More generally, build fault-tolerant experiences for your users when building NLP applications. Your model will fail in ways that you may never have anticipated, and, unless your application gracefully handles the failure, the model's failures may frustrate or anger your users. For example, Google Assistant asks users to confirm a question that is being asked when Google is not sure, and Google responds with a "I'm not sure I can help with you that" when it is truly befuddled. This softens the poor experience for the user.

Lesson 8: Pair Yourself with Really Great Engineers

If your strongest skill set is in developing NLP models, pair yourself with really great engineers to help you more robustly and easily productionize your NLP models. Great engineers will bring much needed systems thinking to your NLP pipeline, designing tests, managing MLOps, and more. In general, pair yourself with others who complement your particular skill sets best because you will not be able to master everything on your own.

Lesson 9: Ensemble

Ensembling is the closest thing to a free lunch in machine learning. Once you have a good model in production, design more models to complement what you have and include all the models together in an ensemble. To the extent the models have similarly good performance but uncorrelated errors, the ensemble will outperform any of the standalone models in the ensemble. It's one of the easiest ways to improve the overall performance of your application in the enterprise.

Lesson 10: Have Fun

This brings us to our very final piece of advice: have fun and enjoy the journey you are on. NLP is hard, and the path to mastery is long. Much like neural nets learn layer by layer to solve pretty complex problems, you will learn how to master NLP a step at a time. Just be patient, start simple, and, most importantly, celebrate the small wins along the way. The more you allow yourself to experience joy, the greater the sense of flow you will experience and the faster you will become a true master of NLP.

Final Word

With that, we truly thank you for taking the time to read our book and to share a bit of your journey with us.

Please stay tuned for more content at *https://www.appliednlpbook.com*, and we hope to see you again soon!

Scaling

As we've mentioned several times in this book, large language models have had a big impact on the field of NLP, and current trends suggest that this isn't going to stop any time soon, as Figure A-1 suggests.

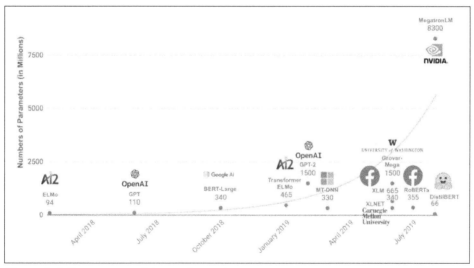

Figure A-1. Language model growth trend

The great thing about this, even if you're not particularly enthusiastic about training a large model yourself, is that most researchers are generally interested in open sourcing their code and releasing the trained model weights as well. Better language models trained on larger datasets for longer means that you, the developer building NLP applications, has a stronger baseline to work off of. It's almost like a free performance boost![1]

Because of this rapid progress and general interest in open sourcing the best models, we generally wouldn't recommend training your own large language model from scratch. It is often counterproductive when many researchers have spents years of GPU time optimizing a specific language model on an existing large dataset. Our very first lesson in Chapter 2 was that being prudent with fine-tuning can reap huge rewards. In practice, you *always* want to use transfer learning wherever you can.

However, if you *do* have the luxury of being able to access large amounts of compute, there are some things you should know about scaling your model training to ensure optimal performance.

Multi-GPU Training

If you have multiple GPUs accessible from the same machine (typically found in high-end workstations, academic compute clusters, and AWS p3.XLarge instances), setting your network to use them is fairly straightforward in PyTorch.

All you have to do is wrap your model in an `nn.DataParallel` class, and PyTorch automatically takes care of the multi-GPU complexity for you:

```
from torch import nn

model = nn.Transformer()
model = nn.DataParallel(model)
```

One small, somewhat annoying detail with this is that if you plan to then use the exported weight of your model, the keys in the state dict will all have a pesky `model.` prefix in front of them that you'll need to remove manually. (There are also scripts to do this automatically, which you can find online.) Various PyTorch users also have suggestions on the forums. This might save you a lot of trouble. Thank us later!

Distributed Training

Most workstations and data centers have *some* fundamental hardware limitation that makes it impractical to scale above a fixed upper bound on the number of GPUs. More often than not, that number is 8. The reality is that CPUs have a fixed number of PCIe lanes, which limits the number of GPUs it can connect to simultaneously.

---

1 Not accounting for the cost of running a larger model, of course…

Apart from this, there are other hardware constraints, such as size, availability, power consumption, and cooling.

Most practitioners shouldn't face this challenge. You should always try to avoid using extra hardware to solve your problems. Even *if* your model becomes unreasonably large, you can often decrease the batch size accordingly, to a point where everything fits on the GPUs that you can fit into a single machine. But if you ever find yourself in a situation where scaling across multiple compute nodes is the simplest path forward, PyTorch has the tools to accommodate that.

The language surrounding distributed training is intentionally a bit abstract. We say "node" instead of "process," "computer," "GPU," or "cluster" because, technically, a node can be any of these!

The key idea with distributed training is that you can scale your computations across multiple *things that can compute*, whether that's multiple GPUs on a single machine, data centers communicating with each other over a high-bandwidth network, or maybe even a completely decentralized collection of low-powered, independent computers. The challenges with all of these are the same:

- How do you communicate information like gradients, loss, etc., efficiently across nodes?

- How can you minimize the amount of expensive message passing between nodes?

- What happens if one of your nodes fails? Do you end training and lose all progress, or find some way to continue?

- Do you split your model weights across multiple nodes, or do you split your batches?

- How do the training dynamics of your model change at very large batch sizes?

If there *is* a silver lining to the complexity of distributed training, it's that many people have already done it before. Distributed training is a very common practice at most research labs where researchers often train on the largest academic datasets routinely to benchmark new ideas. More generally, the paradigm of distributed systems is something that's very important outside of deep learning—scaling databases across regions for high availability and fault tolerance is one example.

Because of the demand, there are now tools you can use to simplify distributed training, and the entire process is relatively straightforward. One setup that is particularly powerful is Docker and PyTorch distributed.

What Makes Deep Training Fast?

Contrary to popular belief, splurging on the latest Nvidia GPUs isn't always the smartest thing to do if you want to speed up and scale your training jobs. In practice, there's a *lot* you can do in just software, and GPUs are *not* the only component of your computer that is used during training.

But let's assume that you've done everything you possibly can to make the most efficient gains in PyTorch or a higher-level library. You're confident that you have the perfect model, the perfect amount of data, the perfect hyperparameters, and so on. Is there anything else you can do?

The answer is yes. There are a number of small improvements that you can implement in your training pipeline to speed things up. Here are some suggestions:

GPU preprocessing
Try to move as many preprocessing steps onto the GPU as possible. This allows you to apply transformations to batches in parallel. Many codebases we've seen still use CPU transformations when it could easily work on the GPU. Look for libraries to help with this.

Use archives
Use HDF files if you have a very large number of small files in your dataset. If your training loop involves reading a large number of files very quickly, your I/O performance can also become a bottleneck. HDF files are a format that allows you to archive a lot of data into a single file. This means that your system doesn't waste time acquiring a lock for every new piece of data it has to load.

Mixed-precision training
Mixed-precision training is a great way to speed up training, and it doesn't even require too many changes to your codebase. Implementations differ from framework to framework, but the general idea is that you use a lower floating-point precision for some steps during training. Nvidia's most recent GPUs also include "Tensor Cores" that are explicitly designed to make these lower-precision matrix multiplications faster.

Eliminate native Python code
Try to remove Python control flow from your code and use libraries like PyTorch and NumPy instead. These libraries use much faster, fine-tuned implementations of different functions. Whenever you can avoid writing something from scratch, it's usually a good idea to do so.

Use a faster language/framework
Finally, no matter what libraries you use, interfacing with Python is still, unfortunately, a bottleneck. Python was a language designed to be easy to use first and foremost. Performance has always been a second-class citizen. Many people in

the community have realized this, and there are now efforts to develop new programming languages and compilers that help speed up general-purpose tensor computation like the type we do in PyTorch. Julia is the most prominent and fastest-developing example of this.

 Implementing many of these sounds like a lot of busy work, and it probably is. But thankfully, the fastai library implements almost all of them by default. This is one of the reasons we recommend it so highly—it allows researchers to quickly implement new ideas and iterate fast and abstract away all the engineering effort that's not related to deep learning.

CUDA

Throughout the book, we've mostly been using PyTorch or tools built on top of it, such as `fastai` and Hugging Face transformers. When we first introduced it in this book, we pitched PyTorch as a low-level framework, where you build architectures and write training loops "from scratch" using your knowledge of linear algebra.

But PyTorch may not be the lowest level of abstraction you deal with in machine learning.

PyTorch itself is written in C++, to which the CUDA language is an extension. CUDA is self-described as a "programming model" that allows you to write code for Nvidia GPUs. When writing your C++ code, you include certain functions called "CUDA kernels" that perform a portion of the work on the GPU.

Who's That Pokémon? CUDA Kernels

A kernel is a function that is compiled for and designed to run on special accelerator hardware like GPUs (graphics processing units), FPGAs (field-programmable gate arrays), and ASICs (application-specific integrated circuits). They are generally written by engineers who are very familiar with the hardware architecture, and are extensively tuned to perform a single task very well, such as matrix multiplication or convolution. CUDA kernels are kernels run on devices that use CUDA—Nvidia's GPUs and accelerators.

PyTorch and many other deep learning frameworks use a handful of CUDA kernels to implement their backend, and then build a higher-level interface to a language like Python. This allows you to run super-fast, hand-tuned code on specialized hardware that experts have spent years optimizing without having to think about memory, pointers, threads, etc.

There are many other similar platforms, like AMS's ROCm,[1] SYCL (an open source alternative from the Khronos Group), and, with AI hardware startups showing up in every nook and corner, many more.

But CUDA is, by far, the most mature and well-developed GPU programming interface available today. In fact, it's mostly the reason that we're all forced to use Nvidia's GPUs—its software stack is just so much better than everyone else's, which makes it easier to develop libraries like PyTorch on top of it.

Unless you have the bandwidth, it's not always a great idea to look for kernel-level improvements. This is probably very low on the list of things you should do if your focus is on deploying an NLP application using existing tools and technology.

But...it *is* useful to understand how such a critical component of the infrastructure that powers deep learning today works, and it's certainly interesting and fun. An understanding of some of the ideas in CUDA may also help you debug obscure errors in your deep learning framework, and can help you make more informed purchasing decisions for hardware.

Threads and Thread Blocks

The fundamental atom of CUDA is the thread. A thread represents a single unit of execution of a computation. Every instruction that runs in a single thread will be executed sequentially. To get massive parallelism, CUDA devices usually have a *lot* of threads, which all run independently.

Crucially, communication *between* threads is hard (even on regular CPUs), and so we try to avoid this as much as possible. If you don't believe this, try to get a hundred people to agree on whether or not pineapples belong on pizza. It's *hard*, which is why CUDA attempts to sidestep the problem to a large degree, and is much better suited for problems that are embarrassingly parallel.

Yes, "embarrassingly parallel" is a somewhat widely accepted technical term that you'll likely hear in a few situations. In general, it means that the problem you're trying to solve is composed of multiple smaller tasks that don't depend on each other. This is true in deep learning, where we have natural parallelism across hyperparameter sets, samples in a training batch, and even across tokens in a sequence for transformers.

Threads in CUDA are arranged into what are called *blocks*, which are themselves arranged into *grids*.

---

1 PyTorch recently added support for this, so it might be a great option to keep your eye on in the near future!

Writing CUDA Kernels

Before you start writing your own CUDA kernel, it's a good idea to gain familiarity with C/C++ and some of the ideas that are common in low-level programming languages, such as the memory model, pointers, and static types.

CUDA kernels are interleaved with C++ code, and are implemented as functions with the special __global__ decorator. Here's an example of a kernel that adds two vectors:

```
__global__ void add(int n, float* a, float *b, float *b)
{
  int i = blockIdx.x * blockDim.x + threadIdx.x;
  if (i < n) c[i] = a[i] + b[i];
}
```

Some of these constructs might seem a little strange and new, especially if you're coming from just Python. But the main logic here is intuitive: c[i] = a[i] + b[i] isn't very different from what you'd write in Python. Given this information, how would you modify this kernel to do an element-wise multiplication instead?

The answer is probably what you'd expect:

```
__global__ void mul(int n, float* a, float *b, float *b)
{
  int i = blockIdx.x * blockDim.x + threadIdx.x;
  if (i < n) c[i] = a[i] * b[i];
}
```

That seems simple enough! Time to write an ultra-parallelized operating system? Unfortunately, no.

There are other things you need in your code to run CUDA kernels.[2] The kernel code itself, marked with the __global__ keyword, is run on the GPU, but we still need to have *something* that instructs the CPU to invoke or launch the kernel with the right data.

A lot of this code is boilerplate, and you'll see it repeated again and again. But such is the case with low-level code that aims to provide fine-tuned access to hardware.

First, we should initialize the vectors (arrays) we want to add:

```
N = 256
for (int i = 0; i < N; i++) {
    a[i] = 1.0f;
    b[i] = 2.0f;
}
```

---

2 The technical term is "launch" a CUDA kernel.

Since a and b are on the CPU, we need to move them to the GPU. This is done through cudaMemcpyHostToDevice:

```
cudaMemcpy(d_a, a, N*sizeof(float), cudaMemcpyHostToDevice);
cudaMemcpy(d_b, b, N*sizeof(float), cudaMemcpyHostToDevice);
```

After we finish the computation, we'll need to fetch our result back from the GPU. This is done with cudaMemcpyDeviceToHost:

```
cudaMemcpy(c, d_c, N*sizeof(float), cudaMemcpyDeviceToHost);
```

To actually launch the kernel (which is the equivalent of a function call from the CPU to GPU), we use a kernel launch:

```
add<<<(N+255)/256, 256>>>(N, d_a, d_b, d_c);
```

The things inside the funky-looking triple angle brackets are called *launch parameters*. We won't be going too much into what they mean, but the short version is that they tell the GPU how many threads to use. Tuning these parameters can lead to *big* differences in the final performance of your kernel.

Putting it all together with a few memory allocations and frees, your final code might look something like this:

```
__global__ void add(int n, float* a, float *b, float *c)
{
  int i = blockIdx.x * blockDim.x + threadIdx.x;
  if (i < n) c[i] = a[i] + b[i];
}

int main(void)
{
  int N = 1<<20;
  float *a, *b, *c, *d_a, *d_b, *d_c;
  a = (float*)malloc(N*sizeof(float));
  b = (float*)malloc(N*sizeof(float));
  c = (float*)malloc(N*sizeof(float));

  cudaMalloc(&d_a, N*sizeof(float));
  cudaMalloc(&d_b, N*sizeof(float));
  cudaMalloc(&d_c, N*sizeof(float));

  for (int i = 0; i < N; i++) {
    a[i] = 1.0f;
    b[i] = 2.0f;
    c[i] = 0.0f;
  }

  cudaMemcpy(d_x, x, N*sizeof(float), cudaMemcpyHostToDevice);
  cudaMemcpy(d_y, y, N*sizeof(float), cudaMemcpyHostToDevice);

  add<<<(N+255)/256, 256>>>(N, d_a, d_b, d_c);
```

```
    cudaMemcpy(c, d_c, N*sizeof(float), cudaMemcpyDeviceToHost);

    cudaFree(d_x);
    cudaFree(d_y);
    free(x);
    free(y);
}
```

Finally, you can compile your kernel by invoking nvcc, the Nvidia CUDA compiler. The syntax is similar to compiling C code with gcc or clang:

```
nvcc -o kernel kernel.cu
```

CUDA in Practice

Writing CUDA kernels, profiling them, and tweaking your code can be fun, but you don't always need to work at this level of abstraction to extract the benefits of CUDA. The examples we showed you are *much* simpler than the CUDA code that is currently deployed in the real world.

In Python, when we want to do matrix multiplication, we look up the docs. Maybe there are a few syntax variations, like a.matmul(b), matmul(a, b), and a@b, but that's about it. We generally don't give these methods too much thought.

CUDA is on an entirely different plane of existence. There are multiple competing matrix multiplication algorithms, with complex heuristics for deciding which kernel to call in which scenarios. The implementation of matrix multiplication that's used can vary significantly depending on the shape of the matrices, memory bandwidth, and other hardware-specific details.

Thankfully, there's a slightly better abstraction layer for general-purpose GPU code: CUDA libraries. This includes cuFFT, cuDNN, cuSPARE, and more. The CUDA libraries contain highly optimized implementations of the most common algorithms you might want to run on a GPU, like convolution, Fourier transforms, matrix multiplication, and more.

There's also the PyTorch C++ library, libtorch, which provides even higher-level primitives like torch::Tensor. PyTorch C++ code looks surprisingly similar to PyTorch code in Python. Here's an example of a layer from the official guide (*https://oreil.ly/IEdxH*) to custom extensions that the PyTorch documentation refers to as *long long-term memory* (LLTM):

```
#include <vector>

std::vector<at::Tensor> lltm_forward(
    torch::Tensor input,
    torch::Tensor weights,
    torch::Tensor bias,
    torch::Tensor old_h,
```

```
    torch::Tensor old_cell) {
  auto X = torch::cat({old_h, input}, /*dim=*/1);

  auto gate_weights = torch::addmm(bias, X, weights.transpose(0, 1));
  auto gates = gate_weights.chunk(3, /*dim=*/1);

  auto input_gate = torch::sigmoid(gates[0]);
  auto output_gate = torch::sigmoid(gates[1]);
  auto candidate_cell = torch::elu(gates[2], /*alpha=*/1.0);

  auto new_cell = old_cell + candidate_cell * input_gate;
  auto new_h = torch::tanh(new_cell) * output_gate;

  return {new_h,
          new_cell,
          input_gate,
          output_gate,
          candidate_cell,
          X,
          gate_weights};
}
```

This is still much higher-level than the pointer manipulation you'll do in CUDA, but it can actually be very useful if you need to implement a new custom layer and find that cobbling up Python code incurs a significant performance penalty. The act of simply writing your layers with libtorch, linking into Python, and using that instead can produce a noticeable speed improvement, and this is an optimization that may definitely be worth your time.

If you want take the first steps toward writing low-level GPU code in practice, but *don't* want to burn your precious hours trying to figure out what the most efficient access pattern is for a half-precision Fourier transform in shared memory, CUDA libraries and libtorch are wonderful tools that you can use as you craft your next NLP creation.

Index

About the Authors

Ankur A. Patel is an AI entrepreneur, thought leader, and author. He is currently the cofounder and head of data at Glean and the cofounder of Mellow. Glean uses natural language processing to deliver vendor spend intelligence within an accounts payable solution. Mellow develops easy-to-use natural language processing APIs for developers to use as part of their product build.

Previously, Ankur was the vice president of data science at 7Park Data, a Vista Equity Partners portfolio company. Ankur used alternative data to build alternative data products for hedge funds and developed a natural language processing-based entity recognition, resolution, and linking platform for enterprise clients. Prior to 7Park Data, Ankur led data science efforts in New York City for Israeli artificial intelligence firm ThetaRay, a pioneer in applied unsupervised learning.

Ankur began his career as an analyst at JPMorgan, and then became the lead emerging markets sovereign credit trader for Bridgewater Associates, the world's largest global macro hedge fund. He later founded and managed R-Squared Macro, a machine learning–based hedge fund.

A graduate of the Woodrow Wilson School at Princeton University, Ankur is the recipient of the Lieutenant John A. Larkin Memorial Prize. He currently resides in New York City.

Ajay Arasanipalai is a deep learning researcher and student at the University of Illinois at Urbana-Champaign. He has extensive experience in building and training deep learning models for a variety of computer vision and natural language processing tasks such as text/image classification, object detection, semantic segmentation, language modeling, and more.

For two consecutive years, he achieved state-of-the-art results on the popular Stanford DAWNBench competition, where he trained an image classifier on the CIFAR10 dataset to 94% accuracy in under 10 seconds, setting a new speed record for 4 GPU training time.

In 2020, Ajay worked with members of the Event Horizon Telescope collaboration to apply deep learning and computer vision to solve the problem of parameter extraction in black holes, which includes recovering quantities like spin that to this day are not measurable with astronomical observations.

Ajay has authored multiple well-received technical articles published by industry-leading deep learning startups like FloydHub and Weights & Biases. In them, he breaks down the latest, most important papers in the field and helps readers implement cutting-edge algorithms like GPT-2, making deep learning research more entertaining and accessible.

Colophon

The bird on the cover of *Applied Natural Language Processing in the Enterprise* is the southern hill myna (*Gracula indica*). This member of the starling family (*myna* comes from the Hindi word for starlings, *maina*) is native to the forests of southwest India (the Western Ghats) and Sri Lanka.

This glossy, iridescent black myna has bright yellow wattles on its head, of a distinct pattern and size that distinguishes this bird from other hill myna species. It also has an orange bill, legs, and feet, and small white patches on its wings. Adults average 9 inches in length, including the short tail. As with other starling species, the southern hill myna travels with others of its kind, whether in pairs or flocks, vocalizing in its shrill natural voice.

Their diet consists mainly of fruit and nectar, including figs and sapu berries, though they are omnivorous and will also consume insects and other small prey.

In the wild, these mynas have a wide variety of calls, learning some of these from other flock members. Hill mynas have long been known as an excellent mimic of the human voice, and because of this are bred by humans but also regularly removed from the wild (sometimes by the thousands every year) for the international caged bird trade.

Though numbers of southern hill mynas are declining, these birds are still currently listed by the IUCN as being of Least Concern. Many of the animals on O'Reilly covers are endangered; all of them are important to the world.

The cover illustration is by Karen Montgomery, based on a black and white engraving from *English Cyclopedia: Natural History*. The cover fonts are Gilroy and Guardian Sans. The text font is Adobe Minion Pro; the heading font is Adobe Myriad Condensed; and the code font is Dalton Maag's Ubuntu Mono.

Lightning Source UK Ltd.
Milton Keynes UK
UKHW030226030921
389824UK00008B/25